CAMP WILLIAM JAMES

BY JACK J. PREISS

argo books
norwich, vermont

Wipf and Stock Publishers
199 W 8th Ave, Suite 3
Eugene, OR 97401

Camp William James
By Preiss, Jack J.
ISBN 13: 978-1-62032-972-6
Publication date 3/28/2013
Previously published by Argo Books

Distributed and managed by Wipf and Stock Publishers.
For all orders and inquiries please contact us at:

http://www.wipfandstock.com
info@wipfandstock.com
orders@wipfandstock.com

sy Fund, Inc.

rica

Books in cooperation with The Norwich
cerned with the future of such volunteer
book. The Norwich Center was founded
Camp William James. Persons interested
ch Center, Norwich, Vermont 05055.

ock-Huessy published by Argo Books may
ch, Vermont 05055.

Front cover picture shows Camp William James in Tunbridge, Vermont (the Rivers place); back cover picture shows campers at work, January, 1941.

So far as man stands for anything, and is productive or originative at all, his entire vital function may be said to have to deal with maybes. Not a victory is gained, not a deed of faithfulness or courage is done, except upon a maybe; not a service, not a sally of generosity, not a scientific exploration or experiment or textbook that may not be a mistake. It is only by risking our persons from one hour to another that we live at all. And often enough our faith beforehand in an uncertified result is the only thing that makes the result come true.

- William James

Two sons of William James, Alexander and William Jr., formally give their father's name to Camp William James at the dedication ceremonies in Sharon, Vermont on December 14th, 1940 (see pages 99-101).

Contents

Preface - 1977	ix
Introduction - 1977	xi
Foreword - 1949	xiii
1 Something of William James	1
2 The First Gilded Youth	6
3 Tenderfeet in Tunbridge	25
4 The Rally	41
5 Field Maneuvers in Washington	49
6 Internal Crises	63
7 At The White House	92
8 Signs and Portents	103
9 Sharon	114

10 The Battle is Joined 138

11 Interim Camp 157

12 Rebirth in Tunbridge 169

13 The Downward Path 183

14 Obituary Refused 202

15 Postscript, 1945 219

Epilogue 240

Footnotes 247

Index 252

Illustrations vi, xvi, 48, 168

Preface - 1977

In the depths of the Great Depression, the New Deal devised the Civilian Conservation Corps to put unemployed young men to work on reforestation and conservation projects. Before it was over, the CCC enrolled three million young Americans in hundreds of "camps" around the country, gave them some sense of order and purpose and, in the process, among many permanently useful projects, planted half the trees planted in the United States since the beginning of the Republic. The results of that remarkable undertaking have not yet been adequately assessed.

Even during the Depression there were many Americans, prominent among them the President's wife, Eleanor Roosevelt, who believed that the CCC should be more than an emergency relief program — that every young American should be encouraged to serve his (and now her) country, much in the spirit of William James' famous essay, "The Moral Equivalent of War."

Mrs. Roosevelt engaged the interest of her husband and in the winter of 1940-41 a group of Harvard and Dartmouth students, recently graduated, who had served their apprenticeships in regular CCC camps, came together in Sharon, Vermont, to establish Camp William James, an experimental leadership training camp whose purpose was to explore the means for turning the CCC into a form of national service.

The sons of William James attended the camp's opening ceremonies; his biographer, Ralph Barton Perry, wrote in support of the enterprise. And articulate leaders as varied as Senator George Aiken, Stuart Chase, Dorothy Canfield Fisher, Ralph Flanders, Eleanor Roosevelt and Dorothy Thompson became close friends and admirers of the "college boys" and their fellow enrollees from Civilian Conservation Corps camps across the country who, together, shared in one of the most fruitful episodes of the New Deal era.

President Franklin D. Roosevelt adopted the camp as his chosen instrument for transforming the Civilian Conservation Corps from a makeshift relief agency to what he hoped would become a permanent and positive feature of the educational and environmental landscape. The onrush of World War II understandably eroded the camp's support as the President and Administration, as well as the original members of the camp, turned from moral equivalents to the grim requirements of war itself.

When John F. Kennedy became President, he created a Peace Corps by an executive order dated March 1, 1961. Sargent Shriver, the Corps' first director, has described in a vivid article* how much this initiative owed to the tradition represented by Camp William James.

Today, when the Congress of the United States considers proposals to re-establish, along new lines, a corps of young people volunteering for national environmental service, it is instructive to note that many of the issues as to the proper role, recruitment and organization of an "ecology army" were first confronted and debated by the founders of Camp William James. When the State of California set up, in 1976, its own "California Conservation Corps," it helped to draw attention once more to the issue of service by young people as "The Moral Equivalent of War." By then it was clear that a peacetime army of young men and women was badly needed to help restore a badly abused environment.

Moreover, the country was facing a serious problem of unemployed and demoralized youth. In response to a growing awareness of the seriousness of this problem, a number of youth employment bills have now been introduced into the Congress. The avowed failure of the so-called volunteer army has also helped to focus attention on the notion of "universal service" — the idea

**The American Peoples Encyclopedia, 1962 Yearbook*, pp. 499-500, Grolier Incorporated, New York, 1962.

that all young Americans should be required to perform some service for their country, one option being military service. There could therefore be no more appropriate time to retrieve the history of Camp William James, the first practical effort to give effect to the idea of national service in time of peace.

Jack Preiss, himself a member of the camp, has written an unvarnished account of its genesis, growth, struggles and demise. That the episodes described in this book have had more than a negligible impact on our institutional history is of less significance, perhaps, than the promise which a dramatic example still holds for our social and environmental future.

Page Smith
Santa Cruz, California

Introduction - 1977

Why is a manuscript written nearly thirty years ago being published now? Part of the answer is that in 1950 I failed to convince a publisher to print it. Subsequently, the few typed copies slipped from view — I had given mine to Professor Huessy* — and it seemed probable that the Camp history, like the Camp itself, would survive only in the memories of a few whom it had touched.

Then, in the late sixties and early seventies, some stirrings could be detected: the idea of work service, often moribund but never quite dead, revived and sporadically grew in public and private ways. As part of this modest renaissance, portions of the manuscript turned up in cellars and attics, and eventually it was possible to assemble a complete copy.

Several former members of the Camp read it and responded positively. Apparently, some of the concepts and experiences

*Eugen Rosenstock-Huessy, professor of social philosophy at Dartmouth College, who gave both intellectual and practical leadership to the Camp. Huessy had tried to foster a democratic work service in Germany after World War I. He left the country when Hitler came to power. Many of the college men who were part of the original group had been in Huessy's classes at Dartmouth. He was unquestionably the most important figure in the life of *Camp William James*. He died at his home in Norwich, Vermont, in 1973 at the age of 84.

of the 1940's remained valid and important — at least they might be. I remember receiving a copy of the history: it was a strange, almost unsettling experience to see again one's words of a long gone time and place. Each chapter brought forth anticipation and apprehension. The critic's eye was now my habit. Words, phrases, whole sections seemed to shout for revision — updating, condensation, clarification, excision, and so on.

What should be done? Most of those interested felt strongly that the history should be published. Young people who had recently read it found it comprehensible and not too tedious. Some even found a spark somewhere. Since regular commercial publishing remained out of reach, it was decided to print it on a smaller scale. For this effort and commitment we owe most to Frank Davidson and Clinton Gardner, who still believe the "maybe" is a risk worth taking. Were it not for them, via Argo Books, this volume would not be in your hands. After some discussion of rewriting, ranging from almost total redoing to an editor's "smoothing up," it was agreed that the most appropriate stance was to disturb the original as little as possible. It would then have its legitimate place, warts and all, as a part of the Camp rather than as a distant view of it. This seemed congruent with a central thesis of the Camp, namely that ideas have survival value, and the significant ones do not require alteration to "fit the changing times." The people who make contact with such ideas will, if they wish, create their own translations and transitions.

I feel the need to make only one further comment. In his magnificent letter (p. 221) to Goldsmith lying in a field hospital in France in 1945, Huessy said that the history of Camp William James had never been written, and he implied this might not be possible. I believe that his letter is actually the core of that history. Even more, it places the Camp in its widest and most significant context — the union of heart and mind. The present volume hopefully complements the scope of Huessy's trenchant and humanitarian analysis and provides the background for appreciating it.

Jack J. Preiss
Durham, N. C.

Foreword - 1949

Throughout this book, I have tried to use facts, events, dates and names with accuracy. Since most of the notes and data on Camp William James were not originally set down with future publication in mind, there is considerable variation in both the content and style of the documentary records. There was no single biographer or diarist. There were dozens — a letter here, a fragment of observation there, a note of a conversation, the minutes of a meeting, a newspaper article. And it is better that this is so. For in no comparable manner could the many moods, personalities, and activities of the Camp be so authentically expressed.

On the debit side, the burdens upon the editor of such a collection are heavy. The difficulty of placing events in their proper chronological order is in itself formidable, since many written items were not dated, or even signed. Furthermore, not all of the material could be used. Some selection was necessary, based largely on my own conception of the relative importance of each contribution. However, the reader may be assured that the following pages contain the most accurate account I have been able to make at this date. I have not concealed or glossed over any conflicts, unpleasant incidents, or failures in which the Camp was involved. Wherever feasible, actual letters, documents, speeches, and records of meetings will be quoted in full or in part, insofar as they appear pertinent to the story.

My chief hope is that the book will cast a little light on some of the paths we may yet explore in our search for social truth and understanding.

* * * * *

This story began for me just after my graduation from Dartmouth College in June, 1940. Many young men in those tense, uncertain times were assailed, even as they now are, by doubts about everything from international politics to their prospects of getting a job. The approach of some overwhelming calamity was heralded by the outbreak of hostilities in Europe. In a world which had become accustomed to discord, the shooting war appeared inevitable. The reasons proclaimed by men and governments to rationalize their hate and distrust of one another sounded even more ominous than usual because of the mounting pitch and tempo in which they were uttered. Americans, still spectators, could feel the cleavages being made and watch the opposing battle lines being drawn.

In this triggered atmosphere, a group of former college students, most of them recent graduates, embarked upon an adventure which was not to terminate in a few months, as was first anticipated, but which was to spread itself over several hectic years. Having been a participant in the first half of this adventure, I have a rather proprietary interest in telling about it, and in trying to discover the useful substance in it. I am sure that like sentiments are shared by many former members of the Camp. It has simply been a question of which one would get to the task first, and I am positive that fully a dozen other names could replace mine as narrator. Furthermore, in fairness to the Camp, I think its recapitulation had to be undertaken by someone who, like myself, believed in its worth and shared in its spirit. The appraisal of a reporter would have been not quite enough.

The life of Camp William James was animate in the true sense of the word. As with many creative works, large and small, it was hardly separable from the identities of those who authored it. Its development, often stormy, was a wedding of idea and deed which is infrequently achieved in similar circumstances. The Camp founders were convinced that they were dealing with a theory which was not only worthwhile in concept, but which was also capable of practical realization. This indispensable concreteness was one of the attractions which drew many otherwise hostile elements into the Camp's orbit. Groups of men can expend great physical energy and endure much privation for tangible goals in which they believe. But if the objectives are amorphous, or lacking altogether, the strength of any united effort is rapidly dissipated. Its tangibility of aim, which was far from being an idle dream, held the Camp together through an almost constant series of ordeals. And perhaps this very quality constitutes its chief survival value for the present day.

The fact that the Camp did overcome its early difficulties, and did establish itself as a going concern, was primarily the result of the perseverance, loyalty, and courage of its members. Any peacetime endeavor which can inspire these three qualities in a group so varied in temperament, racial background, religion, education, and economic status as this one was, is worth careful scrutiny.

We will soon perceive that the Camp tried to unify men for a common cause. Today, by contrast, there are many powerful forces at work which aim at segregating men for exclusive causes. All of us who are interested in finding ways and means of strengthening democracy realize that this modern divisive trend must be stemmed. For it is now clear that the degree to which human beings can link themselves in common identity and aspiration will govern their chances of survival. Within the past ten years, many people have become convinced that they must do their thinking about the future of society on this unfamiliarly broad scale. That is a healthy sign. Yet we must remember that no matter how encompassing or complicated our plans for world order may be, the basic individual relationships which one man has with another will prescribe our success or failure. How we get along with our next door neighbor is still the root factor in determining the course of human affairs.

That is why Camp William James has a universal message which is pertinent, and why it can bridge the gap of communication between one generation and another. The validity of its experience is not altered by the passage of time, and it can be translated into any language. It focussed sharply on a small number of people, living in several small towns, in a small state, in a rather remote section of the nation. During its brief hour it was seldom unaware of the local basis of its nourishment and function. But there was always the possibility that its example might initiate action and have influence far outside its own limited sphere. This was the duality without which the Camp would have been devoid of real meaning.

What the principles of the Camp were and how it tried to articulate them is the story which follows.

Above: At the White House in Sharon, December, 1940. Front row, starting 3rd from left: Alfred Eiseman, Arnold Childs, George Flowers. Back row, from left: Frank Davidson, Enno Hobbing, Louis Schlivek, Page Smith, Jack Preiss, Roy Chamberlin, unidentified, William Uptegrove, Russell Greenlaw.

Below: Tunbridge, summer of 1941. From left: Lee Knowles, George Phillips, Nathan Dodge, Edward Flint, Robert O'Brien.

1. Something of William James

In order to comprehend the significance of "Camp William James", we must first speak briefly about the man for whom it was named.

William James was an American teacher, philosopher, and man of letters who lived during the latter half of the nineteenth and early part of the twentieth centuries. He was a man of great vitality and wide scholarship, whose influence upon his own and later generations has been considerable. His work and interests covered many fields of activity, and included important contributions to psychology, education, and philosophy. However, there was nothing of musty intellectualism or humorless pedantry in his character. His greatest love was for people, and he thrived on his contacts with human beings. He also loved the outdoors, and was overjoyed when he could leave his city home for a trip to the woods and mountains. His restless and eager spirit, coupled with an incisive mind, could not help but live on through his friends and co-workers. Here was a man who was able to make traditionally "dry" philosophical subjects sound and read like an adventure novel, and who was as much at home talking with a teen-age student as he was corresponding with his learned contemporaries throughout the world.

For all of his forceful thinking, he never shut himself off from the ideas of others. He relished criticism of his own works, particularly if the critic had a suggestion or alternative to offer. Quite often, said critic was surprised to find his contribution incorporated in one of James' later works. It is truly a rare man who, like James, can sincerely love an ally and an opponent with equal fervor, and who can profit in great measure from both. To an unusual degree, James was the living example of the precepts he taught and developed, and these precepts have much value for us today.

The question we are chiefly concerned with in this volume is whether or not we can eliminate the practice of organized predatory war from our social structure. And before we go into this momentous problem, and James' answer to it, it is well to define as precisely as we can exactly what we mean. The word "war" is a broad term which can characterize an amazingly large number of human endeavors. There are wars against disease, wars against ignorance and intolerance, wars among businessmen (called competition), the war of sport, even the humorists' war between the sexes. It is evident that the concept of war is one of the bases of a comprehensive field of activities. The man who ceases to have something to "fight" for, whether it be his country, his family, or whatever, is the man who withers and becomes extinct. But of all the "wars" we engage in during our lifetime, those which involve the destruction of our neighbors and their works are the most horrendous and unjustifiable. The practice of mass killing by whole nations and groups of nations is one kind of war which it is imperative for us to efface from our civilization. This is our question of survival, and for its solution we must look, as William James did, into the nature of war itself.

History repeatedly shows us that the highest productive efforts of nations, the greatest sacrifices by citizens, the finest courage exhibited by individuals, occur during wartime. The paradox of this is that man exhibits his virtues at their peak only while attempting to kill and subdue his neighbor in battle. The tragedy of this situation was quite apparent to James. He realized that, fundamentally, any method which resolved the war question would have to rescue the virtues which war stimulated, while at the same time doing away with the chaos and destruction. He put forth his views on this subject in a remarkable essay called "The Moral Equivalent of War," which was published in 1910. As with many discoveries in the fields of natural sciences, politics, and religion, his answer to this societal question was amazingly simple. Therein lies its great appeal, and its ability to be understood by the majority of people. James admitted, primarily, that the numerous values of the military life are worth preserving and fostering — "intrepidity, contempt of softness, surrender of private interest, obedience to command, must still remain the rock upon which States are built."[1] He also realized that these values have meaning only when applied to concrete instances, and not while remaining mere platitudes. War is consciously destructive of man, and is therefore wanton and immoral. It is a perverted creation because it can exist only by feeding upon itself. The end product of such a process is extinction.

How then, said James, can we take the sterling qualities exhibited by men during wartime and turn them to meaningful ends. The task will be to change the *concreteness* by which these qualities are expressed. High-sounding phrases will not do it. Appeals to "reason" and "peace" will not do it. These have been tried many times and have failed, simply because the glamour and appeal of war have been greater than the appeal of peace. The anti-militarists have consistently ignored this simple fact, and have refused to meet the militarists on their own grounds, which are largely emotional. In the end, the peace-lovers have always been swallowed up in the military parades.

Therefore, reasoned James, if we can but direct the vigorous human craving for battle into constructive channels we shall be that much nearer the elimination of destructive war. Whatever else they may be, these constructive goals must assume a large measure of the appeal of war, and must elicit the same response from the people. The human imagination will not be fired by discussion groups and committee meetings, necessary though they are. Regardless of what the new aim is to be, it must call forth the discipline, both mental and physical, of a crack parachute battalion. For only by emulating the battalion, can we substitute for it.

Let James himself tell what he has in mind:

> If now—and this is my idea—there were instead of military conscription, a conscription of the whole youthful population to form for a certain number of years a part of the army enlisted against

> *Nature*, the injustices would tend to be evened out, and numerous other goods to the commonwealth would follow. The military ideals of hardihood and discipline would be wrought into the growing fibre of the people; no one would remain blind, as the luxurious classes now are blind, to man's relations to the globe he lives on, and to the permanently sour and hard foundations of his higher life. To coal and iron mines, to freight trains, to fishing fleets in December, to dish washing, clothes washing, and window washing, to road building and tunnel making, to foundries and stoke-holes, and to the frames of sky scrapers, would our gilded youths be drafted off, according to their choice, to get the childishness knocked out of them, and to come back into society with healthier sympathies and soberer ideas. They would have paid their blood-tax, done their own part in the immemorial human warfare against nature; they would tread the earth more proudly, the women would value them more highly, they would be better fathers and teachers of the following generations.
>
> Such a conscription, with the state of public opinion that would have required it, and the many moral fruits it would bear, would preserve in the midst of a pacific civilization the manly virtues which the military party is so afraid of seeing disappear in peace. We should get toughness without callousness, authority with as little criminal cruelty as possible, and painful work done cheerily, because the duty is temporary, and threatens not, as now, to degrade the whole remainder of one's life. I spoke of the 'moral equivalent' of war. So far, war has been the only force that can discipline a whole community, and until an equivalent discipline is organized, I believe that war must have its way. But I have no serious doubt that the ordinary prides and shames of social man, once developed to a certain intensity, are capable of organizing such a moral equivalent as I have sketched, or some other just as effective for preserving manliness of type.[2]

There you have the kernel of James' idea, stated candidly by him, and retaining its freshness after forty years. He visualized a kind of universal work service, the only qualifications for participation being of age and physical competence. Groups of young men from all walks of life, all creeds and colors, all sections of the country, would be working on common projects, learning to get along with and understand the problems of one another. After a year in such an environment every individual would gain an appreciation of his own dignity as he saw it reflected in his fellows, and life would have new meaning for him, whatever he chose to do in the world. At the time James conceived his idea, he did not express it on other than the national level, but it is easy enough to see the logic of its application on a globe-wide scale. Here at last may be a way of breaching the walls of distrust and ignorance set up by nations against each other.

The inspiration of this possibility was the seed from which "Camp William James" sprang. It was an attempt to find out whether this "moral equivalent" for war was really applicable to life, or whether it was just another exercise in rhetoric. The Camp represented the kind of test which James himself would have heartily approved, since he felt that the criterion of truth for an idea was how well men could live by it.

However, one assumption which would be incorrect is that the Camp began, from scratch, with James' concept firmly in everyone's mind. This was not the case, and only after a preliminary period of trial, error, and groping did the union of the Camp and the theory actually occur.

It is probably true that similar camps with similar aims have been established before, many of them quite unaware of their like method of approach. But the distinction is that these other efforts were largely specialized in their nature, and were based upon the available leisure time of the members. To my knowledge, Camp William James grew into the only "all-out" project ever undertaken in the United States which consciously tried to breathe life into the "moral equivalent of war," as James expressed it.

I leave it to your judgment as to whether or not it achieved its goals.

2. The First "Gilded Youth"

It was 1939, in a world on the threshold of war. As is usual in such times, people were troubled and confused by world events and were unable to anticipate the shape of things to come. The question of whether the United States could remain neutral in the coming European holocaust seemed to be the crucial issue. Although subsequent events proved that there wasn't much of an issue here after all, it was difficult at the moment to turn anyone's attention away from current events. There was no longer time to worry about the causes of war and how to eradicate them, for the war was already upon us and it appeared ridiculous to be concerned about anything except our chances of staying out of it. This apprehensive public opinion, addicted to its daily papers and hourly newscasts could not be changed overnight, if indeed it could be altered at all.

However, there were slight stirrings here and there in other directions. There were still efforts to solve the riddle of war, whose latest shadow was growing ever more menacing. One of these efforts involved a young college graduate named Frank Davidson, who had been troubled during his student days by the widening conflicts and segregation within American life.

A boy on a farm in the Ozarks had about as much connection with the son of a Chicago banker as a grain of sand in the Sahara had with a snowflake in the Arctic. Their chance of ever having a conversation together or sleeping under the same roof was equally remote—except possibly in an army barracks or in the belly of a B-17. Davidson's university life at Harvard had furnished few answers to this problem. Yet he was not one to shrug off his misgivings. He believed something was amiss in the social fabric of America and he determined to find out what it was.

Among the people he knew in Cambridge was Mrs. Henry Copley Greene, a woman of great vigor and high intellect, who was a member of one of Massachusetts' oldest families. Mrs. Greene was much interested in Davidson's dilemma, not merely as his personal problem, but because it reflected the unrest and indecision of the whole generation. Within her circle of friends, she numbered Eugen Rosenstock-Huessy, a professor of Social Philosophy at Dartmouth College. Years before, following the first World War, Professor Huessy had taught in his native Germany and was instrumental in founding the German work camps during the Weimar Republic. The purpose of the camps was to provide a medium through which disillusioned soldiers of the defeated nation could reform their shattered lives on a plane of fellowship and cooperation with each other. Furthermore, the soldiers had to be absorbed back into the civilian community and to re-establish contact with farmers, clerks, and factory workers. However noble the idea, it could not rise above its surroundings. Besides, the German republican government was weak, and the German people, so lately under the iron discipline of war and Prussian rule, did not respond enthusiastically to ideas of equality and democracy. The demagoguery of Hitler soon arose to give the Germans a simpler answer to their defeat—namely, blaming it on someone else. The Germans grasped eagerly at this fictitious excuse and accepted it as gospel truth. Once the scapegoats had been found, and accepted by the people, it was easy for Hitler to instill the spirit of vengeance and to foster the craving for power and glory which had so recently been denied. The work camp movement, as conceived by Huessy, was no match for Nazi passion and hate. As Hitler became more powerful it was evident that the democratic work camps would soon be destroyed or turned to less admirable uses. When he could no longer buck the totalitarian wave, Huessy came to the United States with his family. A man of great scholarship, and with considerable literary achievement to his credit, he was not unknown in this country. After a short tenure teaching at Harvard, he was appointed to the Dartmouth faculty, where he has remained ever since.

Knowing of Professor Huessy's experience with youth in the aborted German camps, Mrs. Greene arranged for Davidson to meet him and talk over these questions. From that meeting many more resulted, and soon Davidson began to see some glimmerings of light. The two agreed that a great leavening and unification of American youth was imperative. The segregation and classification of young people had been gathering momentum for several years, and the social structure was becoming solidified on economic and racial levels. Each segment of the population was drawing more to itself in its country clubs, its company-towns, its ghettos, its movie colonies, its college campuses, and colonial villages. People came to know and care less than they used to about their neighbors. It became possible, in our large cities, to live in an apartment house for years and not have even a speaking acquaintance with those who lived on the same floor. Business was carried on by ticker tape and typewriter. A man bought and sold shares in a copper mine and an oil well which he would never see. An executive of a large concern in New York carried on daily phone conversations with a partner in California whom he would fail to know if he met him on the street. There were farmers in Virginia who looked in wonderment at Vermont license plates because they had never heard of the State. These and many others were examples of the myriad, unconnected lives of Americans. Despite all the great mechanical advances, and the improvements in literacy and education, the differences among people, rather than their common interests, were being emphasized. This wasn't healthy for the individuals or the nation. The great melting pot that was America had cooled off considerably since 1919, and the ingredients were not mixing nearly so well.

During the great depression of the early '30's, many government bureaus and agencies were set up to help ease the economic distress of the country. Because of the large numbers of unemployed, some means were necessary to provide work for young men who had never held jobs, as well as for former wage earners. As a result, the Civilian Conservation Corps was established in 1933 to take care of the unemployed youth. Utilizing the army system of corps areas, a large number of camps were constructed all over the country to house the enrollees. The central administration of the corps was in the hands of a civilian director and his staff, located in Washington. Through an arrangement with the War Department, the commanders of the camps were Army officers, whose subordinate work superintendents, educational directors, chefs, etc., were civilians. It was intended that army-type discipline should prevail in the operation of the camps, although no training in military procedures, or issuance of weapons were permitted. The work engaged in by each camp varied somewhat with its location, but the chief types of projects included soil conservation, flood control, tree planting, and road building, mostly on State and Federal owned land. Any work which would conceivably interfere or compete with private enterprise was strictly avoided. It was hoped that the "CCC" would enable its enrollees to obtain means of supporting themselves until economic conditions improved and more private employment became available. At the same time, these enrollees would have the feeling they were of some use to the country instead of simply receiving a dole. The natural resources of the nation also figured to benefit through the conservation projects of the camps.

As stated by the government, these objectives were worthy, and enjoyed wide popular support. In fact, of all the "alphabet" agencies established by the New Deal, the CCC probably had the least amount of public criticism.

However, upon close examination of the qualification of the enrollment, and a detailed look at the actual day by day running of many of the camps, the need for changes and improvements soon was apparent. For instance, according to an official CCC publication "no applicants are to be selected, whether with or without dependents, whose family or personal circumstances permit them to maintain better than a normal or average standard of living in their respective communities."[1] The purpose of this provision was to make sure that the limited enrollment of 300,000 men, as provided by Congress, was made up of those who most needed the work and the limited pay which the CCC offered. This qualification was undoubtedly instituted with good intentions, but in practice its ultimate effect was to accentuate the poor economic circumstances of the boys and to make them more conscious of themselves as a group apart from society. The CCC uniform told the world that its wearer was unemployed, was usually lacking in higher education and family position, and was practically a ward of the government due to his poverty and lack of vocational skill. In addition, the camps had sparse contact with the communities in their areas, and little effort was made to have the enrollees and local citizens meet together on equal and friendly terms. The camps were like small islands, their chief contacts with the outside world being the supply trucks and the newspapers. For obvious reasons, a feeling of mutual hostility often developed between the camps and their neighboring towns. After promising starts, many boys lost interest in their future in the CCC and either resigned outright, or sank into moods of despondency and laziness. Discipline was not easy to maintain, and morale suffered greatly.

In the face of this condition, which existed in 1939, Davidson decided to enroll in the CCC to find out at first hand about this "lost battalion" of American youth. He had not originally planned to make such an enrollment, believing that it would be better to start a new organization on a private basis. To this latter end, he and a Harvard friend, Richard Davis, had drawn up a prospectus and an organizational blueprint, and they were getting ready to solicit funds. Professor Huessy opposed this idea. He pointed to the existence of the CCC, with its vast machinery and personnel, and its large enrollment. It would be foolish to begin all over again and to build a movement which would duplicate many of the facilities already at hand. Besides, it would take years, and time was not unlimited. Therefore, "if you are really serious in your intentions," he told Davidson, "join the CCC as an enrollee and work for improvement within the framework." Somewhat reluctantly, Davidson agreed to change his approach, and, after much contemplation, he decided to follow Huessy's advice.

Accordingly, he wrote a letter to Mr. J. J. McEntee, then CCC Assistant Director, stating his case:

> My desire to enroll in the Civilian Conservation Corps comes from my belief that the type of training it offers is valuable and even essential for the young men of America, regardless of their economic and social status. As a college graduate, I feel that the experience of living and working with other young men from all walks of life is necessary to complete my education. Manual labor is a needed

complement to intellectual labor.

Beyond this, there is my conviction that every young citizen should, before taking up his specialized job, devote a certain length of time in service to the common interests of the country. Military service in time of war should have its civilian counterpart in time of peace; the conservation of our moral and material resources is not less vital than the defense of the nation against foreign enemies.[2]

Upon receiving Davidson's letter, McEntee decided to approve his request. There was nothing in the application to indicate any ulterior motives on Davidson's part, nor any hint that he was interested in changing the organization of the Corps. He appeared to be just a college boy, perhaps a little unusual in his point of view, but certainly harmless. Nevertheless, granting him permission to enroll was an unprecedented action, especially since it would have been just as easy to refuse him. The Assistant Director probably had ample opportunity to regret his decision on subsequent occasions.

Davidson filled out the necessary forms, took the various tests and innoculations, and formally entered the Corps on October 12, 1939, the first college man in the history of the CCC to be accepted as a regular enrollee.

After the preliminaries of induction were over, he was assigned to a Maryland camp, not far from Washington, D. C. During the weeks in which he worked in the ditches and drain culverts which were the camp projects, he ate, slept and talked on equal terms with the rest of his company. His early premonitions were borne out by the facts. His first letter to Huessy described his initial days in camp.

CCC Co 3313 D-3
Vienna, Md. Friday, October 20, 1939

Dear Professor Rosenstock:

Well, I have been here eight days now, and I feel I can write you something definite about my first impressions of the CCC. The first shock is over. It was a tremendous one, but having survived it, I am confident that the crucial time is over.

Seven of us "rookies" signed on at Washington. It was an odd assortment; one fellow ran away from an orphan's home and joined the merchant marine when he was twelve years old; he has since been in prison, the Coast Guard, and the U. S. Marines. Another fellow was absolutely ruined in a "reformatory"; he is twenty years old; but life at the reformatory and on the road has made him look thirty or forty. And so on.

I have had to forget a vocabulary and learn a new one. But the change has not been a difficult one. A few Anglo-Saxon monosyllables constitute half the necessary language. Beyond that, I have had to invent and stick to a "hard luck" story. I am probably the only person in camp (excepting the educational director) with a college education. Mr. McEntee advised me even before going to camp, that I should not let my background be known. I disliked this idea, but the experience here makes it absolutely crystal clear that it would be nearly impossible to enlist as an enrollee on any other basis. I have made friends here already, and the aggravating thing about my masquerade is that I must continue to fly false colors. But there is a responsibility also to the CCC directors, who let me under the bars as the first such exception in the country; if others are to be allowed in under the same conditions it will be necessary for me to succeed here as an ordinary enrollee. One exception will be necessary, however; in a few days, after I am known definitely as an average, hard-working fellow, I shall inform the Commanding Officer of my reasons for being here. I hope to convert him to our view of things and then it may be possible to try out several of our ideas in this camp during the winter. There is an utter lack of *integrated* intellectual or recreational activities. The fellows think and talk only of sex. A few men have mentioned the situation as a sad one, and I hope to get them to cooperate, eventually, to initiate some voluntary activities in the camp, and perhaps later in one of the nearby communities.

It is absurd for anyone to think it difficult for a "well-bred" person to get along in the CCC. Silence is the sure road to acceptance; once you are accepted, then the sparks begin to fly. Democracy is an impossibility here, but I hope to persuade the Lieutenant, our commander, to select some of the more promising young men and put them in charge of a voluntary activity, such as building a swimming pool or repairing the camp entrance-way. There is a mimeographing machine in camp, and perhaps we shall be able to get out a newspaper. The main thing here as everywhere, is to make a *few* people consent to *do* something.

The remarkable thing about this place is that fellows tell you their entire life history and their philosophy within the first three minutes after you meet them. Incidentally, there is an utter lack of class consciousness, at least in the political sense. I have never met such a conservative group of young men. Of course that does not mean that they are not excellent potential material for a mob; they will not listen to any political or diplomatic or even war news over the radio; they are interested in Benny Goodman and Fred Allen and the football scores.

Our group started by raking leaves; then we graduated to pick and shovel, and now I have been given a temporary assignment in the supply room. You may be sure that I am keeping my eyes and ears open.

You and the Greenes were dead right. There is quite a difference between a Harvard boy with a bright idea, and a person who really lives what he believes. I have never felt so sure of my own personality as I do now. Manual labor *is* a great and important thing, and I am glad to have been forced to get along in what would have ordinarily been an uncongenial group; digging a garbage pit (our work for a day) turned out to be a really dramatic experience. The CCC comes closer than I thought it would to William James' idea of an army against nature. The spirit of the place is really pretty good, despite a total lack of inspiring leadership. I am as convinced as ever of the rightness of our idea, but what I realize now, as I did not before, is that the CCC, if considered against the alternative of no CCC, comes out as a great and important achievement. The framework is here, and perhaps we shall change the face of the organization by persuasion and example. The process will take time, but there is no other way. I see now that working from the inside is a quite different matter from going to the director with a bright notion from the outside.

This letter has been incoherent in places. I'll try to do better next time. Looking forward to hearing from you soon. My very best regards to Mrs. Huessy and yourself.

Frank[3]

We can see from this letter the emergence of the kind of attitude which would eventually result in action. With respect to Davidson's "deception" of McEntee in concealing his real purpose in entering the CCC, (i.e. to change it) it is apparent that he would not have been allowed to enroll if his reform intentions had been made known. McEntee would have been suspicious and would probably have refused the application. This would certainly have been a normal reaction. For although Davidson's motives might be praiseworthy, those already in power could well have regarded them differently. In any event, it was the old question of whether the end justified the means. In this particular case, Davidson felt that it did, and he was prepared to take whatever risks were necessary.

Although there are many occasions when a man can lose heart in an enterprise because of the immensity of the obstacles facing him or because of the loneliness of his situation, Davidson soon found that more and more people were becoming interested in what he was trying to do. Representative of these was Ambrose W. Vernon, a noted American teacher, scholar, and writer. He had heard of Davidson through Professor Huessy, and sent the following encouragement:

> Dear Davidson:
>
> I am so glad that you have had the courage to translate ideas into action. It will make a vast difference in the direction and content of your life. I rejoice with you in your present service. . .
>
> I am also glad that you have now the rare opportunity of coming into close contact with an element of our citizenry which most college men ignore; it will do more for you than many a course in sociology, and you will know what is necessary, and also what is unnecessary, to do to give such men as you are meeting the only abiding satisfaction in our brief but exciting life here on earth. . .[4]

It was this kind of understanding and support which made Davidson feel that his quest was not a solitary one.

* * * * *

Aside from the camp administration, the CCC boys had little contact with other people and even trips to movies and dances were infrequent. For excitement, the enrollees were turning more and more to a life of crime, with organized hold-ups, car stealing, etc., becoming more frequent.

Davidson kept a careful record of his findings and soon forwarded them to Washington, along with some suggestions for change. After receipt of Davidson's report, the CCC officials, now suspecting they may have made a mistake by allowing him to enroll, transferred him to New Mexico, where he made similar observations and submitted them to the main office. Rather than expose Davidson as a "troublemaker" and possibly as an internal "spy" the CCC hierarchy decided instead to hire him as a special investigator to "improve camp practices." Instead of opposing Davidson and his criticisms, which would stir up much unfavorable publicity, it seemed more sensible to make him a member of the team where he could be watched. Accordingly, word was dispatched from the Director's office to all eastern area CCC commanders to receive Davidson cordially and to offer him their cooperation. At first, this appeared to be a stroke of good fortune. Davidson believed he had made some headway and that he might now be in a position to further his ideas for improvement. Among his accepted recommendations, surprisingly enough, was the removal of the restriction of enrollment based upon pauper standards. Henceforth, the only qualification necessary in this regard was to be the unemployment of the applicant, regardless of his economic status or that of his family. Certainly, Davidson argued, there would be few men entering the CCC in order to live off the government. In fact, this would be much less likely among middle-class and wealthy boys than it was among those poor ones who were inclined toward laziness and "gold-bricking." The CCC was not attractive enough to cause any great rush for enrollment by prosperous and well-educated men, even if restrictions were lifted. This reasoning subsequently proved correct, and to its very end, the CCC could never point to more than a handful of college graduates or professional men among its enrollees. However, removing the bars did perform one important function. It enabled several of Davidson's friends from Harvard to follow his example. Students Enno Hobbing and George Phillips both made plans to enroll in June, 1940.

During his term as an enrollee, and later as an investigator, Davidson was not idle as far as the future was concerned. Through his father, a member of the New York State Power Commission, his faculty friends at Harvard, and some of his college friends, he gained access to important officials in various government departments in Washington. He therefore had a good chance of being heard, and was quick to capitalize on his political opportunities.

At Harvard, on hurried week-end leaves, he discussed with such men as Professors William Y. Elliott and Ralph Barton Perry[5] the possibilities of getting large numbers of Harvard men interested in the idea of voluntary work service. His arguments gained validity through his own enrollment in the CCC, a fact which impressed many of the students. However, it was slow work—there were many people to see, numerous doubts and skepticisms to be eliminated, and much lethargy to overcome.

On January 4, 1940, Davidson sent Paul Appleby, Assistant Secretary of Agriculture, a copy of his report on the CCC, presumably for circulation in the Department. The suggestion had been made in the report that the educational advisors in the camps be directly responsible to the CCC Washington office rather than have them subject to Army authority at each camp. Unofficially, Davidson also mentioned this suggestion to Fred Lukens, Chief Educational Adviser for the New England area, who was much interested in putting it into effect. On January 11, Davidson saw Appleby, who had by this time read the report and was most enthusiastic about it. However, Appleby's foremost concern was to eliminate Army control of the Corps and then divide the camps between the Department of Agriculture and the Department of the Interior. To Davidson, such an arrangement did not appear to solve the problem of divided responsibility. On the same day, Professor Elliott of Harvard arrived in Washington, and took the CCC report around to other high officials, including Paul McNutt, Federal Security Administrator. These sympathetic Washington hearings convinced Davidson that it would now be well for him to get into the CCC Director's office, in some official capacity. It seemed essential to build up a good central organization if the camps were to be properly serviced, and Washington was the place to begin the job.

* * * * *

At the same time that Davidson was pushing forward his political program, Professor Huessy was active in New Hampshire and Vermont. There existed, at Sharon, Vermont, a so-called CCC "side-camp," situated in the Downer State Forest. This camp was smaller than a regular CCC unit, both in size and equipment. Its main project was the improvement of a relatively untraveled highway from the state road in Sharon village up to the camp. For several years, Huessy had been telling his classes the same things which he had told Davidson, namely, that here was the tremendous CCC organization, spending hundreds of millions of dollars every year, and which, in spite of some conservation of public forests and highways, was failing in its larger purpose of conserving young men. He further told them that he believed the CCC, if improved, could supply the framework for a great movement, to reaffirm youth's faith in democracy.

Huessy then proposed a concrete plan to his students. He offered to take them on a series of visits to the Sharon camp to meet with the enrollees for social and athletic activities. Many of the students were eager to try this, and so the meetings were arranged. It was decided to first have an evening basketball game in the Dartmouth gymnasium, followed by dinner and a tour of the College. The game proved to be a material success, particularly for the CCC, which had the winning side. After the game, the groups intermingled, and began to find out about each other. The following are excerpts from the observations of some of the Dartmouth students. In these comments, some penetrating and some superficial, we can discern the mixed reactions of the hosts to their guests:

> His name is Bob Arnold, and he comes from Lowell, Mass. It began in the gym, sitting against the wall together, just talking about the camp and fighting forest fires. We showed him the squash courts and the swimming pool. He stopped and stared when he saw the cool green water, and was impressed, as we knew he would be, by the bigness of it all.
>
> We had been talking about colleges, and about Harvard in particular:
>
> *Alex:* I don't see how those fellows can get up day after day and look out over the roof tops of a city. They must get sick of it after a while.
>
> *Bob:* Yeah. And you get awfully sick of gettin' up every morning and lookin' at the woods, too. Like I always say, when you leave Vermont you're entering the United States.
>
> *Ed:* Ever fight any forest fires, Bob?
>
> *Bob:* No. Nothin' worth braggin' about. They had a big one up at Plymouth (Vermont) a couple of years ago, just before I came in. Four days and four nights. Almost had a strike after that one. They didn't pay 'em time and a half overtime. Just straight. What a rookin'!
>
> At this point, the conversation led to a discussion of morale improvement in the camp:
>
> *Alex:* Did you get knocked around much when you first got there?
>
> *Bob:* Yeah. I found out that it only goes one way. . . . . on pay day it's 'Bob, how about a butt on the cuff' or 'Lemme use your towel', but next day when I ask for some shoe polish it's 'G'wan, bud, pull a sneak,' and when I was in the infirmary with my appendix they stole my new

pair of shoes. Two seventy-five, they cost! Y'gotta put your stuff in a trunk with a lock. . . . buy 'em in the canteen. . . . double guaranteed against jimmies and sledgehammers. If you left your eyes hangin' outta your head they'd swipe 'em from ya. They think it's big-time stuff, swipin' everything they can get their hands on.

Ed: A lot of them come from the cities, don't they?

Bob: The camp is just a place for big hauls for 'em. Everything's a racket there. The mess steward starves ya, and makes little dough. The guy in the canteen gyps ya on the butts. Yeah, that's what it is. . . . dog eat dog.'

It is a pity that these boys, involved in such a social venture, and working in conservation for the benefit of the entire nation, fail to see beyond themselves, and live in a world of distrust and loneliness.

As the truck rolled away down the white, icy road, Bob waved to us from the darkness of its canopy. 'Thanks a lot for everything, fellows,' he called. We started walking back to the dorm, each knowing that we had done nothing more than give a little friendship, and that it was really we who should be doing the thanking. Frankly, we both felt like climbing in the truck with Bob to see if, perhaps, over a period of weeks we could help a person, who, in a sense, had never been born. But that is not in the pattern. . . . yet.[6]

* * * * *

But it was the complete difference in position that impressed me. One fellow's amazement at the size of the college, which was 'bigger than his high school.' The quick little laugh of some when I asked if they had come over in a closed car. The general curiosity about the college, the surprise when they found I lived in California — all these incidents pointed to a complete separation of their life from mine.[7]

* * * * *

If this camp could have the prestige of a college, its workers would show a new urge to create. If he (the enrollee) had an organization about him like a family or a college, he would feel free to grow instead of being stuck. It is a drudgery which will fail to bring out the best in a boy's character. But since he must have expression, he will find it elsewhere. They say there is much sneak-thievery in the CCC camps.[8]

* * * * *

My experience with a CCC camper frankly left me a little puzzled. He described his day to me. It wasn't so much what he did during the day that impressed me, but the attitude toward the camp life as a whole. He said that they would waste as much time as possible in going to and from their projects. His attitude seemed one whereby he thought he was out for a good time and that there was no need for overexerting himself. It is an attitude similar to the college student's, the only difference being who supplies the money. For the CCC it is the government and for the college student it is his father.[9]

* * * * *

He was treated as one more CCC camper, a body to be fed and clothed and worked, and not a soul which would have the ability to laugh and cry and love and be happy. All of his praise of the camp was more or less of a bravado to cover up his inner feeling. All in all, it seemed that for him life was merely going through the motions of living to keep himself alive, but no-one cared whether he was dead or alive, and he knew it.[10]

The students generally found the inner life of the camp to be lacking in direction and productivity. Here were two groups, CCC and college, vastly different in manner, appearance, and even speech—yet so alike underneath. For their part, the campers exhibited varying degrees of wonderment, callousness, and despair, and they were not quite sure how to accept the proffered hand of fellowship. On their side, the college boys became aware of their own reflections as mirrored by the enrollees.

Many of the Dartmouth students did not fail to get the point. They saw that they, too, were suffering from the disease of over-isolation and segregation. Many of them were eager to lend their help in bridging the gap between the CCC and the college. However, lacking any tangible means, it was difficult to know where to begin. The college community as a whole was not aroused to the necessity of helping a few boys in a remote CCC camp. Too many other problems appeared more pressing. And so a few students did the best they could, exchanging visits, and trying to foster a real fellowship. But it seemed a long way to go. . . . and there was not much time for the journey.

* * * * *

In March, Davidson and Huessy learned that the CCC was preparing to abandon the Sharon "side-camp." Davidson attempted to prevent this, and at the same time tried to arrange for the Department of Agriculture to take over the camp for experimental purposes. This campaign represented the first real effort to get such experimental work under way. Davidson and Huessy both felt that a practical program of making improvements in the CCC could be conducted at Sharon, and that the camp would provide a testing ground for new ideas.

Below, Davidson describes the elaborate bureaucratic maneuvers entailed in trying to achieve this experimental status for the Sharon camp:

> This morning I gave a full description of the situation at the Sharon camp to Paul Appleby, who is chief assistant to Henry Wallace. Appleby was very enthusiastic, and sent me to Mr. Stauber, one of the top men in the Land Use Coordination Office, and Stauber thinks that the collaboration of the local people in planning the use of the camp labor force is an important suggestion; he (Stauber) suggested that I talk the Sharon situation over with Fred Morrell, who is head of the Forestry Service, which has charge of the Sharon camp. Stauber suggested a joint conference next week with Morrell to see if the camp cannot be held, and if it cannot be designated a special experimental unit to try out the idea of using camp labor to help save the communities from disintregration. Appleby sent me also to Mr. Eisenhofer, who is, I believe, head of the Land Use Coordination Office, and Eisenhofer arranged for me to see a Dr. Bush Allen, early next week. Allen is in charge of the whole pyramid of planning committees (from county to nation) in the department. Eisenhofer thinks that Allen should try to incorporate our broad viewpoint into the general thinking on agricultural planning. Undoubtedly, some of these men from the Department of Agriculture will want to come up and see the situation 'on the ground' before very long. But I feel fairly sure that the Sharon camp will be considered by all the Agriculture people as a very important thing to keep going, as an experimental unit. Since I have the implicit backing of Secretary Wallace (through Appleby), I will not need one single bit of encouragement from my own (CCC) office.[11]

And several days later:

> Today I had lunch with Stauber and Fred Murray (Assistant to the Chief of the Forest Service). In general, Stauber is sold on your idea of a flexible labor force turned to different kinds of work. But at present, as you know, camps are given by the CCC, not to the Departments of Agriculture and Interior, but to *bureaus* of these Departments. Each bureau is jealous of its sphere of influence, and so we have Forest Service camps, Soil Conservation camps, Reclamation camps, Wildlife Restoration camps, etc., etc.; but we have no camps which perform integrated work, such as you suggest. Now, I believe I have 'sold' the Department of Agriculture on the idea of using the camps to save

disintegrating communities, and to do various kinds of work, according to an integrated plan, *but* the chances of saving the Sharon camp are lessened because of the fact that it is a forest camp, and the Head of the Forestry Service (Morrell), who has a bureaucratic interest in seeing that only forest work is done, happens to be the Agriculture Department representative on the CCC advisory council. I believe that the Agriculture planners will take over the idea of turning CCC labor to various kinds of work, but I will have to depend on Appleby to save Sharon. . . .

Another difficulty is that integrated social planning is only in its first stages: one county in each state (Chittenden in Vermont) has been chosen for the demonstration of integrated governmental planning (using all the departments and bureaus concerned), but there is a lack of plans. And CCC labor could never help the farmers on their farms; there would be a tremendous howl, and there would be too much pressure, I believe.

Stauber suggested that I ask you to submit a brief report on the locality, emphasizing the types of work which need doing, and which could be done by CCC labor. If you could present good reasons for a particular set of projects, then there would be something concrete to go on. As it is, I think Stauber will use the idea, and let it seep into the scheme gradually, but I think he will avoid a tangle with Morrell by 'forgetting' the Sharon camp. Moreover, if you could give me an idea of the work which needs doing (in addition to the road), I could talk more forcibly with Appleby next week.

I had a short talk with McEntee yesterday, and I believe he will be in favor of a flexible labor supply, once I get the opportunity to explain it to him. But then he will have to fight all the bureaus. I am inclined to believe that we will need the President's help, eventually, since the present law may not allow such a flexible program as we desire. But at present, the main thing is to get the actual experiment going at Sharon, and for this reason, I hope you will try to set down a specific program of works for the Sharon 'side-camp'; then, I may be able to induce Appleby to issue an order setting up the experiment. In any case, your idea has started percolating in the Agriculture Department, and will have real results, unless the bureaus defeat the coordinators. . .

P. S. I *must* learn how to do things *with* people; it's often better to *get around* red tape than to try to cut it. I hope to achieve a lot by making friends with the several excellent and influential people in town who believe as we do. We are not lone wolves—except in the CCC. Because of the organization of the Corps, I expect to be able to do quite a few things, by dint of my rapidly widening circle of contacts.

Here we have seen something of the intricate workings of

bureaucracy. The strategy of Davidson, who was learning how to find his way through the labyrinth of Washington politics, was to get the Department of Agriculture to take over the Sharon camp by one means or another.

However, he did not have enough "guns" at this time, and the urgency of setting up the experiment was not apparent to enough government officials to induce them to take the necessary risks. Furthermore, there had not been sufficient development of the local scene in Vermont to prove such urgency. This was the weakness of the Davidson campaign. It was true that the economic problems of the communities around Sharon were dire, but the power of the local people had not been well organized, nor were they articulate, as individuals. It was impossible to write up a program of works, and have the required amount of local opinion behind it in so short a time. There was also serious doubt as to whether the Vermonters would subscribe to such a program if it were formulated.

Professor Huessy understood the situation, and had indeed been instrumental in bringing it to the attention of the governmental agencies through Davidson, but their combined efforts were not yet strong enough to initiate any action. In addition, Davidson was just beginning to make himself known in government circles, and besides, he was still attached to the CCC in an official capacity. These two facts limited the steps he could take with propriety outside of his own bureau. Besides, the entanglements of the departments, bureaus, and personalities were almost too much to unravel in the first try. It was an accomplishment just to get a clear picture of a given situation, without even thinking of doing anything about it.

A month after the Washington maneuvers began, Davidson tried to interest President Conant of Harvard in sponsoring the appointment of four men from Harvard to the CCC as enrollees for nine months to a year. He also tried to get McEntee to agree to pick officials for CCC administration jobs who had spent two months as enrollees before embarking on their official duties. Neither of these attempts was successful.

In the midst of his lobbying, Davidson was sent on a New England tour of inspection by the CCC central office. He visited several camps and took the opportunity to write several letters to McEntee touching upon the Sharon question. However, in his position as a subordinate, it was difficult to do more than make suggestions. He decided that a direct request by himself to hold the Sharon camp open would be his only course, since to openly court outside officials would certainly make McEntee angry. Davidson did not want to overstep his authority to such an extent that McEntee would prevent him from doing anything at all, as long as he remained on the CCC payroll. In his memorandum to the Director, he emphasized the value of the meetings between the Dartmouth students and the enrollees, and mentioned (in a casual way!) that perhaps the CCC would contact the Department of Agriculture to work out an experimental program, with the ultimate goal of benefitting the CCC in general. He hoped that McEntee might thus be led to get in touch with Appleby, Stauber, etc., who were quite in accord with the Huessy-Davidson ideas, and who might be able to carry McEntee along with them, provided he took the first step.

However, McEntee was probably aware that something was afoot, specially since Davidson had written him in such detail about Sharon, and had also mentioned some "college professor." At any rate, he did not rise to the bait, and the procedure of abandonment of the camp was allowed to take its course.

* * * * *

At the end of May, the annual conference of the CCC educational advisers for the New England area was convened at Dartmouth College. In the course of the five day meeting, Professor Huessy gave two lectures, designed to help the advisers gain a new concept of their job. He pictured the unemployed youth as a great asset to the nation, rather than a liability. These young men, he said, need to "re-immigrate" into society through the CCC. Immigration has been America's life-blood throughout its history. Now it is imperative that such immigration be carried on *within* the country. In his words:

> The boys in your camps must take the place of the eternal immigrant of the last one hundred fifty years. Immigrants have always represented the future of America. The unemployed must now

reproduce the 'immigrant faith' which has built up this country They must reproduce the promise and fulfillment of the melting pot.[12]

Davidson attended the meeting in his official capacity as Investigating Assistant, and circulated freely among the delegates, pointing up many of the things which Huessy had said. The conference was deemed a success by nearly all who attended, and much eagerness was shown by the advisers to achieve something constructive in their work at the camps. But, unfortunately, this was not the level upon which such decisions were made.

* * * * *

Although this particular battle to save the Sharon camp was lost, many new converts (as well as some new enemies) had been made for the reform of the CCC, and Davidson had opened numerous political doors which were to prove accessible in later negotiations. He had also learned a good deal about Washington tactics.

3. Tenderfeet in Tunbridge

In June, the fall of France was still shockingly vivid in everyone's mind. The significance of traditional university commencements and diplomas paled beside the impact of world disasters. It was not easy for many of the college graduates to decide what to do. Every occupational choice seemed bound to be an interim one, and there was little hope of permanency in any enterprise. However, several of the Dartmouth graduates did make some tentative plans. One of them, Robert O'Brien, of Framingham, Massachusetts, had decided to strike off hitch-hiking into the hills of Vermont, and take his chances on what might come his way. Several of his college friends, Alfred Eiseman, Arthur Root, Louis Schlivek, of New York City, and Jack Preiss of Hackensack, New Jersey, made arrangements to follow him, after short vacations at their homes. Early in July, they received word from O'Brien that he had landed in a village called Tunbridge, situated along one of the branches of Vermont's White River. He invited them to come up and join him. So, packing their sport coats, electric shavers, and golf clubs, they headed north in Schlivek's car.

Arriving in Tunbridge, they found O'Brien at the farm of Lawrence Bowen, who was then Master of the Tunbridge Grange, as well as the town's chief electrician and plumber. It turned out that O'Brien, with a desire to know more about rural life, had simply presented himself at Bowen's door one day and asked for a farm job—at no pay. Just room and board for the privilege of learning. Bowen had been somewhat non-plussed at the novel spectacle of a college graduate offering himself as a hired man, without wages. But, seeing that O'Brien was sincere in his offer, he took him in. Like most other farmers in the area, he was desperately short of help, and even the prospect of inexperienced labor was welcome. By the time his friends appeared, O'Brien had managed to "break in" his new work shoes and dungarees, and he at least looked the part of a farmer. News of his presence had quickly spread around the town, and many were the questions the local people asked one another. "Who was this fellow? A Communist? A Fascist? A spy? Or just a college boy 'missing some of his buttons.' "

In spite of their misgivings, various farmers were persuaded by Bowen to hire the other newcomers, who were now joined by William Uptegrove, a Dartmouth sophomore who had come for the summer. Schlivek joined O'Brien at Bowen's, while the other four went to places in Tunbridge, and the neighboring town of Chelsea. Everyone plunged into the work with much enthusiasm, if not skill. For most of the "hired men," this was the first time they had been within several hundred feet of a cow, and they soon discovered that using a pitchfork all day in a hay field could make a fellow too tired to even lift his dinner fork at supper. They also found that retiring by 9 o'clock was a prerequisite for answering a 5 o'clock reveille the next morning.

Without doubt, this new life created difficulties for the farmers, as well as the boys. The "tenderfeet" had to be taught from scratch, and their education took considerable time. It was hard to explain to a person, no matter how willing, exactly how to milk a cow. It was something you had to learn for yourself, and you couldn't become proficient overnight. That went for cleaning out a bull-pen or chopping down a tree. A man could be shown how to swing an axe, but there was no guarantee that he wouldn't cut off his toes on the next stroke. On top of this, many farmers were not good teachers, and were inclined to be a little impatient with beginners' mistakes. A few were downright mean, and used their helpers somewhat in the manner of dray horses. It so happened that the experience of Eiseman and Preiss on the B. farm was something less than a picture of contentment and good fellowship. The following are some of Eiseman's notes on his two weeks at the

B.'s and several succeeding weeks at the N. farm, also in Tunbridge:

Have proved to myself conclusively—at least in this particular instance—that I am adaptable to a new environment, new techniques, to meeting and getting along with people whose existence and way of life have hitherto been foreign to me. The mere fact of physical labor, of working with my hands eleven or twelve hours a day, after sixteen years of school-chair polishing, has been healthy—mentally and emotionally.

I can see very definitely, however, that without the stimulus of contact with a group of boys educated as I am, and without the drive toward a worthwhile objective, I could very easily be lulled into the perpetual working routine of chores, meals, job, sleep, and so on.

I've always thought that Nature was a big thing. In past summers, and in Hanover, I've often indulged in semi-mystical musings. But I've been too busy at present, and too sweaty to look past the trees and the sky in Vermont. During my most leisurely job—pulling kale in the potato piece—I've deliberately tried to admire the view. Maybe I've begun to approach the farmer's simple acceptance of good and bad weather, his animals, his crops. . . . his family. It isn't fatalism, but a wonderful ability to push on past any setback or disaster, many instances of which I've seen around me in this short time.

I've sincerely been 'in' with the N. family in all of its problems, and have only pulled out of the circle when those 'college fellers' have gotten together. I've been on the job, as far as work goes, nearly all the time. I tried my damndest to swing in the same way at B.'s, the farm from which Preiss and I were fired two weeks ago for suggesting that a little more courteous treatment might not be amiss. At least town opinion is on our side, what with the B.'s reputation for losing hired men. Still, because the thing happened, Jack and I are even more definitely on the spot than the rest.

About the B.'s, while I'm on the subject—it was pretty tough. All the way round, it was the closest to living in slum conditions that I want to come. However, I could have stuck it out if it had been absolutely necessary for the reputation of the whole group. Our room was hot and stinking, the food was putrid—week-old cake, pies and bread, and the everlasting crackers and milk for supper. Sanitation just wasn't, as far as I was concerned. There was a flush toilet, Mrs. B. boasted. She omitted to tell us that the toilet was enclosed in a small, lightless, airless closet, which could only be reached by going through her daughter's bedroom; that musty corsets, underwear, and nightgowns were hung in there; that food was kept on the shelf above; that the bowl was seldom flushed. Almond (Mrs. B.'s son of twenty-one) was impossible to work with. Our presence was resented, and although we were working for room and board, somehow or other our services were measured against the value of her food and bed, as estimated by Mrs. B.

There seem to be reasons for farm degeneration and abandonment other than economic and physical erosion. The B.'s were original settlers in Tunbridge in 1763. The present Mrs. B. was a hired girl on the place for a year before John B. married her. They lived in a separate room of the house, and before John's parents died, the young people were compelled to carry out a very rigid agreement as to work and conduct, and so on, before the property was willed over to them.

John B. was a real leader in the community. Besides holding local office, he sponsored state regulations for tests of 'bangs' disease in cows, and as representative of the Tunbridge cooperative creamery to New England Dairies, he managed to find a market for locally made butter, cheese and other milk products.

Apparently, John B. thought his son should be brought up as he himself had been, but Almond was given even less responsibility on the farm. It was true that for generations boys wanted to leave their farms, and of course, since they were necessary for the continuity of a place, their fathers often made some minor concessions, or would buy them some gadget or machine to keep them amused. At first they might try the good old cure-all of hard work, if the boys got 'uppity,' but if plodding behind a pair of slow-moving oxen increased a boy's contrariness, the father might buy him an old car to tinker with, or put in a milking machine. After all, a son was a good investment, and a small additional outlay, besides the expense of feeding and clothing him, could be put down as money well spent.

So Almond was given one of the first Ford cars in the neighborhood, and in the evenings would tear it down and put it together again. Today, he drives out to the pasture in his '35 Ford. His mother has encouraged him to enter a nation-wide tractor contest, and he takes time off to attend demonstrations and meetings, and to parade a mass of literature, buttons, and badges before the hired hands. And everything is alright with Mrs. B. who directs operations from the front porch. With the aid of a mariner's long brass telescope and a stentorian voice, she can easily broadcast how much work the neighbors are getting done cross the valley and put the pressure on her own family.

The change from the B.'s to the N. farm was certainly as revolutionary in a different way, as coming to Tunbridge originally. I had been afraid, until recently, and I am sure that these rough notes reflect it, that I could only see the blackest side of things. On this farm there are four people: Mr. and Mrs. N., fifty and forty, respectively, a very lively, beautiful six year old daughter, Holly N., and Mr. N.'s father, eighty-six, who, I think, is the oldest inhabitant of the town. They all work together. The old man, 'lame' and deaf, is only disagreeable when he isn't permitted to help out, or when his health is questioned. He still mows by hand a little, works in the garden, cleans and waters the horses, shows me little short-cuts. Glen N., while not too pleased with his lot as a farmer—I think there was once some talk of his owning a dry goods store—is a good father and husband, is very patient with me, and has the ability to make most of our work very pleasant. He dabbles in politics—Republican, of course—but doesn't seem to be more than an errand boy for the local branch of the machine. At first he was suspicious of our intentions as a group coming in here, and was shocked when I mentioned connections with a German professor whose name he could not pronounce. Until I gave him the answer he wanted, he probed, in what he believed to be a very subtle manner, as to my racial and religious background. He is very tolerant, he says. But such suspicions as these are to be expected, and we've watched for them and met them very well so far.

The point is that Glen N. needs somebody like me, or my equivalent—a willing laborer, not necessarily skilled, who can afford to work for just board and keep, or whose living arrangements will be managed by some outside agency. If I hadn't been available at this particular time, he would have had to exchange services with a neighbor, which, while in itself a good traditional form of cooperation, would have put him further behind than he is.

Glen needs to be yanked to his feet, and his wife is trying very hard to do it. She is the most intelligent and the most courageous person I have met in Tunbridge. Admitted to me the first day that she used to be the old maid aunt in her family; she is Glen's second wife. Born in England, well-educated, she taught school around here for perhaps ten years, still teaches Sunday school, and is president of the Tunbridge home economy club. If there is any community assistance to poorer families, she leads it. She has founded the equivalent of the P. T. A. to assist the local school. She works very hard around the house, and before I came she used to do heavy work in the fields, although she is quite frail. I don't think her husband thinks of her any more as a person, but just sees the work that she can do. He forgets that she had the first Caesarian operation in the neighborhood to have her baby, and that she needs a little recreation and more fun, never having had much of either.

The most wonderful thing about this family is the daughter, Holly. The old man reads to her and tells her stories of old Tunbridge. Glen takes her berrying, lets her sit on his lap while riding the horse-rake, wants her with him while he hays. Mrs. N. is an extraordinarily sensible mother. Though Holly is her life, she can be severe with her, and insists that she make herself useful. They all feel that, because of the child, any struggle and sacrifice can be worthwhile, and they're not just grubbing in the dust.

All the rest of the Tunbridge group, as they came to be known in the area, had similar experiences. Recovering from the first impact of their new life, they found that the present Vermonters bore little resemblance to the colonial pioneers of either fact or fiction. The locale was probably the same, and some of the buildings and stone walls were authentic. You could even uncover a few examples, among the inhabitants, of the storied virtues of courage, hardihood, and love of independence. But looking beyond the clean, white cottages of the summer residents from the big cities and the rapturous prose of the travel folders, one could see that here was a region in decline. The little-used meetinghouses and town halls, the sparse congregations at church, the mildewed rafters of abandoned farms, all emphasized that the best days had gone. There seemed to be at least two people over sixty for every one under twenty. Tunbridge once had a population of around two thousand—now it was about nine hundred. Those who were left tried to carry on, if for no other reason than the tradition of generations. Even a few weeks on the farms made this whole picture vivid for the Tunbridge group. Meeting together in twos and threes on week-day nights, and as a whole group on Sunday afternoons, they exchanged accounts of their experiences and mulled them over. A couple of the boys had been interested in the effects on Tunbridge of a proposed flood control dam, one of a number of such dams which the United States Army Engineers had been planning for the White River tributaries. In spite of the fact that the local citizens were opposed to such a dam, on the grounds that it would wipe out a good share of the remaining valley farms by raising the water level of the stream, this didn't strike home as the real issue. It was obvious that unless a nation, a region, a state, a village could replenish its human resources faster than they were lost, its survival was impossible. In Vermont, the losses were far greater than the gains. Rural New England had for many years sent her young people to colonize and invigorate the new West, and now she could not compete, in size or in wealth, with her offspring.

Large numbers of the new towns and cities in Ohio, Iowa, Nebraska, and Illinois were named for their New England counterparts. But there the similarity ended. Many parents whose sons and daughters struck out for the new frontier never saw them again.

And yet there were still those left in Tunbridge who could remember some of the "better days." For a long time they had seen the downward slide and had been powerless to stop it. By good fortune, the Tunbridge group met one of these men soon after their arrival. His name was Nathan Dodge. He was a tall, spare man, with white hair and a Yankee profile. Like many Vermonters, he had lost his teeth early in life, but unlike the many, he disdained the use of artificial ones. As the boys grew to know Nate Dodge, his goodness, honesty, intelligence, and capacity for leadership amazed them. Here in this sleepy town was a man of stature, whose slow speech and quiet dignity were in the Lincoln mold. Nate Dodge became intensely interested in the boys and the spirit that moved them. He recognized that the infusion of new blood into the community was of signal importance. If nothing else, the people were reacting, and the Tunbridge group gave them something to talk about. However, it was more than that. These boys, coming voluntarily, were replacing with living bodies the shadows of those who had long been gone. Some of the other farmers could feel it, too, but it was not easily expressed and Vermonters are not notoriously verbose. Yet Nathan Dodge could see the spark, and he was determined to help fan it. The Tunbridge group found him to be that person in town to whom they could talk with most confidence. Throughout the weeks of haying and milking and cutting wood, the interplay of ideas and contacts between the Tunbridge group, Professor Huessy, and Nathan Dodge was fermenting, and soon, like a yeast, it began to rise into definite shape.

The boys had established contact with Professor Huessy, whom some of them had known while at Dartmouth. His home at "Four Wells," in Norwich, Vermont, became the scene of many of their Sunday gatherings. In these sessions, Huessy listened with interest, and encouraged them to continue their efforts. He was similarly close to Davidson and his Harvard friends, and thus occupied a central position between the two groups. Although each group was doing different work, Huessy knew that their integration was inevitable, since they were each exploring a different aspect of the same problem—the conservation of human resources.

Meanwhile, the CCC camp at Sharon, which had been the initial meeting-ground between the Dartmouth students and enrollees, was now officially closed. Most of the equipment was removed and the camp was, to all intents, abandoned. However, this abandonment was, in a sense, a piece of good luck, because the facilities were not assigned to any specific use, and could therefore be listed as "available."

* * * * *

As the Tunbridge group worked and learned about rural Vermont, the Harvard men had pursued their own course. Enno Hobbing had gone to Wyoming and had quickly adapted himself to the demands of forestry and fire-fighting. He soon became a group leader, and was one of the best-liked members of his company. George Phillips had enrolled in a camp in Plymouth, Vermont, birthplace of Calvin Coolidge. James Lanigan, who had graduated with Davidson the year before, had taken a job on his own hook as an educational adviser in the CCC. He now quit his job in disgust, after trying vainly to buck the entire organization for half a year. After leaving, he sent a letter of criticism of the CCC to Washington, and the President had somehow seen it and had been much impressed. Lanigan temporarily took a job with the Wages and Hours Administration in Boston, but later transferred to Washington, where he was destined to be of great future assistance to Davidson. Having failed to keep the Sharon camp open, Davidson himself saw that his usefulness in the CCC organization had ended, and that he would be freer in movement and expression if he resigned. However, Davidson did not want to precipitate an open break with McEntee, and he did not actually hand in his resignation until early in September, 1940.

As the summer went along, the Dartmouth and Harvard boys began to get acquainted with each other. The Tunbridge group visited George Phillips several times at his Plymouth camp. They also corresponded with Hobbing, who was, of course, out of reach in Wyoming, and they saw something of Davidson during his sporadic visits with Huessy at Norwich. In trading opinions and ideas, it became clear to everyone that the work in Washington and the work in Vermont had direct connections. The Tunbridge group supplied the necessary local base of operations, which could be pointed out to the Federal officials. It provided the concreteness which had been lacking during Davidson's first attempt to keep the Sharon camp open. Furthermore, the presence of Phillips and Hobbing in the CCC ranks maintained the important linkage to that service. Consequently, all the elements of a union were present.

* * * * *

It should be noted here that during these summer months of 1940, the boys secured the support of three valued and sincere friends. One was Dorothy Canfield Fisher, famous writer on Vermont and its people, whose deep-rooted affection for her state and its welfare drew her into immediate sympathy with the Tunbridge group. Although her health was delicate and her activities numerous, she was anxious to give her time and energy to helping where she could. Not the smallest of her contributions was the mere fact that she identified herself with the boys and their objectives. This support aided them immeasurably in combatting the numerous suspicions and doubts about their activities which many Vermont people felt. Her personal integrity was accepted without reservation, and if she was "for" something, why that was enough proof for a good many Vermonters.

At this time, the nationally known Dorothy Thompson adopted Vermont as her home state. She had bought a farm at Barnard, and was now spending as much of her time there as she could. A woman of vitality and intelligence, her newspaper columns and magazine articles exerted considerable influence on American public opinion. Strangely enough, she had originally met Professor Huessy in Breslau, Germany, back in the early 1930's but had not seen him since then. Dorothy Thompson had public spirit, as well as insight, and she soon perceived the many evidences of economic decline and human despair in her new home town. Learning that

Professor Huessy had lived in Norwich for several years, she visited him, both to renew an old acquaintance, and to find out what, if anything, was being done to revitalize life in the region. Huessy told her of the work in Tunbridge. As she listened, her enthusiasm grew. She was convinced that the boys were on the right track and she determined to assist them whenever and however she could. Pressed as she was for articles, lectures, "deadlines," and conferences, she nevertheless gave the Tunbridge activities a high place on her schedule. She offered hospitality of her home to the boys on many occasions, and kept abreast of what they were doing and thinking. From then on, she was one of the group.

Last, but certainly not least, was the backing given by Mrs. Roosevelt. Long known, and often criticized, for her interest in youth activities, she became another friend "in deed." Through their parental connections, Davidson and Lanigan were able to get in touch with her, and she invited them to Hyde Park for the Labor Day week-end. This was a perfect opportunity for them to tell her what they had in mind with respect to the CCC. She had probably already heard about some of Davidson's work, and may have seen Lanigan's report on his experiences as an educational adviser. A summary of the Hyde Park visit will follow shortly on a subsequent page.

The gathering of this influential outside support had an accelerating effect on the unification of the Harvard and Dartmouth groups. In a series of long and earnest meetings the plans and strategy of future campaigns were jointly mapped out. For operational purposes, the existing division of labor and function was deemed excellent as it stood, but it was felt that the united effort had to be directed toward a specific and desirable goal.

The Vermonters were not interested in platitudes of speech or in monetary doles, and neither, it seemed, were many of the Federal officials, especially in the Department of Agriculture. It was decided that fresh initiative to reopen the Sharon camp should come from the local communities, rather than have it offered from Washington. This reasoning proved most sound, since the traditional independence of Yankee farmers, plus their inherent dislike of "Washington fellers" in general, would have made them automatically hostile to any Federal proposals. Although it may now strike us as curious, the very idea of politically combining rural New England Republicans with urban New Deal Democrats did not seem at all absurd at the time. If anyone thought that this was an incongruity, he certainly did not mention it. Perhaps this was because the Tunbridge group had become quite acceptable to the communities, and thereby provided an effective bridgehead. The boys had not wilted on the farms, but had actually increased their strength of body and of purpose. Their baptism was successful, and with it came new confidence in themselves, plus some well-earned respect from their employers. In addition to their farm labors they had participated in church suppers and square dances, and had attended church regularly. Arthur Root had even preached a sermon one Sunday in the absence of the local minister.

As plans developed, it was agreed that the town of Tunbridge alone was too small an entity to enter into any rapprochement with Washington. Furthermore, most of the surrounding towns were in much the same economic and social predicament, and their inclusion in any comprehensive program was an advantage. Using Tunbridge as a base of operations, the boys began to meet leading farmers and businessmen in nearby Chelsea, South Royalton, South Strafford, Sharon, Randolph, Bethel, and Hartford. Nathan Dodge, Edward Flint, manager of the Tunbridge Cooperative Creamery, and Lawrence Bowen arranged many of the introductions, and lent the weight of their presence and opinions to the discussions. The citizens of these surrounding towns were generally receptive. While several of them always remained uncertain about the exact nature of the aims of the Tunbridge group, the quality of the backing which the boys had in Tunbridge usually converted them to at least lip-service. Once this verbal sanction was gained, the next step was to mobilize these people to *do* something.

* * * * *

The Sharon CCC camp was, as we have noted, closed, although it had not yet been dismantled. The Harvard and Tunbridge groups now decided to try to re-open Sharon on an experimental basis, with the impetus for this action to come from the communities. This was to be the limited objective which the boys wished to achieve. In order to explain the idea to the Vermonters fully and impressively, a mammoth (for Tunbridge) rally was planned to which all the people from the surrounding townships were to be invited. This step was in keeping with the old traditions of town meeting. It was the best way to get a large number of people together to reach a common decision. From the beginning, everything was to be "above board" on the Vermont scene and there were to be no undercover maneuvers. The reason for this strict integrity was that there had already been much vague talk among the citizens about "work camps," and "CCC boys" and "college professors." This vagueness and gossip, had been the constant source of many fantastic rumors about the Tunbridge group. The boys were willing and anxious to stand on their record, and they believed that the rally would certainly clear the air and establish their good faith. So a joint statement was drawn up of their aims and experiences. It is worth repeating here because it states, honestly and simply, the history and purposes of the Tunbridge group:

REQUEST FOR A HEARING

Tunbridge, September 11, 1940

To Citizens of Vermont:

Most of you who receive this invitation have heard of a proposal to establish a work service camp at the abandoned CCC site in Sharon. Most of you have also heard that interest in this idea, and plans for acting on it, have been initiated by a group of six college boys working as hired hands on farms in the Tunbridge area. Five of them have just graduated from Dartmouth this past June; the other is in his third year. This statement is written by these boys in an attempt to make clear why they came to Tunbridge and how they became devoted to the cause of establishing the model camp. We realize that especially in times of war and crisis people naturally hesitate to trust others who are considered outsiders. And our hope in writing you this is to tell you our story, briefly and truthfully, from beginning to end.

No one reason brought us all to Tunbridge. Some of us had studied problems of flood control and wanted to continue this study by work on some specific project. At the suggestion of Mr. Phillip Shutler, Vermont State Planning Commissioner, who visited us at Dartmouth, we planned to make a report of the effects of the proposed Tunbridge dam on the life of the town. Others of us simply desired the experience of farming, feeling that such an experience, quite for its own sake, would make for a healthy and interesting summer. All of us got our places on the farms through the help of Lawrence Bowen, Master of the Tunbridge Grange.

But regardless of why we came, our plans were all alike in at least one respect. None of us looked beyond the summer, none of us expected that we would be in Tunbridge today. We are here today because, coming from four years of classroom work and out of city homes, we were unable to foresee just what life on a farm would mean to us. For the whole summer we did the chores, we pitched hay, we helped at odd jobs, we had fun learning to square dance at the grange. For the first time we felt the thrill of getting close to the land, of building our bodies, and of sharing the good times and the worries of the sturdy folks of the Vermont hills. And because we shared this life so fully we began to see it in a different light.

Through our work we made our friends, and from our friends we came to see that our work was much more than simply the means to a healthy summer or a chance to study flood control. Work was much needed. Our work was important to the farmers with whom we lived. Moving off the highways into the back hills, talking to the folk, we learned of the tremendous need for labor in this area, labor to improve rural roads, to build and repair houses and barns, to do painting, and to work on the farm itself. We were six. We might much better have been sixty.

College men from the city, who had never before done manual labor, worked and lived with Vermont farmers, and both groups enjoyed a profitable experience. Because we actually lived this experience together, because it came to us first-hand and unexpectedly, it seemed much more real and much more important than any of the original plans that brought us here. And through talking over our life here with local citizens and with one of our teachers at school, we came to realize how the benefits of our experience, both to us and to the townsfolk, could be ensured for the future on a much greater scale.

We learned that whereas there once used to be a thriving CCC camp at Sharon, it had finally been closed down. The official reason was lack of work projects, when really there was work crying to be done everywhere. We learned that farmers around here had little regard for the CCC because this camp had spent its time on wasted and unnecessary projects. In addition, the townspeople and the boys in the camp had little contact; each group distrusted the other. Under such conditions the camp failed to help either its own boys or the region in which they were working.

Our Proposal, therefore, is:

1. That the government reopen this abandoned camp.

2. That instead of having only the poor and unemployed in the camp, there be boys from college, factory and farm; in other words, boys from all walks of life. Why? Because in America we do not believe in separating rich from poor, section from section. Because in America, regardless of wealth, religion, political opinion, we all want to live together in peace and prosperity. And because as young people, upon whom rests the future of American freedom, we are willing to bear the hard labor and sacrifices required to serve our country.

3. That these boys in the camp, instead of working merely in state or national forests, building so many picnic grounds, be a labor force to work in the towns surrounding it, - on the roads, on maintaining schools, on farms, on all needed community projects.

4. That this work be directed by the communities themselves.

We believe this plan to be practical. The camp already exists. The equipment is already on hand. Wages will be paid from regular CCC funds which are already appropriated. There would be no local expense involved in running the camp.

We believe that such camps will be duplicated throughout the country, but that they cannot be duplicated without first trying this camp, on a smaller scale, to learn from experience. We think, further, that this is a way to preserve and to extend the values of democracy by building loyal citizens and by making every community a stronger and happier place to live in.

This is what we want to talk about at our Rally on September 25.

Will you come and hear for yourself?

Alfred Eiseman
Robert O'Brien
Jack Preiss
Arthur Root
Louis Schlivek
William Uptegrove

This statement was mimeographed, and several thousand copies were distributed by hand throughout the area. Whatever else might happen, the rally would not fail for lack of good publicity.

Careful attention was given to the program. Jack Preiss was chosen chairman of the meeting, and Arthur Root was to give a short speech as spokesman of the Tunbridge group, emphasizing that it wanted to be of further service to the local people. Enno Hobbing, on leave from his Wyoming camp, was selected to speak as a CCC enrollee, and to express the wishes of CCC members to become valued members of the communities in which they were stationed. Then Nathan Dodge and Ed Flint, as leaders of the community, would tell why they were supporting the project. The main address of the evening would then be delivered by Dorothy Thompson, who would point out the national implications of the proposal. Music was to be furnished by the town band. The climax of the rally would be the mass signing of a petition to the President urging authorization of the new camp. Dorothy Thompson had volunteered to deliver the petition in person.

* * * * *

While all these preparations were going on, Davidson and Lanigan had their Labor Day meeting at Hyde Park with Mrs. Roosevelt. They informed her of the impending rally, and also presented some specific suggestions in writing for improving the CCC. They described the low morale and poor leadership now found in the camps. They said that the college men now in the CCC could provide a nucleus for a demonstration and training camp, which would test new methods of training and leadership development. They recommended to Mrs. Roosevelt (as they had some months before to Appleby and McEntee) that the Sharon camp be made available to the Department of Agriculture for these general purposes. This first camp would then attract other young men of high caliber, and would be an initial step toward an adequate personnel training program. It would be a staff training center, providing equal advancement for all enrollees exhibiting technical ability and qualities of leadership. Finally, they suggested that a Federal advisory committee be formed at once to study the personnel problems of the CCC and to work out some solutions (among which they hoped would be the Sharon camp.) Among those proposed for the Committee were Paul Appleby, about whom we have heard; Wayne Coy, Assistant Federal Security Administrator under Paul McNutt; James M. Landis, then Dean of Harvard Law School; Harold Lasswell, of Yale Law School; and Professor Huessy, of Dartmouth. As Davidson's nominees, these men could certainly be counted as sympathetic to the Sharon idea. All of these descriptions and suggestions were drawn up into a single memorandum to be submitted to the President.

The net effect of this interview upon Mrs. Roosevelt was extremely important. She now had a clear idea of the entire project, and she had become acquainted with the actual individuals involved. Her affirmative reaction to Davidson's visit was most heartening, and the Tunbridge group now felt that if they could elicit a positive response from the local citizenry at the rally, the Washington end of things would be in strong and capable hands. If, for any reason, the boys failed in Tunbridge the hopes for the experimental camp would probably be squelched for good, for the fate of Davidson's CCC reform was also in the balance. The night of September 25, 1940 was vital—and everyone knew it.

4. The Rally

Some of the events of that day were interesting, and will bear repetition.

Dorothy Thompson had been invited to the Noyes' farm for supper on the evening of the rally. Previously, the news of her prospective appearance in Tunbridge had set the people agog for days in advance. Members of the Ladies Aid swept out corners of the town hall which had been undisturbed for years, and arranged carpets and flowers on the stage. Through the efforts of Lawrence Bowen, an electric amplifier was rigged up to carry the proceedings out into the street, on the remote chance that there would be an overflow crowd. The band put in a few extra licks of practice, and members of the Orange County 4-H club got dressed in their Sunday-best to act as ushers. Regardless of any other outcome, this was surely going to be one of the biggest social events to engulf Tunbridge in a long time.

* * * * *

As word of the Tunbridge project had been propagated throughout the country by Miss Thompson, Mrs. Fisher, and others, the boys received a steady stream of letters from many people and organizations, asking for information, and offering services and monetary support. If at all possible, each one of these inquiries was answered, although no money was ever accepted. One of these incoming letters was from a certain Edward Holton James (no relation to the William James family), who asked, innocently enough, for data about the project. He was answered in some detail, and the date of the rally was mentioned. An immediate and emotional reply from James came in the next mail. He called the boys "heroes" and offered to sleep in a hayloft if necessary just to be with them for the rally. His "Yankee blood was stirred," he said, and he rapturously offered the prediction that "we will all soon be on the march together." He then sent a telegram on September 24th, announcing his arrival the next morning. His second letter had given a clue as to the type of character he was, and his motives were all too plain. He was out to build up an army of storm troopers. As if there weren't excitement and worry enough, there was now this ticklish problem of dealing with a fascist-minded bigot, who might very well ruin the whole meeting by jumping up and giving a speech of his own.

Most of the preparations were completed on the morning of the 25th, when E. H. James made his appearance. It had previously been decided that Arnold Childs, a Dartmouth graduate who had joined the Tunbridge group in August, should take James in hand for the day to keep him out of the way and to prevent anyone from thinking he was a supporter of the Tunbridge project. Shuttling between Hanover and various points in the White Mountains, Childs performed a classic diversionary action, including a detailed inspection of every building on the Dartmouth campus. It was learned later that James had given him the full treatment, and had urged that everyone be outfitted with red tunics and black patent leather boots.

Dorothy Thompson arrived in the late afternoon, and was escorted to the Noyes' farm for dinner. Her appetite was excellent. Not so the other members of the party, who were suffering from varying degrees of stagefright and anxiety. Miss Thompson broke the sometimes oppressively long pauses in conversation by recounting some of her experiences as a correspondent in Europe, and by engaging Mrs. Noyes in spirited talk about domestic affairs. As the meal dragged on, Eiseman, Preiss, and Root, who were also present, were becoming more and more anxious to get down to the town hall. Finally, under their none too subtle prodding, the drive to the village was begun a good hour and a half before the scheduled start of the rally. A quarter mile from the hall, a continuous line of parked cars appeared on either side of the road.

These led directly to the front of the hall itself, where a crowd of about twenty people were clustered about the entrance. Going around to a back door, Miss Thompson and the boys entered the building looking incredulously at each other. Inside the hall was an amazing sight. Every inch of space was occupied, including the seldom-used balcony. People lined the walls and jammed the aisles. Even the wings on either side of the stage were filled, and a few spectators were perched on ladders outside the open windows. More kept coming, and the crowd fanned out across the road, and overflowed onto surrounding lawns. Many went back home when they saw the hopelessness of getting inside. Word soon flashed around that both George Aiken and Ralph Flanders, opponents for the Republican Senatorial nomination, would make an appearance and would support the Tunbridge petition.

By any yardstick, this proved to be the largest gathering, except for the annual Tunbridge Fair, that any of the old-timers could remember. Ed Flint later made the straight-faced claim that after the festivities were over, the measurements revealed that the balcony was three inches nearer the main floor than it had been before. At any rate, the meeting would not fail for want of attendance.

Thus fortified, the chairman got things underway a half hour ahead of time. The crowd received the speeches with considerable interest, in spite of the universally cramped conditions. Some jokesters claimed that they heard the entire show over the loudspeaker system while seated on their porches half a mile away. Mr. Flint was in especially good form, and told some local anecdotes which shook the building with laughter. After Miss Thompson's keynote speech, which she delivered vigorously and with feeling, the members of the Tunbridge group circulated among the audience with the petitions. This last activity was somewhat difficult because of the congestion in the aisles, and it was further complicated by the almost simultaneous arrival of the two Senatorial candidates, who hurriedly began greeting old friends and making new ones. Nevertheless, in spite of the confusion, pens running dry at crucial moments, and the shortage of trained "petition circulators," a total of 321 signatures were affixed. It was estimated that nearly half of those present did sign, and this was an excellent percentage, considering the adverse circumstances.

When it was all over, and the hall had become normally quiet again, the boys felt tired, but relaxed. Even E. H. James had been forgotten in the rush of events. He had stared balefully at the speaker's rostrum for the entire time, but had uttered no sound. His only sign of life came at the end of the meeting when he offered a $50 contribution for "expenses." This was politely refused and the gentleman turned heel and left. He was never heard from again.

As can be well imagined, the rally was a local topic of discussion for weeks. Although many people had learned more about the Tunbridge boys and Dorothy Thompson than they had previously, a good many of them were still hazy on the broad ideals of the new kind of camp. They could readily associate the farm work that the boys had done with their own economic requirements, and some of them were familiar with the history and location of the Sharon camp. The rest of the program was still "just so many words." A lot of folks never did resolve their doubts completely, and retained their skepticism and distrust of things they did not thoroughly understand.

This problem of making themselves clear was always one of the main barriers which the Tunbridge group had to surmount. Hurdling it was even more than normally difficult because the boys frequently did not agree among themselves on precisely what it was they were after. Their own ideas and objectives were often slow in forming. Their activities were more or less on a day to day basis, at least as far as tying the work in Vermont to the Washington strategy was concerned. There were no precedents to fall back on, and paper predictions were not reliable.

For in spite of a dedication of mind and body to a common purpose—establishing the experimental camp—there was much disagreement as to tactics. This disagreement grew out of more than just a rational discussion, of a kind which might be found in a class room. In the first place, all the boys were making tremendous personal adjustments—giving up scholarships and jobs, doing strange (for them) kinds of manual labor, eating unaccustomed foods at unfamiliar hours, living with new people whose attitudes and manner of speech were different from their own, and being cut off from their accustomed environment. In the second place, there was the ever-present family pressure to come home. Many parents found their sons' activities incomprehensible, and some were vociferously angry. At best, they adopted an attitude of worried resignation, and moodily sent up packages of canned sardines and woolen socks.

The internal group conflicts were of the most harrowing type; but, in a sense, were the most rewarding. For the boys learned to respect each other as fellow workers, *regardless* of opinions expressed. Everyone acted within the framework of the joint cause, no matter how spirited the debate. The lesson being learned was that no true unity could be born without trial and adversity. They discovered a new sense of "family," in that any two individuals might be arguing fiercely one minute, and presenting a solidly united front to any outsider the next. This was the same sense of loyalty which is bred in armies under fire, and it served notice that the boys were on no picnic or camping party.

The disputes centered chiefly around emphasis and methods. The Tunbridge group felt that the work in Vermont was the main strength to be built up and preserved. They believed that too much energy was being sacrificed in dealing with the Washington bureaucracy. But the Harvard group felt that the larger goal of CCC reform was the primary consideration, and that Tunbridge, although important, was simply one manifestation of a larger movement. This dichotomy of approach was a constant source of friction and irritation at meetings, and it seeped into the personal relationships. Yet each side did exert a powerful influence on the other, and both were consequently saved from their own prejudices and short-sightedness. It wasn't that either group was wrong. It was rather that both were right. One side was always a check and balance on the other, and usually after the smoke had cleared away a sound course of action would result. This was a kind of give-and-take democracy which did not claim to be perfect or unemotional. It stemmed from honest convictions and was not opposition purely for its own sake. On the other hand, the boys were never afraid of losing "face" or prestige with one another by agreeing on many points *without* a verbal battle.

We have gone into some detail on these matters on inner struggle because it is essential to realize that such struggles are an indispensable part of any group endeavor. They are usually hidden from public view, and often tend to be overlooked because they are sometimes unpleasant, but they are basic to the growth of any social enterprise. No man could have alone mastered all the buffetings of circumstances beyond his control, but as part of a group he could endure them, and eventually triumph.

* * * * *

As has been previously pointed out, there was a certain political incongruity about this whole undertaking which defied conventional analysis. Many professional politicians were perplexed by this fusion of Republicans and Democrats, and they distrusted such unorthodox deviation from the standard rules of partisanship. Furthermore, no member of the Harvard or Dartmouth groups acted from a desire for political plums or government positions. In truth, many offers of bureaucratic jobs were turned down with a positiveness which frequently left the officials dumbfounded. Here was a rarity on the American scene—a group of intelligent young men, bound together on a purely voluntary basis with no visible ties, and yet impervious to the appeal of personal profit on any grounds whatsoever.

However, the boys were realistic enough, and knew enough people of political influence to make their combined weight felt where it counted most. Yet they scrupulously avoided the furtherance of any party doctrines. It so happened that the Democratic party was in control of the government at this particular time, but *any* administration would have been approached in the same energetic way, whether it were Republican or Bull Moose. The boys functioned just as well with the Democrats on the national level as they did with the Republicans on the state and local level. The group seldom forgot the cardinal political principle that in the last analysis it was dealing with specific people, places, and institutions, and it tried to operate in this milieu as capably as it knew how. It is important to remember this non-partisan flexibility, because it accounts for a major share of the camp's political power. It didn't make any difference how a person voted politically, as far as his acceptance in the group was concerned. There was rarely any talk among the boys of "liberals" and "conservatives," of "radicals" and "reactionaries," of "workers" and "capitalists." As judged by the common definitions of these terms (which are by no means explicit) there were many shades of opinion represented in the group. This refusal to be side-tracked by labels, which later made it possible for some Vermont Republicans to voluntarily cooperate with Washington Democrats, was a strong influence among the boys themselves.

There are people, including some who saw it happen, who will still not believe that such a unique combination can be successful in modern American politics, except in wartime. On that score, the record speaks for itself. The Tunbridge project was a unique kind of political "bunny" and very few of the old-line politicians were ever quite sure how to deal with it.

Above: Tunbridge, 1940. At right Nathan Dodge. Between him and Mrs. Dodge is Eugen Rosenstock-Huessy.

Below: Lawrence Bowen, Master of the Tunbridge Grange.

5. Field Maneuvers in Washington

The unqualified success of the rally boosted the hopes of the Vermonters and the boys, especially when Dorothy Thompson left for Washington a few days afterwards to present the petition to President Roosevelt.

Several weeks previous to this, Frank Davidson had returned to Washington to prepare the ground for these new efforts to secure the Sharon camp-site. This trip had been predicated on the belief that the Vermont citizens, through the rally, would voice their support of an experimental CCC unit. His main objective was to activate the advisory committee on CCC personnel, which he had recently described to Mrs. Roosevelt, so that plans for the camp could be ready soon after the end of September. This was extremely important, because a long and enervating time-lag between the date of the rally, and the opening of the camp had to be avoided. The following letter gives an account of his strivings in this direction:

Dear Eugen,

George Phillips and I have come back here[1] in order to try to hasten the President's decision. This morning we (including Lanigan) had a half hour with Mrs. Roosevelt, and she agreed to speak to her husband tonight and urge him to sign our memorandum (which had been submitted through Department of Agriculture channels.)

Last Thursday, the President, apparently trying to adopt our plan, told McEntee to establish one training camp for 'senior leaders' and another for 'educational advisers.' Luckily, George and I persuaded Wayne Coy (McEntee's superior officer) to regard our memoranda, if they are signed, as superseding the Thursday discussion. So, if Mrs.

Roosevelt is successful tonight, we will have our preliminary demonstration camp at Sharon, and we will have a committee to plan a CCC staff college to grow out of this camp. Coy, Appleby, and Alexander (Chairman of the National Defense Commission) are eager to have our plan succeed. The committee we proposed to the President consists of these three men (who possess all the necessary administrative power) plus yourself, Lasswell, and Dean Landis.

Hoping to have definite news soon—as ever,

Frank[2]

The primary result of these efforts was the following memorandum:

The White House
Washington

September 18, 1940

MEMORANDUM FOR PAUL McNUTT

The Army is at the present time withdrawing many of the ablest reserve officers who have served in the Civilian Conservation Corps. This raises the question of the future personnel of the Corps, their recruiting and training.

I desire that there should be created in the Corps a special training agency to prepare this leadership--perhaps in one or more of the camps not now in use. I suggest that you set up a small committee competent to study the needs of the CCC and to work out a plan for recruiting and training this personnel. Your committee might very well include Will Alexander, as Chairman, together with such men as Paul Appleby, Wayne Coy, Jim Landis, Professor E. R. Huessy of Dartmouth, and Professor Harold Lasswell of Yale Law School.

(signed) F D R

At the risk of deviating a bit from the narrative, it might be interesting to dissect this memorandum and analyze it because it illustrates graphically the sort of performance which won for Roosevelt his reputation as a master politician.

The content of the memo and the seeming casualness of expression belie the care which went into its preparation. It condensed Davidson's entire CCC report into a dozen simple lines, which omitted nothing of importance. It contains not a single word which could injure anyone's feelings, no matter how sensitive. Roosevelt had a great knack for getting controversial things done in this "friendly" way. He was well aware of the real reasons why the CCC was in dire straits, but he chose to give, for public consumption, a non-partisan reason which would not offend members of his administration, and would not give his opponents anything out of which to make political capital.

In his short first paragraph, he clears the whole field for action by attributing the plight of the Corps to national defense. He then "desires" (i.e., orders) that a special agency be set up for personnel training, and adds, almost as an afterthought, that such an agency might "perhaps" be housed in an abandoned camp. He was referring, of course, to Sharon, though he did not mention it by name, and his real intent was the formation of the staff college, as recommended by Davidson's memorandum. He further suggests the appointment of the advisory committee which Davidson had requested, and in the clever phrasing of the last sentence he actually gets around to naming the men he wants (most of them Davidson's choices). McNutt could not take offense at any item in the memorandum, yet he could not help but comply with it as an order. The President had by-passed McEntee by ignoring him completely, and by treating the staff college as an entirely separate problem, seemingly divorced from daily CCC operations.

It has often been said that Roosevelt seldom made a frontal attack on a subordinate whom he desired to replace; but he was a master at making such a person impotent by isolating his job, by setting up new agencies and procedures which gradually took over his functions, and by giving him the silent treatment. He was so adept in this technique of "painless firing" that he could almost kick a man out of office, and then have him turn around and say with real feeling, "Thank you for the promotion, Mr. President." The memorandum of September 18 was a small but perceptive example of this administrative technique.

* * * * *

Shortly afterwards, Davidson himself did manage to see the President, personally, and in a half hour interview he reiterated the proposals he had already submitted in writing. The President then directed Davidson to get in touch with Will Alexander to explain his plans, and to see whether the advisory committee could be formed at once. The following was his letter of introduction:

The White House
Washington

September 24, 1940

Dear Mr. Alexander:

The President, in an interview with young Frank Davidson, instructed him to go and see you and explain why he, the President, thinks a study of a plan for a Staff College of the CCC should be begun as soon as possible. This would of course necessitate the appointment of a committee by you, or some other authority, to start the work. Young Davidson will bring this note to you, and give you any additional information that may be desired.

Sincerely yours,
/s/ Edwin M. Watson
Secretary to the President

As Davidson left the White House with this note in his pocket, the road ahead appeared bright. As in the past, however, this optimism was short-lived. It now seemed to be the intention of the CCC officials and the Forest Service to hamstring the formation of any experimental camp by calling for numerous conferences, studies, meetings, etc. The diversionary movement was designed to keep matters in the talking stage until the boys' enthusiasm died down, and until the President became absorbed in weightier matters. This tug of war between those who wanted action and those who wanted delay assumed many forms, and the advocates of the camps were frequently threatened with defeat through calculated indecision alone.

Another point, somewhat technical, but none the less troublesome, was the fact that part of the Sharon camp-site had reverted to the jurisdiction of the Forestry Department of the State of Vermont. This made it necessary to secure the support of State Forester Merrill before the camp could be re-established on state property. Since Fred Morrell, the United States Forestry Service representative on the CCC, was cool toward the Sharon project, it appeared likely that Merrill would be influenced by his attitude. It was hoped that the counter-pressure generated by the Vermonters themselves, as well as persuasion by the Tunbridge group, would be sufficient to secure state approval. However, this matter would not become urgent for at least a month, so no direct request was made of Merrill at this date.

In order to leave no relevant paths unexplored, George Phillips resigned from the CCC as an enrollee, and subsequently left for Ohio to join in the work of the Rural Resettlement Administration. This move was designed to gain some knowledge of how the Department of Agriculture was handling the problem of submarginal communities in the midwest, and to acquire some practical experience in agency field work. It was also a means of exhibiting to the government officials that *their* efforts to solve social and economic problems were being taken seriously and were worthy of study.

Davidson visited Boston again, along with Enno Hobbing, recently returned from Wyoming, in order to enlist further support in the Harvard and Cambridge area. Mrs. Greene, ever a staunch supporter of the camp idea, and of Davidson personally, arranged several interviews at her home. She again brought in Professor Ralph Barton Perry, along with Mr. Nat Sage of the Massachusetts Institute of Technology, and James Landis. These men were all most encouraging, and urged the boys to "dig in" in Vermont, where they could reasonably expect to ride out any political storm which might arise.

Simultaneously, in Washington, Paul Appleby wrote a letter to Paul McNutt, outlining in some detail, his conception of what the Sharon project might achieve. This letter was rather unusual, in that it illustrated the deep impression which Davidson and his ideas had made. It was not the perfunctory or gratuitous sort of letter which often characterizes correspondence between government departments. It was more the kind of frank statement one conscientious person might write to another on a subject of mutual interest. Here are a few excerpts:

> We (Department of Agriculture) are interested in the proposal to establish a staff school for the CCC, and I was particularly pleased to learn from Wayne (Coy) that you've been considering the establishment of a special committee[3] headed by Will Alexander to work on the proposal. We want to cooperate in the undertaking by making available the facilities of this department.
>
> In the broader implications of Will Alexander's committee, let me suggest some of the things that need to be studied. First, the kind of CCC we may all be striving for might be a sort of training ground for a representative cross-section of American post-school, pre-work youth

> rather than a parking ground for young people. Whether for defense or constructive citizenship, the training CCC could provide would make better democratic men out of a great many boys.
>
> Next we need to think about the permanent contribution of the camps to rural community life. This is a phase in which Agriculture is particularly interested. The countryside needs flexibility of works, according to seasons, and it is possible that the camps could supply many localities with a flexible work force for desirable community projects, public and private.
>
> Reconsideration ought to be given to the selection and training of staff personnel. This provides a real opportunity to get the right kind of leaders and train them in the right way. The broad problem of finding and training high caliber administrative personnel is important to all our programs, and one that our agencies are trying to meet. The camp commanders, the project supervisers, the educational supervisers should be more than technical specialists. Each should know the broad principle of conservation, and be trained in educational and administrative methods. More than that, they should be men who can transmit an awareness of American ideals of constructive citizenship, as well as skills of mind and hand. I think of no better source from which to draw such leaders than the camps themselves, once the enrollment has been reconstituted on a broad basis.[4]

Shortly after this letter was sent, although probably not because of it, McNutt appointed the committee which Roosevelt had suggested a month before, and including several important membership changes. The roster included W. W. Alexander, Chairman, Wayne Coy, Virgil W. Simmons, Floyd W. Reeves, James M. Landis, Harold B. Lasswell, and John A. Fox, Secretary.

The new committee soon decided to hold some hearings on the questions of training CCC personnel, and the formation of a staff college. Davidson feared, quite rightly, that these hearings could drag on indefinitely, and that his hard-won initiative would be lost in endless discussions and investigations. Alexander and Coy were both immersed in their own large responsibilities for parts of the national defense program, and they could not be counted on to give him much help in getting things done outside the committee room. On the other hand, McEntee and his friends, who now saw the new camp as a definite threat to their official existence, could be expected to give a good deal of attention to the task of preserving their own jobs. In appointing other committee members, Coy and Alexander had insisted that Professor Huessy's name be left off the list because they feared the political vulnerability of anyone connected with the German labor service, even during the days of the Weimar Republic. However, Huessy was designated a "consultant," which simply meant that he had no power whatsoever.

The first meetings of this committee provided some unexpected "fireworks," with numerous strategies and passions vying for supremacy. Fortunately for the Sharon project, Davidson and Hobbing had been invited to address the assembly, and to act as a source of information for any questions the committee members might have.

Before presenting the graphic and interpretive report of the sessions which Hobbing made, a few explanatory remarks about one of the committee members will make the proceedings more comprehensible. Floyd Reeves was selected presumably because of his experience in the field of administrative education, and not because he was a close friend of Alexander, with whom he served on the National Defense Commission, or because Reeves was Director of the American Youth Commission, of which Alexander was also a member. The Youth Commission (AYC) was a private organization, appointed by the American Council on Education, and it had just completed a study of some high school and college work camps, which had been operated under the auspices of the American Friends Service Committee, a Quaker group.

The man who had done most of the field work for the AYC was Kenneth Holland, who had observed youth camps in Europe and the United States for several years. The Quaker-led camps which the AYC fostered were limited as to membership, being only on the college or high school level, with no mixing of the two. They were summer ventures, lasting about eight weeks, and the campers paid from $125 to $200 for the term. Work was attempted which would be of community value, but most community relationships were primarily on the social level, rather than on the work level. These camps had been successful, as far as their limited objectives were concerned, and the AYC had supported them wholeheartedly. However, the chief criticisms of them were that they appealed only to vacationists, and that they remained rather insulated from their surroundings. Furthermore, they were consciously "educational" and there was little feeling of organic participation in the long-term life of the communities. They had more in common with the summer visitors and city campers, who would be back home and in their classrooms long before the cold weather came. In short, the AYC type of camp was certainly better than none at all, but it was a long way from solving many of the social and economic problems of either American youth or American agriculture.

The Tunbridge and Harvard groups had been in some contact with the AYC and the Friends Committee, but the basic differences in their approach did not encourage active collaboration. Nevertheless there had been no acrimony on either side, and each appeared content to go his own way. However, with the growing strength and prominence of the Sharon project, which had become a source of public interest after Dorothy Thompson's speech at Tunbridge, certain officials of the AYC began to show signs of irritation. This may have been due to a fear that the AYC could be eclipsed in its own work camp program, and to Davidson's relentless Washington campaign, which had culminated in Presidential approval of the Sharon camp.

The proponents of Sharon were full of energy, and had exhibited remarkable tenacity. They had little of the spirit of compromise which is often so highly regarded in government circles. They would not take "no" for an answer to any question, and kept searching until they found some individual or agency which would say "yes." Many people found this insistent vigor to be quite alarming, and in the case of Reeves and Alexander, there was a distinct desire to tone it down. Therefore, the presence of these two men on the committee made some kind of conflict likely.

The following is an account of the committee meetings as seen and interpreted by Hobbing:

> It was to be expected that the committee meeting would provide a real clash between the American Youth Commission and our group, but even more expected was the complete exposure of the CCC. We believed that we could urge on the committee the need for a model camp and have that camp approved on the basis of the Tunbridge experience, with Floyd Reeves as the only dissenter. We felt that the committee should be fairly narrow in its field of operations, since it had so little information at its disposal. We believed that the committee had no definite structure. We believed that attempts at 'sabotage'

would be verbal, and that no definite obstructionist program was under way.

In the main, we were wrong.

The first indication of sabotage was the news that Alexander had invited Holland to speak at the Saturday luncheon; this was simply a declaration of his adherence to Reeves. The second omen was that Fox was instructed to tear from the agenda the page containing the names of the committee and the consultants. This had its sequel later on. Omen three was the fact that the men from the CCC, Army, etc. appeared in a bunch, instead of testifying before the committee separately, under which conditions they might have made some interesting contradictions. Even so, John Fox reported at one point that the CCC men were telling more than they wanted to. Landis was evidently very effective in cross-examination.

We went to the Cosmos Club where the committee had luncheon, and Fox called us in to hear the end of Holland's speech. There was nothing in Holland's remarks that directly refuted our point of view.

After Holland had indicated that the results of his study (Quaker work camps) would soon be available, Alexander suggested that two young men who had spent some time in CCC camps would like to make suggestions. Frank discussed our objectives in entering the camps, and gave a general picture of the low morale there. Enno described the inefficiency of the work projects and the consequent lack of training and spirit. Alexander asked about the process of recruitment, and Enno described his experiences at Shoshoni, Wyoming, and the absolute lack of articulation and relationship among the people there. Simmons said only one of ten camps that he investigated was as extreme a case as we discovered. Enno replied that we had ample confirmation, and Simmons said that the truth probably was that some projects could never be interesting. We refuted this by the argument that it all depended on the camp organization, and that problems of personnel readjustment from the top would have to wait until a more satisfactory camp routine is worked out. Frank jumped in and said that to solve the work and morale problem, the model camp was essential, with its principles of useful service, cross-section of enrollees, community relations, and reorganization of daily routine.

At this point Alexander asked whether there was anything else we had to say and we continued the model camp subject. Reeves asked how many towns were interested, and we named eight. Fox read the letter from Nathan Dodge to the committee, but Alexander squelched his effort to read the Tunbridge petition. Then Lasswell, referring to the group, asked why so many fellows had made sacrifices to get this thing going. . . . Frank had introduced this note. Enno described the Tunbridge history and its benefits to the farmers in detail, and got very good attention from Mr. Simmons, very suspicious glances from Mr. Reeves. Alexander again attempted to end the discussion, but Landis spoke up and said that he had felt from the whole evidence that the CCC camps, by being allowed to do only one thing, defeated the idea of any comprehensive area plan. Enno popped up with the description of the past failure of the Sharon CCC camp precisely because of this departmentalization, and reiterated the need for such an area plan as the Tunbridge group envisaged. Alexander suggested that most of the Tunbridge services would be beyond the law of the CCC, but Lasswell replied that enough work might be left that would fall within the law. Coy said that the forestry branch alone had enough work for twenty-five years, an irrelevant statement, but it settled the work project issue at Tunbridge.

We were through, and got kind handshakes from Simmons, and Frank tried to whisper something about a general resolution into Alexander's ear, but that gentleman obviously had no intention of passing any resolution. We made sure that Holland came out, too, and he told us how much of a stir we had created, but that we shouldn't expect everything we wanted and that he hoped we would go into CCC work; he wound up with an anti-Rosenstock speech, describing him as too intellectual and too vague to be of any practical use. Frank and Enno got the impression that Holland was content to remain a consultant.

For the rest of the afternoon, the committee dug into the question of the model camp. Although this had been the first item on the agenda, it had been completely passed over until Frank had very energetically proposed it. We had thought that we would probably be asked questions on Tunbridge on the basis of what had appeared in the agenda, but it turned out that the agenda was distributed only while we were there. However, after its mention, the question of the camp was kicked around. It appeared that at least two camps would have to be set up, according to Lasswell. (This part of the account is based on Lasswell's information.) Reeves' suggestion that NYA[5] take this business over was ignored; his generally slighting remarks in the direction of Tunbridge were noted. Interestingly enough, when Landis suggested that Holland might write the personnel policy of the CCC, Reeves was the first to question his capability.

The impression of the Saturday session was that Simmons was fond of us, that Coy was on the fence, that Landis would plump for us on the basis of a moral uprush, that Reeves and Alexander were hand in hand.

Frank, Jon, and Enno had dinner with Lasswell and surveyed the situation. Reeves was sore at us for our unmeasured language and lack of judicious approach, but Simmons was quite moved. Coy and Simmons were going to be together that evening. Lasswell's guess was that in one form or another Tunbridge would go through, but it would obviously be put under some department. It would not be given to the Tunbridge group for supervision. The choice seemed to be between the Department of Agriculture and Wayne Coy. If Coy ordered McEntee to make a camp available, proper administrative procedure would require him to allow McEntee to inspect and regulate the camp. There was a grave question whether Coy could be trusted anyway. Giving it to the Department of Agriculture meant a further consideration as to what bureau chief would get it. Morrell[6] would knife it by having a senseless work project prepared. The necessity was clearly to trust Appleby, or rather to press him. He could probably not appoint a special assistant to handle the camp, but he might locate it with a reliable man. This was agreed on, and Fox drew up a tentative resolution which he would like the committee to approve. The resolution called for approval of the Tunbridge principle, and for handing the camps over to the Department of Agriculture.

* * * * *

Sunday morning the committee met at the Cosmos Club. Reeves lost his head, and described Frank and Enno as narrow, motivated by self-interest, and incapable of achieving any positive benefits. Landis flatly contradicted him.

The committee finally agreed on these points:

1). Need for a new CCC personnel program

2). Need for a personnel director in CCC

3). Tunbridge project approved in principle under Department of Agriculture

4). Selection of personnel transferred from welfare agencies to U. S. Employment Service, which shall determine whether a boy goes to NYA or CCC

5). Serious consideration must be given to office of Director of CCC

6). The War Department is to be eased out

7). Army not permitted to use camps as training ground for reserve officers, and is not allowed to make any more appointments

8). Entire salary schedule of CCC to be reconsidered

9). Provision made for enrollees to rise from ranks through the staff college to the position of junior executive in camps.

Reeves, Coy, and Alexander have constituted themselves a Washington Committee to handle problems 2 and 3. One of them, presumably Coy, is to wait on the President with regard to 5.

Landis brought up the need for firing McEntee, and Reeves followed with violent abuse of McEntee. Landis further said that the morale of the camps must be raised immediately by the research camp project, and he favored scientific selection (of enrollees) through the United States Employment Service.

After the meeting Landis told Fox that he would see this matter through, and that Frank ought to press Alexander to keep him from writing out a destructive series of regulations for the camp, as Reeves would dictate them.[7]

As far as Davidson and Hobbing were concerned, the determined opposition of Reeves was anticipated, but its vehemence was surprising, as was the apparent defection of Alexander. The latter appeared to follow Reeves' lead consistently. Reeves appeared to be trying to get control of the CCC himself through the AYC, and both he and Alexander resented Davidson's political connections (i.e. the President). The results of the committee meetings were not altogether fruitless, but the actual founding of the camp was still a long way off. The air was cleared somewhat and the Tunbridge project was specifically approved in theory. It was also valuable to learn, at this early stage, of the real feelings of Alexander, who had previously been considered a supporter of the camp.

Several days later, Hobbing had a further discussion with Landis back in Cambridge. The intentions of Reeves and Alexander were apparent to Landis, who disapproved of them thoroughly. He visualized Tunbridge as an experimental camp with an intelligent area conservation plan, but at the same time, advised kind treatment for all the committee members so that a fight would not be precipitated before the issues were clearly drawn. As a result of this advice to be cautious, matters would have remained in a fluid state indefinitely.

It was then that Davidson decided to see Dorothy Thompson, who was in Washington, and who had just visited Roosevelt. This was the trump card which had been held in reserve. He told her of the advisory committee's approval of the Sharon project in *principle,* and urged her to make a direct request of the President to set up the camp in *fact.* Without hesitation, she sent a note to the White House.

Dear Mr. President:

I have been pursuing that matter of the Sharon CCC camp, about which we spoke the other day. Today I came to Washington and spoke at a meeting of the Secretary of Agriculture and the various Bureau Chiefs, and the Secretary committed himself to the establishment of the camp. Frank Davidson tells me that Dr. Alexander's committee has recommended the Tunbridge project *in principle.*

But I have a fear that the matter may be unnecessarily delayed by the pressure of other things, and by lethargy, and that the spirit will evaporate.

Also, I have written a story, with pictures, for *Life*[8] magazine. It lacks, however, a news value to give it reason for publication. . . the opening of the camp would furnish that reason. A good human story on the CCC and on youthful enthusiasm would be excellent for us at this minute when there is so much talk of giving things back to the people. For this whole thing happens to be a people's call.

These boys, Mr. President, who have already given four months out of their young lives to this, out of sheer enthusiasm, ought to have a clear answer. If you would initial one note to Wayne Coy asking for immediate action,[9] we would all be happy and things would be set. And we ought to be *sure* to draft Professor Huessy as training consultant for the camp the moment it is set up. That would tie the camp immediately to Dartmouth College, and would establish that 'blood transfusion' between a camp and the local university, and thence across to the farmers, which would be most desirable.

So won't you initial a note to Wayne Coy, so we can get going?[10]

The effect of this note was electric. The President, about to take the stump for some important speeches on his third term candidacy, had been supported in his campaign by Dorothy Thompson. Her support was not approved by the *New York Herald Tribune,* which printed the Thompson column, and her articles had been "suppressed." She did not change her stand, however, and the President undoubtedly appreciated her sincerity and steadfastness in his behalf, especially since she was jeopardizing her personal security.

He immediately dispatched the following memorandum:

The White House
Washington

October 18, 1940

Memorandum for:

The Secretary of Agriculture,
Dr. Will Alexander,
Mr. Wayne Coy:

Please do what you can at once to open the Sharon CCC camp and go through with the Tunbridge project. Also, please put Professor Huessy in some kind of supervisory or advisory capacity in the camp.

Will you let met know?

/s/ F. D. R.

The positive tone of this memorandum narrowed down the opportunities for discretionary action on the part of the three men to whom it was addressed. There could be no doubt as to the President's wishes, and no official could now flatly reject the Tunbridge project. The only catch was that for the memorandum to be put into effect the Departments of War and Agriculture, and the Federal Security Administration had to sign a "cooperative agreement" to pool their CCC resources. This pooling was necessary to provide for such basic camp needs as food, shelter, and medical care. Both Davidson and John Fox, secretary of the advisory committee, remained in Washington to try to achieve this.

6. Internal Crises

Shifting back to the Vermont scene, we find that the month of October produced several important developments. The sponsorship committees of the eight towns which had supported the September rally now met to consolidate their relationships and to vote for permanent officers. Nathan Dodge was elected chairman, and Mr. McKenzie of Norwich, and Mr. Curtis of Sharon were elected vice-chairman and secretary, respectively. An executive committee, consisting of one member from each town, was also chosen.

The most pressing question before the meeting was the selection of suitable work projects for the camp. Most of those present were confused as to what sort of work could legally be done, as well as who would pay for materials consumed, and other overhead expenses. The most desired projects were soil erosion control and the resettlement of abandoned farms. The resettlement idea attracted the greatest interest, and Mr. Dodge outlined his conception of how it might work. First, he felt that the roads to these abandoned places would have to be improved. Second, the buildings would probably need repair, and the land would require some fertilization. The camp could supply labor for all of these activities. Such improvements should not be elaborate or extensive, but would be sufficient to give any new family a fair chance to get on its own feet. A family to settle on each rehabilitated farm would then be chosen either from among those in town who had met unfortunate circumstances, or from outside sources. With regard to these outside sources, Dodge reviewed conditions abroad. He concluded:

> America should always welcome people from Europe who can become good citizens. We can provide a home for these refugees, and the abandoned farms could be settled by them. Financial arrangements could be worked out. By this project, we would be doing something for America and for universal peace.

After this simple and noble expression, the meeting approved the resettlement project, and voted to send it to the Washington advisory committee. Each town was to make a list of farms suitable for rebuilding, and to recommend the names of good potential settlers. Mr. Dodge suggested that the owners of the old farms could either donate them to the towns, or that a corporation might be organized to acquire the properties selected.

The meeting thus gave real indications of producing a significant long-range project, and its support by the towns was something which no one would have believed possible six months before. However, there was still much to be done to put such ideas into practice, and it was not at all certain that the local enthusiasm could be sustained over a long period of time.

This matter of projects was a problem which was destined to plague the Sharon camp throughout its existence. In Washington, from the President on down, the general idea of what the Harvard and Dartmouth boys wished to do was comprehensible. They wanted to improve the CCC camps internally and they wanted local communities to share in the planning and execution of the work projects. But just how this was to be done specifically was not yet determined. The hybrid nature of the CCC itself, involving so many bureaus, committees, personalities, and spheres of influence made for much confusion. The thread of continuity and the chain of communication were often strained to the breaking point. A further complication was that the work in Vermont, with its wholly different atmosphere and method of approach had to be continuously tied in with the developments in Washington. The Vermont farmers and the Washington bureaucrats were on opposite ends of the see-saw, in the middle of which were the college men, dashing first toward one end, and then toward the other, trying to maintain the balance. The question of what the experimental camp would actually be permitted to do was not being clearly answered. If it operated under strict CCC procedure, as some Federal officials believed it must, there could be no talk of resettlement projects and work on private property, even though the administration and the operation of the camp were made more democratic. This kind of "reform" camp would have satisfied the government people because it would merely have meant an improvement in an existing agency without going outside the CCC statutes. But such a limited gain would not have been enough for the Vermonters or the Tunbridge group. They were interested not merely in revising the CCC personnel structure, but also in changing the type of work to be undertaken. Rehabilitation of its rural economy was Vermont's main problem in the area surrounding the camp, and this was what the local people were anxious to engage in. Simply changing the membership and administration of the camps would not have impressed them. Having lived in the area for several months, the Tunbridge group shared this point of view, and their advocacy of it had been largely responsible for local support. Yet such far-reaching deviations from the usual CCC work pattern would necessitate making the Sharon camp something apart from the law, either by circumventing it in some way, or through a special designation by the President. However, reasoned the Vermonters, if this is to be a true experiment, it should carry through right down the line, and after all, the work projects were the core of the camp itself. How could the idea of resettlement be proved or disproved if it wasn't tested?

In all fairness, it should be said that the timidity of those in Washington was understandable. They were not sure how far the President wished them to go in this affair (there is little evidence that he knew how far he wished to go himself), and they were always on the alert for Congressional criticism. Consequently, they did not want to get too far out on a limb for fear of being stranded in clear view of their critics. The well-known "mountains of red tape," coupled with this bureaucratic hesitancy to take bold action, were the twin crosses which anyone who dealt directly with the government soon learned to bear. The Vermont people, however, were removed from these governmental politics, and the delays and confusion were beginning to confirm their underlying conviction that the government "could never do anything anyway." Reports of the wrangling in Washington did not serve to change their minds. They had a pretty good idea among themselves of what they wanted to do, and could not understand why the Federal officials were wasting so much time.

These two opposite poles, of Washington and of Tunbridge, were strong enough to affect the allegiance of the boys themselves. Those who were in Vermont tended to take the point of view of the local people, and began to criticize the actions of those who were in Washington. The strain of working, and waiting, and trying to keep the Vermonters from throwing over the traces in disgust was wearing down their nerves. On the other hand, the boys in Washington seldom were in Vermont, and most of their contact was by letter and telephone. Moreover, the intricate game of strategy and politics they were playing absorbed most of their thoughts, since they were steering a perilous course at best. They tended to lose sight of the Vermont picture, and to give it less overall importance than the Tunbridge group felt it deserved. As a result, a serious division of feelings and opinion was taking shape, and the rifts which had their start in the discussions leading up to the rally were becoming more pronounced.

Professor Huessy, fortunately, was aware of what was happening. His home in Norwich had become the clearing house and meeting place for the entire company, and he could get a whole perspective, whereas each individual could only know what was happening in his own sphere of activity. Eiseman, Preiss, O'Brien, and the rest could not follow the Washington merry-go-round, and their lack of information made them over-sensitive. Davidson, Hobbing, and their helpers likewise had lost touch with the back hill farmers they were ultimately trying to help. They did not know how Nate Dodge and his committee felt, nor had they captured the real flavor and texture of the rural virtues they were espousing. This cleavage might have become too great if Huessy had not taken positive steps to halt it.

However, before this was done, the President's memorandum

of October 18th, to Wayne Coy, had given promise that the Sharon camp would be reopened in some form. It became necessary, therefore, to secure recruits from within the CCC to help make up the new enrollment. Davidson no longer had contact with the boys in his original outfit in Maryland, and Hobbing had only a few boys available from his camp in Wyoming. So, with most of the heavy summer work on the farms completed, Preiss, Eiseman, and Schlivek joined the CCC in Vermont. Their dual purpose was to live the CCC life as it then existed, and to find enrollees who would be interested in joining the Sharon camp. Arthur Root, who had been previously rejected by the CCC because of acute sinus trouble, joined the NYA. O'Brien and Arnold Childs remained on farms in Tunbridge so that representation would not be completely lost in the communities. Phillips, it will be recalled, was in a resettlement project in Ohio, where he was gathering some recruits from surrounding camps, while Page Smith, another 1940 Dartmouth graduate who had joined the Tunbridge group and had later enrolled in the CCC was doing recruiting in a camp at Garret Park, Maryland. Davidson and Hobbing remained on the Washington scene.

About this time, the President's memorandum began to achieve some concrete gains. The Department of Agriculture, through its representative on the CCC advisory council,[1] dispatched a letter to McEntee:

> Dear Mr. McEntee:
>
> The Department of Agriculture requests your approval for the establishment of a camp of approximately fifty enrollees, at the existing side-camp at Sharon, Vermont, the camp to engage in work authorized by the CCC act and outlined by the Soil Conservation Service, in cooperation with the White River Soil Conservation District.
>
> The purposes for which Agriculture desires this camp established are: first, the development of a nucleus of trained personnel for a staff school, and second, an experimental CCC camp which would be a proving ground for current and future proposals. Agriculture hopes through operation of the camp to assist materially in meeting the need for long-range planning and long-range training essential to the Corps as a permanent and integral part of the governmental and social structure.[2]

The remainder of the letter dealt with supply functions, methods of payment of personnel, and various food and medical services to be furnished by the Army under Department of Agriculture supervision.

McEntee waited several weeks before giving his answer, and inquired specifically into what the project plans were. He well knew that the Agriculture people were flirting with such ideas as resettlement on private farms, and he also knew that they would never propose such ideas bluntly, especially since he had the power to veto them.

During this "waiting period," Alexander's advisory committee finally made a request of Professor Huessy, as consultant, to give his views on what should be done about the work service in the United States. His reply in part was:

> American youth is educationally overfed, and vocationally undernourished. The United States must allow youth an active, autonomous, and spontaneous experience of citizenship. Such an initiation into society is especially needed by the college youth.
>
> In any army, even in wartime, the soldiers spend three quarters of their time waiting. The army wastes time, and work is always done there ineffectually. Whereas the army stands and waits, the work service *performs*. It delivers the goods 'here and now.' It either does a good job today, or it will never do one tomorrow. However, although the army cannot be a model for a work service, a still greater disaster would befall the CCC if it were handed over to social workers, educational advisers, or a civil bureaucracy. At present the CCC camps are an appendix of the army; boredom, playing cards, loafing are the result. Three members[3] of the Tunbridge group who serve in a CCC camp at this moment report that from eight in the morning to four in the afternoon, every day, the problem is how not to work, and from four in the afternoon until eight the next morning, it is how not to do anything else.
>
> The key to a solution is in the hands of the college men all over the nation. These boys are today turned out by the millions into job-hunters. But if they can see their way into a group enterprise and a field of spontaneous group action, in the lull between college and marriage, and if their individual shortcomings could be checked by the solidarity of such a group, then a serious achievement could be asked of them which would furnish self respect and real life experience.
>
> Today, November 6, fourteen young men are waiting to be allowed to do something. They have offered one year of service to their country.

They are not salaried, like myself or you, and so they cannot afford to wait indefinitely. Their availability ends after six months, of which six weeks or more have already elapsed. Their example can only bear fruit if, by June 1, 1941, tenfold or a hundredfold their number have been stirred to follow their examples.

If your committee can set in motion a process that will achieve this growth, it will have added a *quality* to the CCC which its purely quantitative set-up is now lacking.

However, the danger is that a scheme of a universal character will, if improperly handled, produce not a new quality of leadership, not better regulations, not a higher efficiency, morale, and vitality, but a new group of government paid job-hunters. The pampering of youth in the Boy Scouts, Y.M.C.A., the NYA, etc., has reached a terrifying degree already. A scheme that would merely subject all underprivileged American youth to one master plan will only end in ever more boredom and frustration. It would be a great pity if the misery of youth, already faced by too many impersonal jobs, would be increased by the creation of another ten thousand well-regulated CCC offices.[4]

* * * * *

It was apparent that McEntee would try to restrict the new camp in every manner possible, if indeed, he granted it at all. In order to strengthen the hand of Alexander's committee, which was never very well supplied with precise and authenticated information, Eiseman, Preiss and Schlivek wrote a detailed account of camp life to John Fox, for presentation to the committee as a whole. It was hoped that the committee, despite the partially verbal opposition of Reeves and Alexander, could nevertheless offset McEntee's direct hostility. The following are excerpts from their letter:

Almost two weeks ago the three of us enrolled as members of the CCC. We are now in a company with a rather exceptional status in this area (first soil erosion program requested by farmers in Vermont) and we have entered it as exceptional enrollees (as Dartmouth men interested in erosion control). But despite these facts, we have not discovered anything different from the spirit of camp life than we have been told exists elsewhere. We know well that our experiences since entering this camp will have a familiar ring to you. We are sending them along simply as further evidence to support the findings of your committee.

We arrived in camp late in the evening of October 29—three ordinary rookies, as completely incognito (to the other boys) as any enrollee whose entire life history is summed up in a few details scratched on a form sheet.

The system of anonymity continued with vengeance the next day. We found there is no program of orientation in the sense of a common beginning in a big, important thing. What happened seems nonsensical when we look back on it. We were left completely alone in our barracks the whole day. We asked 'Where shall we go, what shall we do, whom shall we see if we want work?', and were told by our bunk-mates, 'Don't worry, they'll come for you as soon as they want you.' Imagine the effects such isolation must have had on the batch of Vermont boys who came in just before us and lay in their bunks for three days, waiting.

Whatever program of indoctrination exists is altogether informal and haphazard, and for that reason disastrous. Your bunk-mate who tells you you'd better get a trunk if you don't want your belongings stolen, the 'chow hog' who grabs the food from under your nose at mess, the veteran 'goldbricking' next to you on the job, the 'straw boss' who shouts 'Get off your ass,' while comfortably seated on his own, the 'rated' man who treats you like dirt until you become a privileged person yourself—all these, by their implicit attitude of nervous uneasiness, by the ever present 'chip on their shoulder' convey to you that you must follow the prearranged pattern of gangsterish toughness, or go under.

One must learn the fine art of suspicion from the very first moment. The word 'suspicion' characterizes all camp relationships. The command suspects the enrollees, the 'rated' men suspect the enrollees, and the enrollees, besides suspecting these two overpowering forces, suspect one another. Very few friendships develop. There are cliques and small groups within the one big gang, and every man is on the alert and can trust no one. One reason for this pervasive distrust is the poor beginning made in a camp career. Another, we feel is the work—or rather lack of work—that is done.

We found out a lot about this in a few days. Our records followed us into camp a day after our arrival at Danby, Vermont. We were three men who, because we had gone to Dartmouth, could not be counted in the same predictable mass as the rest of the enrollees. The C.O. called us into his office and admitted he had no idea why men of our background should want to enter the 'C's'. We told him some of our reasons—that we were interested in practical erosion control, which we are—and he, in turn, asked us to step out for fifteen minutes while he thought of something for us to do. We realized that there was nothing in the code-book to cover such a situation, but we were naturally surprised when assigned to policing the camp. For four hours we were expected to clean up papers and rubbish—a job that would have taken one man an hour, at most.

From then on the command frankly had to invent jobs for us, just as it had to for many other enrollees. Considered too 'valuable' for pick and shovel stuff, we are now being kept in cold storage until the camp moves to Poultney. At Poultney, we will be apprenticed to the surveyors, farm planners, foresters, and other technicians on the erosion control project. In interviews with two of these technicians we explained that we first wanted to do pick and shovel work, with no special privileges.

We asked the technicians what would be done to insure satisfactory relationships with the surrounding communities. We were told that nothing would be done unless *something went wrong.* Well, something has already gone wrong at Danby. A few weeks before our arrival, some town girls were badly 'roughed up' when they came to camp to see a movie, and the morning after we came, two enrollees were apprehended for stealing a 1940 Buick. Holding a hearing to clear up the details of an attempted rape, and the clapping of two bewildered car thieves into jail would seem an exceptionally tardy and distorted way to build a cooperative community spirit.

Likewise, when we asked if they were concerned with the broad economic and social effects of their work, the technicians confessed they saw very little beyond their own specialized jobs. Theoretical overtones were to be handled by the educational adviser—that is, if anyone would take the trouble to perform this task. At present, there is no educational adviser assigned to the camp.

To come back to our daily experiences, after our 'policing' was completed we were assigned to the camp wood pile. Here was gross inefficiency, slackness, and boredom. The CCC enrollee on the job uses all his energy and inventive skill in trying to do the least amount of work. On the wood pile, perhaps one man out of ten will work for a few minutes, but will soon join the rest who are smoking, swearing, tumbling about, and lying on the ground. No one is present to show the boys how to saw, chop, or pile wood. This condition of carefully cultivated inactivity exists throughout the camp.

The disciplinary system used by the commander is one of watchful waiting. The business of discipline from above is all right as far as it goes; it can very capably maintain cleanliness, good order in the barracks, and excellent meals. But when it is not balanced by educational and spiritual leadership, it must inevitably insist on petty obeisance to the law, and then verge over to dictatorial tyranny. We have seen something of this, too, for with us, as with every enrollee, the symbol of authority is the regulation Army pistol that faces us when we line up before the 'C.O.' on pay day.

In our camp there is no recreational, as well as no educational program. Just because this is a temporary camp is no excuse for this gaping hole in the life of the enrollees. After trying to burn up time all day at his despised job, he returns to his barrack and is faced with five more empty hours. It is little wonder that there is no rest, reading, or writing—no real fun or song. The blank haze of after-work hours is only punctuated by fighting, gambling, pay day drunks, and boasts of various 'adventures.' A 'rec trip' to Rutland is just an intensification of these basic things, with the added possibility of temporary satisfaction. The CCC boy who comes from South Boston to a camp situated in the hill country of Vermont is still a slum kid lounging around a city street corner. And the Vermont boys who are here never think of the camp as home or a place they have come to 'work out'—rather, this is an opportunity to 'winter over.' In an amazingly short time Vermonters pick up Boston slang and lose life-time working habits.

This is what it all adds up to—there is no unity, no spirit in the camp as a whole. The day, the week, the month are put in isolated compartments which are never drawn together by anyone. The enrollees' horizon can only be the whistle for work, end of work, chow, 'rec trip,' pay day, or week-end leave. There is no consciousness of purpose or a sense of striving for direction on the part of either the individual or the camp as a whole. . . . .[5]

* * * * *

Some mention has already been made of the difficulty and friction which were developing among the members of the Tunbridge group and the Harvard group. Such difficulties were now penetrating into the intra-group and were further evidence of the increasing pressures and tensions on each individual. Arthur Root had gone to an NYA vocational camp in Waterbury, Vermont. His letter to Huessy captures very well the kind of mood in which all the Tunbridge boys found themselves. For they were beginning to feel the effects of the very events and forces they were helping to create:

Dear Eugen,

This was originally meant to be a long, narrative, and critical letter when I set out to write it almost two hours ago. But until a minute ago, I didn't have the opportunity or the energy to write even a single word. Instead, I have been dictating, to the charming fellow who occupies the lower berth of our double-decker, a most ardent love letter. Little does he know my deficiencies on that score; but, desirous of sending a letter to his love in 'college man's language,' he jumped on to my cot just as I was going to write you. He is now, after lingering on my every word for almost two hours, copying his 7-page declaration of his affections.

Since I tried to recapture the times when I came near to writing such a letter, and since I tried to do the job my friend here expected of me, I am now almost exhausted—but at peace!

Now I haven't been at peace for a long time, almost a month, but especially since the outbursts of bigotry and narrowness I met with at the Larkin's[6] some time ago. I confess, as I said before, that during the summer I built a romantic image of the farm and the rural community Romantic as my notion may have been, it never reached the proportions of an illusion. Therefore, I was never disillusioned, only saddened—saddened by the utter lack of breadth and vitality in the towns, by the petty vanities, jealousies, gossip, by the sluggish politics and complacence. Yes, I say this, tho' I have loved the past few months as I have never loved any similar time period, or any other experience. But after four months, I felt I had enough. I wanted a little more time and opportunity for my own personal whims—reading, letter writing, thinking, idling, solitude. The never-ending series of work - chores - politics - plans - worries - work . . . . . was beginning to wear me down. I was becoming 'selfish.' In addition, we had our own inner group troubles, just among Bob, Jack, Bud, Al, Arnie and myself. Carelessness about community relations, about promptness in our own dealings, hot tempers, and so on were all annoying to us, even tho we usually ended any upheaval with a reaffirmation of mutual concern for the group . . . .

And so I came here with no trepidations and lots of expectations - expectations of experience that will help our camp, and of experience that might help restore my lost vitality. This, the NYA camp has done in the short time of three days (showing that I really wasn't feeling too bad anyway).

It must be added that I am enjoying the camp despite its faults. Three days have passed and the director has not yet made an appearance before the whole group! Nine-tenths of the boys don't know his name. The result is mental chaos - especially the first two days. No routine explained, no hopes engendered, confusion as to what to do and what not to do, and not knowing whom to ask. A tremendous opportunity is thus missed to make a group spirit, a camp solidarity. The administration just assigns work, and the fellows, not understanding, complain. They don't want to be cleaning the grounds, they say, when they came to learn mechanics, carpentry, etc. Already there is talk of leaving. And all day today the most persistent topic of conversation was whether there would be permission to take the week end off. Everyone looks forward to the week end. One fellow says, 'I guess I can bear it if I look from one Saturday to the next.' Only what they learn in the shop interests them, and that's why they came. All other work is obnoxious - a necessary evil.

They are generous, kind, cheerful, honest (for the most part) - really good guys. What worthy citizens of mankind they could make! Please write me, at length if possible. I feel so like conversing.

Regards to Mrs. R-H
Arthur[7]

How similar were these two letters from Danby and Waterbury, although each was written without any knowledge of the other!

* * * * *

The chief political unknown at this date was whether or not Roosevelt would be elected for a third term. If he did, it seemed reasonable to hope that final clearance of the camp would be forthcoming soon thereafter, especially if Dorothy Thompson intervened again. Davidson wrote Huessy that the final draft of the cooperative agreement between the Department of Agriculture and the CCC had been completed and distributed to the proper authorities. Mrs. Roosevelt had also voiced her hope that things would soon be settled, and had indicated of talking about the Sharon camp at an NYA meeting in New York. McEntee was now in a position where he would have to give a specific answer. If he said "no," the alternative would be to have Dorothy Thompson urge the President to order the CCC to accept the arrangement. This would be a last resort.

Then, on November 14th, McEntee replied to Agriculture's request in the affirmative. However, he did not do so without important reservations, and it doubtless would have been more prudent to eliminate some of these reservations before accepting his offer. But the pressure to *do* something was imperative, and it did not seem as though the project could survive another round of frustration and delay. The result was that McEntee's only real concession involved transfer of administration of the camp from the War Department to the Department of Agriculture. In all other respects, such as work hours, projects, pay, and equipment it would "have to comply with the law and regulations governing the Civilian Conservation Corps." The camp was now officially granted, but its status was far from independent, and there was little doubt that McEntee meant to keep hold of the reins if he could. When this limited approval was received, the Department of

Agriculture promptly called for a meeting with some of the boys to set up the organization.

The government officials in charge were Roy F. Hendrickson, Director of Personnel of the Department, and Ralph W. Olmstead, Assistant to the Undersecretary. These two men showed genuine interest in the project from the very beginning of their association with it. They believed that the first task was to formulate a structural plan with regard to camp supplies, finances, and membership, with emphasis on the choice of a commander, or leader, whoever he might be.

However, these matters of organization, especially with regard to the commander, had never been fully resolved by the Harvard-Dartmouth group. Everyone was sure they wanted as much freedom from rules and restrictions as possible, but there was little conception of the services and procedures required to supply the physical needs of the camp. The boys were perfectly willing to leave such "details" to supposedly routine channels. But the main thorn was the problem of command. The Tunbridge and Washington groups had always functioned without any designated leader. This was a result of natural evolution, and a division of labor according to talent and preference. It suited the boys well, but to the Department of Agriculture this situation gave the appearance of anarchy. Yet, even if the *idea* of a single commander were to be agreed upon, the actual choosing of an individual would be more difficult. None of the college boys wanted (or dared to want) the top job because it would always foster awkwardness in his relationship with the others, and the possibilities (now realities) of friction were manifold. On the other hand, the imposition of a total outsider might cause still more resentment and distrust. The process of picking someone who would be acceptable to the boys, the Town Council, and the Department of Agriculture was sure to be a complicated one.

While most of the Tunbridge group were seeking recruits from the CCC and NYA, and Hobbing had gone on a farm in Chelsea, Davidson stayed in Washington a good part of the time. Speaking generally for the group, he tentatively agreed with the Agriculture people on the necessity of a single commander. When the rest of the group were advised of this, a series of angry meetings were held and the whole business of command was discussed from many angles. Professor Huessy advocated *no* commander, at least for the time being, so that the camp could grow in its own way and find its place in the community. It could be governed, he felt, by leaders elected from the group, alternated frequently, and functional responsibility could be divided among several men at a time. The majority deemed this to be the best course, and Hobbing left for Washington to convey the decision to Davidson. Davidson, meanwhile, had specifically proposed John Fox, former secretary of the Alexander committee, as commander, and had asked him to take the job. However, Fox declined, feeling he would be of greater value as a liaison officer between the camp and the various government agencies. In such a position he could get things done for the camp by following them up personally, instead of waiting for regular channels. As a government employee, he knew that a good friend of the camp in such a strategic position would be priceless.

As soon as Hobbing arrived in Washington, he and Davidson discussed the "command" question thoroughly, but could reach no conclusive answer. They next met jointly with Hendrickson and Olmstead, who asked a series of preliminary questions about Vermont farm economy, CCC experience, etc., to get the background of the camp. Getting down to brass tacks, the matter of rules and regulations was reviewed, and Hendrickson believed that despite the narrowness of McEntee's authorization, there would be sufficient flexibility on this score. Olmstead remarked that this was still a CCC camp, and that modification, not a new creation, was the objective at Sharon. The boys did not see eye to eye with this viewpoint, but they had to agree to operate within the present set-up, as far as funds and rules were concerned. They now realized that there had been too much haste in accepting McEntee's shrewd terms. Furthermore, Olmstead would not countenance any formal agreements between the Department and the camp. He pointed out that such agreements were impossible since the new enrollees would be employees of the Department, not on equal terms with it, and that all sorts of administrative difficulties might result if such agreements were put on paper. "You have to trust us," he said.

Davidson then reversed his stand regarding unified command, and said he now favored a camp council instead. He was thereby expressing the ideas of the group at Tunbridge, as conveyed to him by Hobbing. This reversal of position surprised and disturbed Hendrickson and Olmstead. They believed such an arrangement would only foster inefficiency and confusion. They saw in the insistence on a camp council, in the quarrel about money and regulations, in the discussion of work on private farms, a real scattering of objectives. Their position was that they were already in opposition to McEntee simply because they had become responsible for the camp. This being true, they wanted a man in full charge whom they could trust, and through whom all arrangements could be made for camp activities. Davidson's idea of working through Fox in Boston struck them as entirely too vague. It was finally decided that the camp group should get some specific proposals down on paper as far as organization was concerned, but that the idea of new work projects should be delayed for the time being.

After this inconclusive meeting, Hobbing and Davidson again talked about "command." The possibility of finding a person satisfactory to everyone appeared remote, and yet the Department of Agriculture had shown determination that some leader must be named. Hobbing then phoned Huessy, advising him of the dilemma, which might actually block the establishment of the camp itself. Huessy, who had opposed the idea of a commander, now agreed to go along with one, since no other course remained. Hobbing and Davidson then re-visited Olmstead and informed him of their change of mind (if not of heart). This second retreat was a bitter pill for the boys to swallow, but they yielded to what was described as the "logic of the situation." The Sharon camp could no longer be considered untouchable and sanctified. It was now a governmental unit, and consequently was not the sole master of its own fate. This was a transformation which the boys themselves had not grasped, and the meeting with Hendrickson and Olmstead brought it home to them for the first time. Davidson's practicality and his closeness to the bureaucracy had made him see this before the others, but he was still ultimately bound by the wishes of the rest of the group. After their double reversal of form, Hobbing and Davidson headed for New England considerably chastened by the events of the day.

When they arrived back in Vermont, they still had to reckon with the rest of the group. O'Brien and Bagby were definitely opposed to these latest Washington arrangements. They felt that the integrity and unity of the camp would be destroyed, particularly if an outside commander were appointed. They still advocated complete freedom from regulations and restrictions, even if it meant abandoning government sponsorship altogether. Hobbing and Davidson contested this point of view, and said it would be foolish to discard all that had been achieved so far, especially since the way seemed to be clear for the opening of the camp. The "give and take" of argument waxed heavy for the next two days. Everyone was becoming more convinced of his own beliefs, and less ready to accept the beliefs of others.

At a general meeting in Huessy's home in Norwich, the three boys from Poultney came in, along with Root from Waterbury, Arnold Childs, and Roy Chamberlin, a 1938 graduate of Dartmouth who had recently begun working on a farm as a member of the group. The substance of the meeting was a review of the current situation, along with its effect on the individuals involved. There were many shades of feeling, ranging from O'Brien's almost solitary concern with Tunbridge and the *ideal* of work service, to Davidson's conviction that some sort of agreement with the Department of Agriculture on a *practical* basis was necessary. The following is a record of some of the actual conversation which took place:

Davidson: The fact that this is to be called 'Camp William James,' and that James said we should be in it, is important. The main point is that we *are* in it, and we all ought to be familiar with the facts of what we have done. Then we must be clear on principles and tactics, so that we don't contradict each other. This was our trouble in Washington.

Preiss: We have gotten disorganized before, and then pulled things together, and we can do it again.

Davidson: I have two technical suggestions. First, we should keep full records so that we not only know *what* the decisions are, but *how* they are arrived at. Second, we must improve communications among the group. I confess that I have been the chief sinner in this respect.

So far, things have been poorly planned on our end. Now the question arises as to whether we can harness our energies within a special government set-up, because the camp, as conceived by the Department of Agriculture, has definite, assignable limitations.

Preiss: For our approach, I think working through the CCC is the best course. Furthermore, we should start in the place where we will encounter the *most* resistance, not the least. Since we are bound to have a big clash somewhere along the line, let's have it right away, and establish ourselves right in McEntee's backyard. This would be more realistic than trying to set up an 'ideal' and have it filter into high places later.

O'Brien: I don't know. Yesterday, talking with Frank and Enno, I had had real doubts about whether we should go through with this at all. I remember when Jack, Al, and Bud came here to study flood control, and they found out that flood control was not the important thing. Perhaps the CCC is not important, either. I also wonder whether bureaucracy is good, even if it is well-run. I wonder if we shouldn't transfer our allegiance from this camp to a national ideal of service.

Root: In a sense you're right. I'm not for running this as a CCC camp, because that is an initial compromise of our standards. Our whole idea did not start with the CCC, but rather with individual service to the community. I know from experience in NYA that we can not base our program simply on job training. I know that the Vermont people and the college people have as poor an idea of the CCC as we do, although probably for different reasons. However, we want to reform the CCC because they have a large organization, a great physical plant, and a good deal of money. It would be foolish to disregard these assets. As I see it, our question is how can our camp improve the CCC? If we get the camp, why is it not possible, by emphasis on spiritual values, to create a new kind of work service?

Hobbing: I think we must go back to where we find social disease and eradicate it. Faith must remain without result if it is unwilling to penetrate concrete situations. If we can't do something about what we believe, then our beliefs are a shadow.

O'Brien: We may never get a chance to think of concrete situations. There is always the possibility that America is heading for a tremendous break-down. Our faith must be out of the present time and space if it is to survive.

Preiss: Then you are resigned to a possible break-down?

O'Brien: No, or I wouldn't be in Tunbridge.

Hobbing: I'm still interested in the CCC because every year half a million human beings deteriorate there. Let's not forget that.

O'Brien: We should start at the bottom, and the CCC isn't the bottom.

Schlivek: Why go to the bottom if it isn't necessary? The country has made great strides forward in the last eight years. We must avoid any break-down by preserving and fighting for present gains. My impression of Bob's feelings is that he might not be satisfied with just setting up a camp.

O'Brien: It might be a camp, or it might be simply people in a community.

Schlivek: Perhaps some of us have different aims. For my part, the fact that the government spends a lot of money on institutions as bad as the CCC is frightening. I want people with positive aims to go into this thing.

O'Brien: Maybe we cannot do anything except in the general picture of American youth.

Preiss: I still say your position leads to resignation, and it is much too vague.

Schlivek: Personally, I don't want to see a breakdown such as you mentioned. If there's going to be a breakdown we have to fight it. We have to change the administration of these ideas on a practical level.

O'Brien: The important thing to me is *not* to remain interested in CCC but to go on to something more.

Davidson: But you, with your whole heart and soul here in Vermont, should not strike out what we have seen elsewhere. What you feel here about Tunbridge, we feel about other situations.

Preiss: Bob, you feel we are too concrete and materialistic. Yet don't you see that you have to realize spiritual convictions on a concrete basis?

O'Brien: It all depends on where you start. We are starting in the CCC when we should be starting in Tunbridge.

Davidson: Don't forget, our group has a history dating back a year and a half. The CCC growth is as natural as the Tunbridge growth for some of us.

Schlivek: That's right. Some of us can look after the community, and some after the camp. It needn't be all of one or all of the other.

Root: We are trying to establish the camp, Bob, to help you do what you want to do in Tunbridge. You've got to look at both things together.

Preiss: We agree, I am sure, that our camp won't be a success unless we do enliven life in Tunbridge. This camp will be the guts of this new life, and the members will go out to do the same thing in other places.

Schlivek: Right now the CCC is the only way for us to procure food and supplies through government channels. The important thing is that we get our kind of personnel and objectives into the organization.

O'Brien: I am in complete disagreement. I don't want reform, I want to create.

Schlivek: But if reform is complete, it will be a creation.

Hobbing: Let's stop beating around the bush. As I see it, there are only two choices. Either we become farm hands in Tunbridge, or we go into the camp.

Schlivek: Yes, we have to act. We have to know where we are going.

Davidson: I want to point out that the further danger of institutionalizing the Tunbridge group, though we might create a very beautiful institution, is that we assume less real responsibility than we would in the camp. I feel that we can be decisive in the lives of many young men we meet, and I want to use this opportunity. Your conception, Bob, is more romantic than mine, and I can't for the life of me see it.

Schlivek: Personally, when I am in the CCC I get excited, and I feel something tremendous is happening. I don't think I ever felt as excited in Tunbridge as I do in the CCC. The summer was very important to me, but I felt I had sapped the value out of it, and I wanted to move on. Right now we are in the midst of a great political battle over the CCC. Action has started and we can't turn our backs on it.

Chamberlin: We can still maintain our fundamental unity. We are not going to spend all our lives in a camp. Eventually, we'll all go out into communities.

Davidson: Alright, let's review what has been said. The question is whether it's to be a CCC camp, or whether the group decides to do the job at all. I feel the CCC will be what we make it. If we do a job that's creative, then we have a good chance of success. I believe we can maintain our creativity even under certain limitations.

Hobbing: And don't forget that conditions in Tunbridge are also a limitation, just as much as the camp would be.

Preiss: Above all, I feel our physical unity is important right now. If we all decide to go into camp, then there will be unity in the camp. If we break up, our only chance for unity is destroyed. We've all been spread out, and at some point in the process we've got to get together in one place. After a while we can spread out again.

Root: I disagree with Bob strongly in his emphasis on Tunbridge. However, I do agree with Bob that the camp succeeds only if it uses its substance for real fellowship. The CCC, as it operates now, is completely different from what we want. It does not emphasize service, and it has not suggested a way of furthering such an ideal. We have to establish a camp which will help us to find the way. I am interested only in the establishment of a universal work service.

Davidson: Had I known the group's feeling of doubt about the CCC three months ago, I would have realized that whatever I did could be revoked at any step. Perhaps I wasn't really the ambassador of the group after all. But I emphasize that the consequence of withdrawal at this point is that we let our outside friends down, and we give our enemies an immediate victory. If we withdraw, a reform of CCC will not be possible for several years.

Root: But if we are going to make *any* withdrawal, now is the time to do it. We can't keep changing our minds at our own convenience.

Davidson: We're part of the CCC. I feel, as an individual, that I have an obligation to CCC and I wouldn't like to say to the people in it, 'Your lives are completely wasted. We're cutting out of society, until we can set up an entirely new organization.' If we did that we couldn't get a new Federal start for six months. We'd all be out.

Hobbing: And we'd be out with Dorothy Thompson, and all the private agencies, too.

Schlivek: We must remember that a lot of these people, although they may be bureaucrats, are still people, and they're sensitive. They must have felt we've been unbearably arrogant. If I'd been in their position, I doubt that I would have had so much patience.[8]

And so the conversation continued—arguments, differences of emphasis, varying emotions—sometimes sticking to the point under discussion, sometimes wandering far afield. The consensus of opinion, including that of the Poultney boys, who often did not side with Davidson on other issues, was for acceptance of the Department of Agriculture plan, and O'Brien remained rather isolated. But his rather dogged defense of his individuality and freedom to act was a good tonic for the others, and helped to bring a lot of pent-up ideas out into the open. Davidson felt extremely "let down." It was as if his months of maneuvering were in danger of being repudiated by his friends. The group solidarity was being given a severe test, and although nobody had advocated an open break in the ranks, such a step seemed quite possible.

The sudden culmination of this confusion, as illustrated by the Washington fiasco, and the arduous discussions among the boys, had convinced Professor Huessy that some action on his part was necessary. Therefore, without participating in the wrangling which he knew would follow Davidson's return from Washington, he had gone to Cambridge to visit the Greenes, and other friends of the camp. Upon his return, he found everyone pretty low in spirit. This was what he had expected, and it was the anticipation of it which had provided the reason for the trip to Cambridge. It was clear to him that at this moment the boys themselves were in need of rehabilitation—much more than the farmers or the CCC. In Cambridge, he had raised some funds to finance his own "project," and was now prepared to tell the group what he wished to do. Despite the paucity of their number, he said, there had already been too much personal segregation and too little joint effort, especially on the plane of fellowship. The time had passed for talks with the government on policy, and what was now required was a summing up of the intensive experience of the past four months. The group should ponder *together* the real meaning of the camp, and not argue incessantly over political and technical details. The great need was for at least two weeks in which to read, reflect, sing, and take some long walks in the woods. Only in such a group enterprise, said Huessy, can the strength of each individual be renewed for later tasks.

This proposal came as a complete surprise, but after it had had time to sink in, everyone realized that it was the proper thing to do. This was the restorative medicine which must be administered. Naturally, there were many arrangements and procurements to be made. Eiseman, Preiss, and Schlivek would have to get leave from their Poultney camp, and Root likewise, from his NYA camp. Phillips was to be called in from Ohio, and Page Smith from Maryland. Davidson was to wire the Department of Agriculture that he was "detained" in Vermont, and the men on farms in the Tunbridge area were to give notice of temporary absence to their employers. Huessy desired to use the so-called foresters' house at the Sharon camp-site as the headquarters for this fortnight. The building was a large, white farmhouse, now vacant, but which could be quickly converted for a short-term stay. O'Brien was then appointed to contact state officials for permission to use the house. Various other people were assigned the tasks of renting beds from Dartmouth College, securing cook stoves, utensils, books, blankets, and so on. All was to be in readiness by December 3rd.

* * * * *

Although a strenuous effort was made to avoid it, the question of "command" was again brought to the fore, mainly because Davidson thought that some answer would have to be sent to the Department of Agriculture, in view of their insistence that someone be put in charge. In an attempt to reconcile the factions, Huessy declared that he still believed that choosing a commander at this time was too difficult a task. The camp had no definite shape of its own, and it would be a great mistake to impose outside authority under such circumstances. The commander would have to be a spiritual, as well as a physical partner in the group, and could achieve his position only by sharing experience and friendship with the boys themselves. This would necessarily be a slow process. Huessy criticized Davidson for forgetting these considerations, and for being too willing to bargain away the autonomy of the group in exchange for the physical attributes of the Sharon camp. However, he felt that Davidson, like everyone else, was certainly not infallible, and that this entire matter was being regarded too pessimistically. His final suggestion was that Hendrickson and Olmstead should be invited up to the foresters' house during the two week sojourn. Here they could be met on "home ground," and could see the group at full strength and to best advantage. They would be re-impressed with this unity, and would perhaps change their minds concerning self-government. They would also get an opportunity to meet the farmers, who would thereby be reassured, both as to their own importance in the scheme of things, and by the evidence that the government officials were really doing something.

This course of action was agreed upon, and it was further decided to take a complete recess just prior to the prospective opening of the camp on January 1st. This would permit everyone to enjoy the Christmas holidays at home.

* * * * *

Several nights previous to this group conclave, the representatives of the local towns, with Nate Dodge as chairman, had called their second meeting. There were only four towns represented, in addition to O'Brien and Chamberlin of the Tunbridge group, and William Lowry, a Dartmouth student who had become deeply interested in the project. The local representatives were Slater of South Royalton, Curtis and Gibson of Sharon, Bowen of Tunbridge, and Lyman Burbank of Chelsea. The following is a personalized report of the meeting, as made by Chamberlin. It illustrates once again the difficulty of integrating the towns, collectively, into the camp set-up:

> Conversation was opened up by the naturally ebullient Curtis, who narrated several exciting deer-hunting episodes, chief of which was a beautiful one about a deer who ran a half mile with no internals except a heart and lungs. I didn't watch the clock, but I guess it was close to nine before we turned to the business of the hour. We were, in part, stalling for time, hoping the other representatives would come.
>
> More serious matters began when Slater was questioned about his success in getting hold of council members for this meeting. At great length he told of his conversation with a certain 'Doc' Deering, a South Royalton dentist, in trying to persuade him to be a council member. It seemed obvious that 'Doc' Deering exercised a strong influence over Slater. I may be wrong, but it is my guess that Slater placed great value on Deering's opinions, and that Deering's skepticism of our project worried him. I felt that Slater was conscious of his own reputation being tied up with this project. If it goes through successfully, he gains prestige in his community. If it does not, he will be ridiculed—and that would hurt him more than anything else. I do not wish to be unfair to Slater. I mention this (which some may regard as a product of my imagination) because I think it is important that we understand his feeling. As long as we don't let him down, he is a great friend.[9]

The formal organization of the council was then discussed, and the name, "Council of the Eight Townships" was adopted as official. An executive committee was elected, consisting of Dodge, Curtis, and McKenzie of Norwich. Someone suggested that Vershire, which was reputed to be the most run-down and depleted town in the State, be admitted as a ninth member of the Council, provided a representative could be found. Bill Lowry said he desired to bring as many Dartmouth students as he could to these Council meetings so that, as potential recruits for the camp, they could become more familiar with local people and their problems. Nathan Dodge replied that he felt this kind of relationship would be an excellent one.

To quote Chamberlin again:

> This whole discussion led directly to what seemed to me uppermost in the minds of these Vermonters. Here they were being called upon to be missionaries of the new William James camp. Yet how were they to present a convincing message if they didn't have the facts. Curtis wondered how he would approach the absentee Council members, or how he would get up and speak to his Rotary club. Slater, as we have seen, wondered how he could deal with men like 'Doc' Deering. Burbank was silent, relatively new to the whole thing. Gibson kept reiterating the suggestion that before they could gain broader support, the camp must be set up and demonstrated. Lawrence Bowen said little, only remarking that he would speak if he disagreed with what the others said. Mr. Dodge said he was anxious to discuss plans—concrete plans, such as what part the Council would have in 1) selecting the boys, 2) administrating the camp, 3) securing the proper execution of the work projects.
>
> Bob O'Brien asked him, first, what he meant by 'administering the camp.' Bob pointed out that the actual internal management of camp affairs could not possibly be run by the local people. But it *was* the local people who were planning the work projects, who were holding the properties being rehabilitated, and who were most certainly entitled to a say in what settlers would be brought in. On the matter of selecting the recruits for the camp, the nucleus of the group would be those boys whom the Vermonters had come to know in their communities. The selection of members would be in their hands, O'Brien said, and would not Mr. Dodge trust their discretion? Discussion followed.
>
> After the meeting, which was inconclusive, I rode home with Burbank, and we discussed many topics at length. On the whole, I felt the meeting was pretty much of a flop.[10]

The chronic uneasiness and lack of clarity on the part of the Council members was here again painfully evident. It had originally been hoped that as the project developed, the local people would become a steadying influence on both the camp and the government. But obviously, the Council was now groping blindly for information of the most elementary nature, and did not know what was expected of it. Their ignorance of what was going on made the members feel extremely sensitive to criticism by their neighbors, since they did not have the facts to counteract such criticism. This lag in the Council's efficiency could not endure for long without dire results to the camp itself.

*   *   *   *   *

After the group decision to spend two weeks at the forester's house, Davidson, over Huessy's vehement protests, decided he must return to Washington to "mend fences" during the week preceding the scheduled gathering date. Upon arriving in the Capital, he wrote:

> Dear Eugen,
>
> Yesterday, in New York, I had a forty minute talk with Gideonse,[11] who turned out to be a friend and former colleague of Lasswell's. Gideonse is entirely on our side, is willing to help; but he explained that Brooklyn College is so large, and as yet understaffed, that he, personally, had almost no student contacts. He suggested that one of our group give a little talk before his faculty and some students, but whoever undertook the assignment had better be prepared to repel all sorts of attacks from the Left. Gideonse described his mention of work service in his 'annual report' as a mere 'feeler' to start discussion. He regards development of a labor service as one of the chief continuing responsibilities of over-intellectualized, over-citified colleges.
>
> I was unable to see Samuel Grafton.[12]
>
> I spent most of today trying to find out where things stand, so that we will have adequate information on which to base any administrative suggestions to the White House. Olmstead wanted me to try to work things out with Morrell first, and then only refer back to himself when things went wrong. I had a long talk with Morrell, and it is quite plain that he will move no farther than he is pushed. The positive result of the day's labor is that I will have copies of Agriculture's request for the camp, and of McEntee's reply, to take along to the White House.
>
> Olmstead was re-impressed, naturally, when he heard I might see 'The Chief' this week. But he thinks the only good insurance against sabotage is to have the President direct Jim Rowe (a White House assistant) or some other intimate, to back up the project at every step. There are so many ways to delay or otherwise hinder us that we will need the benefit of continual, high-pressure support. So, in addition to having the President designate us 'Camp William James,' and allow us to change the rules, we must see that the Hendrickson committee gets full, enduring White House support. You may be sure that I will exploit to the full the Tunbridge petition.[13]
>
> Olmstead wrote you a note today which gives you the perfect opportunity to invite him to Vermont. . . .[14]

The net result of Davidson's hinted interview with Roosevelt was that it gave him nothing more than the added prestige of having seen the President, although this fact alone was a considerable asset in Washington. The interview was very short, and produced no concrete assurances about the future of the camp. The White House staff was absorbed in the task of increasing the nation's measures for preparedness, and was more concerned with actual "things military" than with their "moral equivalents."

Implementing these defense measures, the Selective Service Act, had been passed in September, 1940, and the soon-to-be-famous draft boards were being formed throughout the country. Many citizens were vigorously opposed to conscription, and had fought the Act. But it was the opinion of most of the people that a belated effort must be made to build up a strong military force. One of the authors of the Act was Grenville Clark, member of a famous New York law firm, who was prominent in the "inner circle" of Roosevelt advisers. He often assisted in the writing of important pieces of legislation which the President wished to promote. Helping to formulate the Selective Service Act was one of his more ticklish jobs.

Clark had met Huessy shortly after the latter's arrival in the United States, and they had talked about the work service long before the war began. After the present military conscription bill had become law, Huessy wrote to Clark with a suggestion that the law be amended to provide for its post-war conversion to the work camp idea. Clark replied that the Act, as constituted, was only designed as a temporary measure to meet existing emergencies, but he conceded that "it is not too early to begin thinking about a revision of the Act to put it on a longer term basis.[15] Clark envisioned a program whereby every young man would give a year of service to his government at some time between his eighteenth and twenty-fourth birthdays. Some men would go into the military establishment, depending upon current manpower needs, with the remainder, in any one year, to go into the work service. Clark's main idea was that the armed forces requirements should be linked with the *general* idea of service so that the soldiers would not be set apart from the civilian workers by anything other than the nature of their duties.

This was a most important concept, and was definitely worth striving for, but for the time being, the marshalling of military strength, through compulsory training, was the government's most pressing and immediate problem. As we shall see, the Selective Service Act was to have much to do with the personnel problems of the emerging "Camp William James."

* * * * *

In order not to lose track of what was happening in the colleges, particularly at Dartmouth, we will double back over the past half year and bring events up to date in the academic sphere. For after all, the colleges, along with the Federal government, the Town Council of the Vermonters, and the Tunbridge group, were the fourth basic element in the intricate scheme of cooperation which was designed to bring "Camp William James" into being.

Since most of the hoped-for college recruits, who were to supplement and replace those now active in the camp's formation, would naturally come from schools such as Dartmouth, Huessy had long ago tried to get the College to take an official interest in working with the CCC camp at Sharon. He wanted to give the then informal relationships between his classes and the CCC boys the sanction of College approval. This would encourage more students to participate, and would provide a perpetual source of college youth for the experimental project. As far back as May, 1940, he had written to the Administration of Dartmouth asking for this support.

President Ernest Martin Hopkins evinced his interest in Huessy's request:

> Dear Professor Rosenstock-Huessy,
>
> Your letter of May 21st has just reached me, and I am more interested in the particular subject to which you refer than in regard to almost anything else at the present time.
>
> As a matter of fact, I have been going through a good deal of mental stress recently, trying to analyze to myself whether a dollar spent on the so-called higher education of an institution like Dartmouth was as properly spent as it would be if it were donated to further development of such a project as the CCC camps. I should like exceedingly to get clearly in mind how the two projects, that of the

liberal college and that of the CCC camp, could be articulated. . . . .

Yours very sincerely,

/s/ Ernest Martin Hopkins[16]

This concern of President Hopkins at first appeared to be a hopeful sign for College recognition of the purposes of "Camp William James." But under the twin pressures of war and graduation, nothing specific was done. As the summer wore on, and the Tunbridge group became increasingly involved with government officials and agencies, the College became wary of possible entanglements in political controversies.

However, in the fall, thanks to the energy of Huessy and the widening newspaper coverage of the camp, there was a marked increase in undergraduate interest. A considerable number of students attended the Tunbridge rally, and the college newspaper, "The Daily Dartmouth," devoted a large amount of space to the Vermont scene.

Also in the fall of 1940, as part of a national plan for the mobilization of men and resources, Dartmouth had established a so-called "Defense Group" to actively promote such measures and programs in the locality of the College which contributed to "preparedness." On November 11th, Armistice Day, a group of students sent a petition to this Dartmouth Defense Group, which was composed chiefly of College officials and faculty, saying:

> We look upon the starting of this camp (Camp William James) as a real opportunity for Dartmouth to contribute towards and be influential in the beginnings of a great national activity. The liberal college may, by cooperating in this movement, help give it direction and strength, and at the same time graft to itself a new and invigorating relationship to our national life. Here is a great opportunity for Dartmouth to lead.
>
> We suggest that the Dartmouth Defense group take the following steps:
>
> 1). Endorse the principle of this camp.
>
> 2). Recommend that the College cooperate actively with the camp by allowing academic credit to students who participate actively in its work. We believe that a student should be allowed a semester of college credit for a semester and a summer at the camp.

3). Appoint a sub-committee to study what further action should be taken.

Respectfully submitted,

Robert Blood William Lowry
Jon D. LeSeur Hans Huessy[17]
William Uptegrove

Nothing came of this bold pronouncement, although it did highlight the fact that at least a few students took the Sharon project seriously. These students were looking for some means of connecting themselves with the camp without permanently jeopardizing their standing as undergraduates. But more was to occur along these lines a few months later.

7. At The White House

The opening of the fortnight at Sharon coincided with the beginning of an "old-fashioned" Vermont winter, which is another way of saying there was plenty of snow and below-zero weather. The foresters' house, nicknamed the "White House" solely because of its exterior color, did not lend itself readily to the rigors of cold-weather living. The main source of light and warmth was a large stone fireplace in the living-room, supplemented by three kerosene lamps and Enno Hobbing's pipe. The second story served as a repository for frozen meats, doubling at night as a dormitory. Into this unpromising atmosphere were thrust the borrowed beds, books, pots, and furniture which had been gathered during the preceding week. The cooking was to be handled by George Flowers, a native of Sharon, who had some experience running his father's restaurant. The boys began arriving on December 2.

Besides the expected presence of Hendrickson and Olmstead, it was anticipated that many more guests would appear, ranging from old friends to curiosity seekers who had read about the camp in the newspapers. In order to get things done efficiently, a regular schedule of work and study was drawn up. Hobbing was put in charge of outside work (snow shovelling, gathering wood, etc.), Bagby took care of food buying, Chamberlin headed the house-cleaning division, and everyone else chipped in on K. P., bed-making, handling correspondence, and pushing frozen automobiles. There were daily lectures and discussions, led by Huessy, plus research assignments by individuals on camp projects and internal organization. But the real purpose was to live together under one roof, and to experience the fellowship that comes only from common endeavor.

The best way to describe this period is to use the following diary sequence, which is based on notebooks kept by various individuals. It is believed that this form of presentation will give the most authentic picture of things as they happened:

December 3rd

There was a morning lecture by Huessy on the problem of unemployment in America. He said, in the main, that 'Camp William James' must be a reproduction of America. It is an 'opportunity' more than it is a physical entity.

In the afternoon work was done around the house and in the woods. Plenty of wood, but it's all green, and smokes like hell.

At evening discussion, Huessy announced that the Dartmouth Defense Group had contributed 50% toward reprinting an article on the Tunbridge boys written by Arnold Childs for the *Dartmouth Pictorial* magazine this past fall. Davidson reported that McEntee had written President Roosevelt protesting the formation of the Sharon camp. President sent that letter to Dorothy Thompson, who had urged McEntee's removal. Davidson also had seen Mrs. Roosevelt before coming to Vermont, and she gave camp her best wishes and the offer of her services whenever needed. Davidson's interview[1] with the President lasted *two minutes.* President thought camp was already in operation and asked how instructional plans were going.

Questions of rules and regulations brought up again, and it was agreed that Hendrickson and Olmstead should be pressed, during their visit, for a relaxation of CCC rules. All went to bed early—half the fellows sleeping with their clothes on under the blankets.

December 4th

A regular CCC detachment from Bellows Falls, Vermont, arrived today to start rebuilding the Sharon side-camp. This indicates camp is really going through. Huessy gave a lecture on relationship between education and economics. He said the problem of the 'rhythm' of the camp is an immediate one because of the arrival of the CCC boys from Bellows Falls. We must create new camp routines, and work out new regulations for ourselves. If we make our own rules then we will be proud to comply with them. But the camp will be a failure unless everyone can have the feeling that something important and new is happening.

Whole group was invited to Sharon church at 6 P.M. for supper. It was decided to attend, taking Jack's car and Eugen's. At 5:15, Eugen arrived from Norwich and agreed to go, but only after delivering a short address on the 'rhythm' of the camp. A long wait was occasioned by the appearance of some of the CCC boys who are doing the construction work. They walked in as though they owned the place, so Eugen gave them a hospitable and unmistakable welcome, to show them that they were guests. After leaving we had to push Jack's car a long way with Eugen's, until a truck came by and pulled Jack's car the rest of the way into Sharon. At the church hall, which looked very festive and pleasant, no places were set for us. Eugen thought we had not really been invited, since it appeared that the people were not prepared for us and we were only embarassing them. But it turned out that we were only late, and the tables for us had been taken down. A few men, some women, and mostly children were still there. We ate a swell meal, met a number of people, and joined in group singing. It was most enjoyable.

Council member Curtis told Art Root, privately, that many local people thought that Eugen was a spy. When Art and Roy discussed this in the car on the way home, Eugen blew up.

Outside of this, all the fellows thought the evening was a great success.

December 5th

In the morning there was a lecture by Huessy on the problem of leadership. The main gist of it was that our present-day leaders have become managers. We are pre-occupied with routine, rather than with the creation of new things. Real function of leadership is to determine what is the important thing to be done at any moment. Then the leader must identify the group with that thing and work toward its achievement.

After an afternoon of working at wood-cutting, house chores, and assisting CCC cadre on rebuilding camp, we all had supper, followed by short business meeting. There was discussion on Voorhis bill,[2] which proposed universal work service for all U. S. youth, and also on Grenville Clark's letter concerning revision of Selective Service Act.[3]

Bud Schlivek reported on prospective guests, which included Department of Agriculture people, a couple of candidates for camp commander, some Harvard and Dartmouth visitors, and various friends of the camp, such as Dorothy Thompson. Bedding situation was still to be settled. Jack Preiss offered to handle this at Dartmouth. Everybody thought the telephone rang too much, so Page Smith called the operator and told her to discontinue service. Loud cheers. Bud Schlivek brought up question of his car, which had a broken oil pump and burnt-out bearings. There was some argument over whose responsibility it was, and Schlivek said he was getting a raw deal. If group wanted to use his car, it should pay for the upkeep. No conclusions reached.

After supper, Huessy gave talk on real meaning of resettlement. He said that the New Deal had understated the whole problem by only worrying about production and distribution. This isn't the basis of our real problem, which is to find the *balance* between production and rehabilitation. The government has tried to stabilize a temporary condition in economics which cannot be stabilized. In our economy, the giving of land to settlers does not tie them to the land forever. With the first sick cow, the whole of the economic romanticism is gone. We cannot condemn a man, for instance, to have a sixty acre farm stand for his whole position in society. On the contrary, the land which the Vermont farmers received merely symbolized their faith that this was 'God's country.' The farm was the reflection, the mirror, of an internal spiritual order. It was not, of itself, the end product of life.

Following from this, we can see that the faith of a man can survive different phases of his material existence. We ourselves have been in different places at different times, and we are now in a CCC camp. This ability to change location and survive indicates that we still have spirit. If we had just worked on a farm for several months, that would have no spiritual meaning by itself. A man who no longer has the spirit to express himself in different environments is ready to die. Likewise, if we do not give a man the opportunity to express his spirit in more than one manner, then he becomes a cog in a machine.

Today this country lacks spirit because half of it is condemned to industry and the other half to farm labor. The two categories should have a chance to exchange their membership, at least for a short time. This is one of our objectives in the camp. But the people in Washington have not realized the importance of this interchange because they continually force people to be one thing *or* the other, either farmers or industrial workers.

To counteract this, there should be a moment in everyone's life when it is an honor for him to shift his role in society. This metamorphosis explains the true meaning of rehabilitation and resettlement. Therefore, we should look upon our own resettlement plans in Vermont not as a kind of economic relief, but as an honorable expression of the right of every settler to enter a new phase of his life.

* * * * *

December 6th

Worked and wrote letters all morning.

In the afternoon, the problem of the orientation of new enrollees was discussed. It was decided that we should try to keep the foresters' house as a permanent part of the camp so we can use it in our educational program. The house must become the cultural and social center of the camp. Here is where the boys join the fellowship, meet guests, and come in contact with outsiders. The house will be 'home,' whereas the barracks are only a place to sleep. It will not be easy to get the CCC boys to share in periods of study and discussion. This will take time, but it can be done gradually, if the effort is made to draw them into the circle.

The evening meeting was devoted to a survey of the matters to be brought before Hendrickson and Olmstead. Main objective is waiver of rules and regulations so that camp does not have to report back to McEntee. Weakness of our position is uncertainty as to work projects. Communities expect resettlement program to be adopted, yet this is not at all assured. In fact, Department of Agriculture probably wishes to steer clear of so controversial a project. It is a moot question whether these two groups can be reconciled. Success of camp depends on it.

Add to this the knotty and ever-recurrent problem of the camp commander. Davidson suggested we stall on this until the opening of camp on January 1st. Meanwhile, continue to look for and interview candidates.

December 7th

Morning meeting about general matters of camp organization, such as providing for democratic internal rules by elected officers, majority vote, etc. It was decided to have a religious service on Sunday, with Bible reading, and group singing.

December 8th

Had surprise visit from Lieutenant Tierney, who is in charge of cadre building the camp. He didn't know much of what was going on, and was naturally curious. Brought a captain with him who had been dispatched by Boston command of CCC to inspect Sharon. He was 'fishing' for information, too. He said CCC in Boston had no clear idea of what Tunbridge group wants to accomplish. Nobody in Washington did, either. He told of much confusion about kind of buildings required, alterations on existing structures, and so on. Army told him to get ready for a January first opening. This could probably be done, although supplies and furnishings have not come very quickly. Bad weather had hindered movement of goods, so opening could be delayed. Huessy brought up matter of our keeping foresters' house. Captain said he had no jurisdiction over that. Merrill was man to see, since State of Vermont had control.

Some discussion of supply question. Captain insisted that an army man would eventually have to administer supply set-up if Army supplies were to be used. Somebody suggested granting a sum of money to the camp to purchase supplies locally. This was vetoed as too risky. We cannot play around with food and clothing on a hand-to-mouth basis.

Captain wanted to know, confidentially, whether a new kind of CCC will cause 'unemployment' of reserve officers after the war. Said that all men like himself couldn't stay in regular Army. Huessy said supplies and routine functions might still be handled by Army, but new leadership is needed *now*. Explained idea of all kinds of boys being united in CCC. Captain and Tierney agreed this was good program. Captain gave his 'life history' as an Army man. Tedious discourse! He said he was interested in the new camp and wanted to keep track of how it works out.

* * * * *

Noted that articles on the prospective opening of camp were appearing in local newspapers, especially in Hanover, N. H. and White River Junction, Vt.

Five CCC boys from cadre came up for a few hours. They were Wendell Jacobs, from Barre, Vt., and John Brener, Ralph Dumas, Stanley Rack, and Ralph Anderson, from Massachusetts. Really nice fellows. Everyone liked them. Explained aims and purposes of new camp to them. Jacobs, Dumas, and Anderson were very enthusiastic, and wanted to stay on. Will try to make arrangements to keep them.

December 9th

Hendrickson and Olmstead arrived for big pow-wow. Robert McKenzie of Norwich, Vice Chairman of the Council of the Eight Towns, took them to lunch in Chelsea, along with some of his own group and five of the Tunbridge boys. Olmstead very interested in meeting the local people. Asked many questions about social life, economy, future of region. Relations very cordial, if not 'chummy.'

Back at foresters' house, the Agriculture people said they felt uncomfortable about the emphasis being placed on the resettlement project. They said that working on private farms was 'doubtful,' and that reception center raised many 'problems.' They emphasized compromise on objectives, at least at first. They felt camp was too vulnerable yet to engage in controversial work. Preferred to have detailed work plans coming from local people, and then sent to Washington for approval.

Discussion then turned to staff problems. No suitable commander has yet been unearthed. Department of Agriculture plainly irked at this. Hendrickson suggested postponing opening of camp until January fifteenth, so commander could be found. Huessy wondered whether the D. of A. would support the group financially from December 15th until opening, whenever it might be. Olmstead said 'no,' except as regular CCC camp. Huessy again wiggled in request to keep the foresters' house. Olmstead said he would ask U. S. Forestry Service to make request to Merrill. Hendrickson again went back to the superintendent question. Suggested we have a Soil Conservation Service or a Forestry Service man because of familiarity with camp routine. He also wished to keep his own staff people happy by giving one of them the job. Several names were brought up, but none seemed to fill the bill. Qualifications listed as 1) age—40 to 45, 2) know his particular job well, 3) have a 'human' side, 4) be able and willing to delegate responsibility. Hendrickson afraid we were looking for 'Superman.' Hendrickson agreed on need for two foremen and medical officer. Olmstead said Army should be given charge of supply, so they could not claim they were neglected.

Davidson brought up matter of CCC officials inspecting camp. Olmstead replied that clarification of status of camp was being sought from Paul McNutt, who was McEntee's boss. Probably CCC would insist on being allowed to visit camp. This vagueness made us feel somewhat uneasy. Olmstead mentioned difficulty of getting everything taken care of simultaneously. Said we must cross bridges when we come to them. Bagby asked about regulations. Hendrickson wanted to know just which regulations he was referring to. Huessy said 'two whole volumes' of regulations, and that the best way to handle them is not to have them. Olmstead countered that if camp was not under general CCC regulations, McEntee had grounds to say it didn't prove anything. Huessy asked if we could at least keep initiative on what camp did. Olmstead answered that this was one of the questions that the Washington Supervisory Committee could handle. Hendrickson chimed in that we must be 'organized' as a pressure group. Many enemies were waiting for us to make a slip.

December 10th

Discussion continued in the morning. Olmstead wanted to know if non-college boys would really get anything out of the camp, and spread the idea to other people of like background. Schlivek told of slow acquaintance process with boys in Poultney camp. Olmstead continued that he was tremendously impressed about national significance of the camp, both as to the circumstances of its beginning and its place in the minds of the public (he didn't say *what* public). Wanted to hear what kind of instruction is planned. Huessy replied that we must relate work experience to the 'whole man.' Recruits will be judged by desire to come to Sharon, not by their I.Q. Hendrickson said he had been struck by limited opportunities boys in CCC have had. He realized that every American boy should go through such a camp as 'William James.' After a little more talk, Hendrickson and Olmstead left with Huessy for Four Wells.

Mixed impressions after they left. Arthur felt they had been completely 'taken.' Davidson and Hobbing thought a lot of hard work needed to be done. There was a general feeling of relief, as if a crisis had been passed.

December 11th

Final meeting with Hendrickson and Olmstead. There didn't seem to be much more to say. They appeared glad they had come. Said just being on the scene meant a good deal, and could not be substituted for. Huessy's parting shot was that we were interested in human beings, not routines. We wanted to treat youth according to their age, not as old men. Youth is the time for kindling the spark of accomplishment. If we treat CCC boys as unemployed liabilities, we make them 'old men,' and they lose hope and confidence in themselves. H. and O. left to catch train, amid much hand-shaking and mumbling of good-byes.

After they had gone, there was a discussion about food. So far, meals had been unsatisfactory, especially during the stay of H. and O. We must remember that the CCC boys would never stand for this. Mess had really been a 'mess.' This was due to our carelessness, and not planning properly for our guests. Service would also have to be improved. This may seem like a small matter, but guests were sensitive to it. List of table rules should be decided upon before the camp opens. Otherwise there will be chaos at meals, and this would be ruinous for morale. Discipline and community spirit are essential during mealtime, if at no other. This matter cannot be neglected.

December 12th

Eiseman, Smith, and Chamberlin went on a recruiting tour of local communities to see if some Vermont boys are available to join camp. Such representation is necessary if connections with the towns are to be maintained. Statement on rehabilitation project needs to be drawn up and sent to Washington. Look into possibilities of rebuilding Vershire as an entire community project. Perhaps Dartmouth could be interested in such a reclamation. Would afford a wonderful opportunity for students to participate.

Late in the morning, Colonel Alan Hanbury-Sparrow, British friend of Huessy's, arrived. Will stay for a few days. Was in last war, and has 'stood' for Parliament. Talked with group, and emphasized idea of service, along with need to put economic value back into soil. Warned us against too much political planning and control.

Plans announced to have formal dedication of 'Camp William James' on this coming Saturday. All the sons (three) of William James have been invited, plus Mr. and Mrs. Greene, Dorothy Thompson, some Dartmouth and Harvard faculty people, and a host of local folks. Jack Preiss to be chairman, with Huessy and William James 'the Younger' as speakers. Program was outlined.

December 13th

Huessy lectured again. Stressed that people do not have to be alike to be true friends. People can be friends without even speaking the same language. Many groups in America do not have the same frame of reference. He cited the example of Hendrickson and Olmstead meeting with the farmers at Chelsea luncheon. Both groups found they could understand one another, even though mannerisms and speech were dissimilar. This gave hope of unity, for in a group, every man's differences with his fellows can be turned into assets. If each man stood alone, this could not be so. That was why people were being drawn to this camp. It appealed to the spirit of creation, and contained elements of both family and friendship. The apparent frailty of this group, its lack of structure, has been its greatest strength up to now. Camp is like an insect, which, if it loses a leg, can immediately grow another to replace it. Only a living organism can do this.

Rest of day spent in making preparations for tomorrow's dedication exercises. Everybody worked like a beaver—besides, it was a cold day and you had to keep moving.

December 14th

Dedication Day[4]

Dear Mrs. Greene,

I don't know whether this is your first report of the wonderful dedication exercises that were held here on Saturday. William and Alexander James were here,[5] and their presence really made us feel that we were the living successors to a great man. It was really an American festival—from the old, joyous Mr. Gilman and the absolutely unshakeable Judge Stone, of South Strafford, from Lieutenant Tierney (cadre commander of the CCC boys rebuilding the camp), from the Dartmouth faculty, from the softly noble William James, all came that same delight, that same confidence in this work. It was again a proof that we can reach no end of human beings, that untold numbers of men are looking for something of this sort, that we are the meaning of life to the old people of this area, that we are the spark for the young. Mr. Mattison of South Strafford, who spent 40 years in the Chelsea bank, turned to Judge Stone as they were leaving, and said, 'We were born 50 years too soon. If we were young, we'd be in this thing.' William James shook my hand and looked for words, and found them slowly, and then simply spoke, 'God bless you all.'

Our ceremony was more than we expect of ceremonies in this day. Jack Preiss spoke first, and said this living here was like a dream, and he didn't know what to make of it. Eugen told of our efforts and our hopes, our succession to the spirit of William James. 'Perhaps,' he said, 'the boys are too late, but that doesn't matter. They must do this anyway.' It was impossible to hear him calmly.

Eugen then gave our plaque, with 'Camp William James' inscribed on it, to William James, and asked him to present it to the camp formally. William James was troubled for words, for consecutive expression, but from time to time he would speak out distinctly. . . . . 'that great lesson. . . . . fellowship. . . . . unselfish service. . . . . the dictators. . . . . they'll pay.' It meant so much to him that he could not master it.

Bob O'Brien and I accepted the plaque, and we closed with our song. . . . . we had begun the ceremony with 'Nobody Knows the Trouble I've Seen.' We all joined in a buffet lunch, and until 4:30 the room was as full of spirit and warmth as any man could ask his house to be. . . . .

We do not rest on our capital. Frank, Phil, and Bob O'Brien left for Washington to see if Benton McKaye[6] will become commander of the camp. Jack Preiss and Al Eiseman are collecting data on our project. Page is in charge of the list of enrollees. Roy Chamberlin has to keep this house running. Tomorrow night we see ex-governor Wilson (of Vermont), whose land we would like to get for the resettlement project. Wednesday, we visit State Forester Merrill to celebrate his birthday, and to squeeze out of him the right to use this house for six months.[7]

December 15th

A general holiday was declared, to begin on Thursday, the eighteenth, and to continue until about the twenty-ninth. This will give everyone a chance to let off some steam, and let parents know their sons are still alive. Everybody was invited to Hackensack, N. J. for Jack Preiss' 21st birthday party.

Paid a visit in the evening to ex-governor Wilson, who is in private law practice in Chelsea. He was very cordial, and wished to help. His land, on Brocklebank Hill, in Tunbridge, is sparse in vegetation, but would be ideal to use as a reception center and to test various agricultural practices. Wilson agreed to sell 300 acres of his property at from two to three dollars per acre. The property which he will sell, together with Mrs. Noyes' adjoining 80 acres, is admirably suited to a demonstration sheep run. The land is well-watered—good open sheep country. Mr. Wilson also advised that there is an 'island' of two acres of land on his property owned by a Mr. Drohat, a former CCC official: there are two cottages on this land which can be occupied immediately by a shepherd and two farm families. The asking price: about $600 for the Drohat property, and about $600 for 300 acres of Wilson's land at two dollars per acre. A check on the tax assessment on Wilson's land revealed that the asking price was very much below the listed evaluations on file in the town clerk's office. Should expansion be desired, over the original 300 acres, Wilson would sell the other 400 acres of his holdings. This is good, productive woodland, and the price rises as high as fifteen to twenty dollars an acre. In the meantime, Wilson very kindly offered to let us draw out from the woodland plot all the wood necessary for fence posts—free.

It was agreed to send this information to the Department of Agriculture, and that it should be listed as 'Project No. 1.'

December 16th

The morning was spent making up a list of enrollees. Work on camp construction proceeding slowly. Supplies lagging, too. An opening on January 1st is now out of the question. A new liaison arrangement must be found to speed up requisitions and contacts with proper authorities. We cannot run to Washington every five minutes. The circuitous handling of Al, Jack, and Bud's status is an example. They are on leave without pay from Poultney camp, but only for two weeks. At the end of that time they must report back, or be subject to dishonourable discharges. This matter was brought to the attention of John Bowen, Morrell's liaison officer in Boston, but nothing has been done. We should not be left vulnerable in this sort of a situation. It could happen to other enrollees, with more serious consequences. If it became known to the recruits that they were jeopardizing their own position by joining the experimental camp, many would not come. Jack and Al have decided to return to Poultney before going home in order to see their recruits and to tell them of the possible delay in opening at Sharon. We must not let these enrollees think that they have been forgotten.

December 17th

Everybody began preparations to leave tomorrow morning, except O'Brien and Chamberlin, who may stay a few extra days. Spirits were generally high, both for what we have done and what we are going to do. There was remarkably little friction over the past fortnight, considering the pressure of events. There were plenty of gripes, mostly private, about food and the lack of hot water. Also some hot words about policies and tactics, but no black eyes. In retrospect, the two weeks more than fulfilled their purpose. Everyone in the group came to know the others as people. There was no brooding. Any conflicts came out into the open quickly, which was much healthier. Then too, the reception of guests, public and private, in our own 'house' gave us all a sense of permanency. If we could extend hospitality to others, then we were really a part of society, and not outcasts. The dedication of the Camp last Saturday marked the real beginning of things. We assumed shape, confidence, and above all, a concrete unity. How strange and wonderful are the creations of men—and how unpredictable![8]

8. Signs and Portents

After the dispersal of the group on December 18th, Huessy received a letter from Hendrickson, who wrote:

Dear Professor,

It was a pleasure for Mr. Olmstead and me to be your guests, and to learn more intimately of the plans and motivation of the Sharon camp—even though the interrogation, at times, may have appeared somewhat intensive.

First of all, we encountered, as I told you over the telephone Monday, a stumbling block in connection with your appointment (to the Washington Committee of Supervision for the Camp), growing out of the fact that you have not received your citizenship.[1] The Federal Security Agency Appropriations Act, under which funds for CCC activities are provided, specifically prohibits the payment of funds as salary to other than citizens. We are communicating with the Department of Justice, asking if some arrangement cannot be made to hear your petition for citizenship prior to the date Mr. Nicolls has set, June 3rd. I am very hopeful that we can arrange for an earlier hearing. I feel especially bad because of the fact that you have already undoubtedly been to great expense in connection with this project, and certainly adequate means of compensating you for expense from this time on must be found. Meanwhile, we plan to appoint you as a collaborator of the Department, without compensation, so that you may have official status.

You spoke[2] of requisitions for food, clothing, bedding, etc. and suggested 'something will have to be done immediately to allow direct correspondence between Mr. Bowen and us.' I prefer one channel of communication in order that we reduce to a minimum the possibilities of misunderstanding. I realize that in suggesting this it may seem bureaucratic, but Mr. Bowen[3] is, after all, a representative at Boston, of Mr. Morrell, and it is far better to have Bowen's line of responsibility to Morrell uninterrupted. I am sure that by communicating with me, we can move as rapidly as it is possible to do. . . . . As to the foresters' house, Mr. Morrell is proceeding with negotiations with Mr. Merrill, and I feel confident that the negotiations will be successful. If, somehow, these negotiations fail, we will ask that such a (reception) center be constructed.

With respect to regulations, our arrangement with Mr. McEntee is that the Department (of Agriculture) is to have responsibility for this camp. The Department is interested in adjusting all rules and regulations in any way possible which will be consistent with the research character of this camp. I doubt that for the research purposes involved it is going to be necessary to waive all rules and regulations. In my discussion with the boys, I suggested that this procedure be followed: indicate what rule or regulation interferes or threatens to interfere with the camp and its operation from the research, or any other, standpoint, in a communication to me, together with a simple, brief statement indicating why such a rule or regulation should be waived, and thirdly, indicating by what date such a waiver needs to be in effect. We will then attempt to obtain the waiver, first establishing here promptly who has the power to waive.

Now to some of the other points I discussed with the boys:

Selection of Superintendent: It will be satisfactory if McKaye becomes superintendent, provided he is supported in the direct line of unified command by someone who can take over substantial responsibilities in connection with the routines and many of the operating problems incident to the Camp. Mr. Klos[4] might work out very well as assistant Superintendent. The earlier the decision can be made on this matter, the better.

I discussed with the boys the willingness of the Farm Security Administration to assign a man full-time or part-time to work in connection with consideration and possible planning of the project or a community reception center. If you would like to have such a man on hand by January 1st, I will make every effort to arrange to have a good man on the job.

I will be expecting your group to send me as soon as possible the names and addresses of prospective enrollees so that I can make arrangements with Morrell for their induction, whatever such arrangements involve. You need not wait until you have the complete list—if it comes in several installments that will be entirely satisfactory. We are leaving the matter of communicating with prospective enrollees to your group.

I agreed in discussions with the boys to ask Mr. Morrell to arrange, if possible, with Lt. Tierney to stay through the month of January to handle supplies, mess, etc., and also to have George Flowers enrolled as cook. We also discussed the desirability of having an ambulance as well as a doctor on hand from the start, and I will discuss that with Mr. Morrell, and let you know soon.

The matter of foreman will be left to the superintendent. . . . .

I am sorry this is such a long letter, but this camp involves a tremendous number of details and we certainly don't want to slip on any one of them. Please communicate any matter to me promptly.

Sincerely yours,

Roy Hendrickson
Director of Personnel[5]

Huessy's subsequent inability to obtain an earlier hearing on his citizenship application made his financial situation temporarily acute, since the funds he had secured for the two weeks at the foresters' house were exhausted. The group as a whole was now almost completely without money for travel, telephone calls and the various expenses of "lobbying" in Washington. However, Dorothy Thompson helped out generously at this critical time, and in addition to sending a check, she promised to speak to the Secretary of Agriculture with reference to his support of the Camp.

* * * * *

These last two weeks of December represented a period of indecision. Progress toward solving many problems, large and small, appeared to be much too slow. There was a feeling that the Camp was about to be born at last, but there was considerable uneasiness as to just what kind of a "baby" it would turn out to be. In spite of the hopeful signs, there was a general inability to actually get things done. An example of this is Hendrickson's letter, which we have just quoted, in which he was obviously trying to be helpful. However, he only succeeded in creating a feeling of frustration and delay in Vermont Perhaps this was inevitable, and should have been anticipated by all concerned. Yet at the time it was most depressing.

As the following paragraphs will show, there remained several points of difference among the boys, the men in the Department of Agriculture, and Professor Huessy. We know that the Department of Agriculture did not relish its conspicuous position of responsibility, and that it believed the most important questions to be solved were of an organizational and procedural nature. This attitude had been made plain in all negotiations to date. On the other hand, the Camp group, and particularly Huessy, felt that the chief problems were ideological. "Camp William James" yearned, unrealistically as far as the Federal government was concerned, for complete freedom to develop in its own way and to mold its own shape. But the Department of Agriculture, which held the purse-strings, was reluctant to grant such freedom, since the consequences might become politically embarrassing if something went wrong. Thus another tug-of-war developed, with the Camp making "demands" for autonomy, and the Department insisting on "going through channels" as much as possible. There was some validity to the arguments of both sides, and it was simply a matter of which point of view could muster enough pressure to become predominant. In the past, the Camp had always been alert to the dangers of compromise with bureaucracy. This aggressive singleness of purpose was effective when dealing with outright opponents, such as McEntee, but it was now bound to have some unpleasant repercussions when applied in equal measure to the Camp's friends.

On December 26th, Davidson sent Hendrickson a memorandum briefly outlining the Brocklebank sheep-raising and resettlement project, as developed through the conversations with ex-governor Wilson in Chelsea, and the hurried research of Eiseman and Preiss. Hendrickson replied, both to this memorandum and to a further letter from Huessy relative to his insecure personal status in the Camp. Huessy had written that he wished, as a member of the yet unconvened Supervisory Committee, to have a status either equal to, or independent of, the Camp commander, who was still to be chosen. He could not accept less, he felt, in view of his own personal and financial sacrifices and his paramount contribution toward guiding the boys up to this point. Hendrickson's answer was that an official appointment could not be made until Huessy's citizenship was established, and until that time, the Department could not issue him any salary or delegate any authority. He further pointed out that the Department was purposely not taking any initiative with regard to the selection of a commander, so as to give the Camp every opportunity to pick its own man. However, he said that the Department would have to step in and choose someone if it became clear that the interests and property of the government were in jeopardy. In a simultaneous letter to Davidson, Hendrickson advised that the list of future enrollees at Sharon had been forwarded to Morrell for processing, and that the new enrollees should take over on about January 7th. He also discussed the Brocklebank project, which he felt was too sketchily presented, and raised numerous doubts as to whether such a proposal could *ever* be accomplished by the Government under existing statutes. This was further evidence that the Department of Agriculture and the Camp were still far apart in the matter of resettlement. Hendrickson went on to urge establishment of several "clearly legal" work projects for immediate use, until long-range projects could be worked out. With respect to command, he advised that since McKaye had intimated he would not take over the superintendent job,[6] he (Hendrickson) was arranging for a temporary "Acting Superintendent" to take over on January 2. This man could be replaced whenever a permanent commander was selected. McKaye would not be added to the Supervisory Committee, but could, if he so desired, join the staff of the Superintendent to help with planning the projects.

These exchanges of letters convinced Davidson that Hendrickson and Huessy did not fully appreciate each other's point of view, and that, as a result, an open conflict might ensue. Therefore, after receiving Hendrickson's letter of December 27th, he wrote to Huessy as follows:

> Dear Eugen,
>
> I received your letter about the budget and I agree entirely that we must have freedom to spend our savings and plan a *unified* budget. Your statement of the problem is important, and I am copying it to send around.
>
> *But* I think you are unfair in blaming Hendrickson and Olmstead for our present lack of free funds or clear authority. Both of them will be glad, I am sure, to let us spend even more than the average budget (for a camp) and for purposes we may indicate. But they have been handicapped by the fact that the superintendent is not yet appointed

(because we have not found or persuaded one, so far) and there is the further difficulty that the 'Committee of Supervision' has not yet met. This Committee is of our choosing and we have no reason to weaken or belittle it. The question of extra funds for education and music, of extra equipment such as a staff car, and of a paid civilian secretary for the research center might just as well be taken up by the Committee at its first meeting. I have already requested a staff car and funds for education, but the requests just reached Washington late yesterday, and if we find ourselves a bit short of facilities, equipment, etc., that is probably our fault at least as much as theirs. Due to the inevitable timing of our group's growth, we have had to postpone the listing, requisitioning, etc., for specific allowances, or even for general understandings. The CCC regulations have nothing whatever to do with the case, because Agriculture can spend its funds for this Camp, to a great extent, at its own discretion. We ought to admit that the present difficulties (which are certainly not overwhelming) are half our fault. At least at the present time, there is no reason for attacking the Agriculture people as if they were our enemies. It may be distasteful to negotiate, but you have always agreed that there is an 'outer' as well as an 'inner' front, and we will simply have to explain, persuade, bargain when necessary, to achieve our aim. I am making this statement especially strong because I think it is very important for us to keep the good-will we have built up in the Department of Agriculture. We need to concentrate on clarity of communication with Hendrickson so that he may know what we want and why we want it. The committee (of Supervision) will be of great assistance to us in this connection, and the sooner we can get McKaye[7] to say 'yes' to the superintendency, the better off we'll be, because Hendrickson will be satisfied that his chain of command has been established.

Your last letter (or letters) gave Hendrickson the impression that you were trying to 'high pressure' him. Here again, I am absolutely sure that what bothered him was not what you said, but the way in which it was said. I hope you have kept copies of these communications so that we may go over them together. Your letters often assume knowledge on the part of the reader, that the reader simply doesn't possess. Sad, but true.

I told Hendrickson that we hoped to persuade McKaye to take the job during the first days of January. Hendrickson would prefer to defer the appointment of Lawrence Bowen (as foreman) until such time as we have our superintendent—then the superintendent will have been consulted in the choice of his subordinates. This seems to me very reasonable, provided we can find a superintendent before January 3rd. If we can't I'm sure we can arrange to have Bowen taken on somehow or other, anyway. Lieutenant Tierney can be kept on, and Hendrickson will attend to that. . . . .

As ever,

Frank[8]

* * * * *

To further complicate matters, the local Town Council was again showing signs of being restive. As with any organization whose internal structure is loosely knit, and whose specific functions are unclear, the Council frequently felt that it was neglected, and that its influence was minor. The Council members still believed that the resettlement project would be the Camp's first undertaking, and much of their limited support was based on this belief. The individual members were quite unaware of the legal and political complexities involved in this project. Undoubtedly, something should have been done several months before to apprise them of the true nature of the situation. Yet their support was so tenuous that it seemed to be running an undue risk to tell them that the Camp might have to settle for considerably less than a resettlement program. Through their own experience with Sharon when it was a regular CCC camp, and through the information they received from the Tunbridge group about the CCC central organization, the local people felt that they, too, could not compromise with the old regime. When they had been asked to support a "new" kind of camp, and were told they would have a voice in its operation, they took these promises at their face value. Anything that suggested regular CCC practices, real or imagined, would not be condoned. Since community support was absolutely essential to the whole venture, the sensitivities of the Vermonters could not be handled roughly, even though they sometimes led to intransigeance. It was certainly going to be difficult to make them accept the new Camp with any basic deviations from the concept which existed in their minds. The Council members felt that they were personally "on the spot" with their neighbors, who still had many suspicions about the whole idea, and this position made them even less susceptible to compromise.

Evidence of fresh discontent on the part of the Council came in the form of two notes from Nathan Dodge, addressed to the Camp.

The first note stated that at a Council meeting on December 27th (no quorum was present) the consensus of opinion was that the Brocklebank sheep-raising project was not feasible or desirable, although no formal disapproval was voted. This action appeared rather surprising, in view of the broad resettlement plans which the Council had envisioned, and of which Brocklebank was supposed to be the beginning. Probably the underlying reason for disapproval was that the Council did not feel that it had been adequately consulted in the plans. This reasoning is substantiated by the fact that the Council gave no specific grounds for its opposition, but instead submitted a statement on policy, written by Mr. Dodge. He said that while he did not believe that a formal agreement need be drawn up between the Camp and the Council (as long as the Tunbridge group remained in "authority") he did feel that some flexible understanding should be reached by both parties respecting qualifications of the recruits, hiring a superintendent, planning and working out of projects, and fixing responsibility of Camp officials. He thought that responsibility in these matters should be divided equally between the Tunbridge group and the Council. He suggested a meeting of all concerned to discuss these matters. Dodge concluded that unless some such understanding was reached on these questions, he did not feel that he could continue as part of the undertaking.

This communication had serious implications. Unless the Council was pacified, and assured of its importance, its support would probably be withdrawn. Nathan Dodge was undoubtedly the key man in the Council, and it was important that his support be maintained. For if he resigned, the entire Council would certainly do likewise.

Huessy recognized this threatened defection, immediately wrote Dodge a long letter, and thereby assumed the role of "diplomat" in his turn. He replied in considerable detail to the points which Dodge had raised. A meeting was suggested for January 3rd, to include the Council, the Tunbridge group, and Fred Morrell of the Department of Agriculture. Huessy explained that the Tunbridge group had no official status as far as the Camp was concerned, and he stressed the point that the Council itself would ultimately become responsible for the human and economic values connected with the resettlement program. He also mentioned that the Council was already being given a full voice in choosing a work superintendent, and that several unsuccessful candidates had appeared personally before Mr. Dodge and other Council members. In the matter of recruits, the suggestions of the Council members would be most welcome, but the recruiting process would be left to the boys themselves, as much as possible. The largest part of Huessy's letter attempted to bring Dodge up to date on the political aspects of the Camp. For example, McEntee's objections were cited as a threat to the Camp's very existence. It was therefore necessary to engage in strictly "legal" work (which would preclude labor on individual farms) for the time being. In addition, the Camp should be regarded as part of a nation-wide service, and this broad perspective must be maintained. Vermont was supplying leadership in breaking new trails for community-camp integration, but there must be no feeling that the Camp was exclusively a local proposition. In conclusion, Huessy called attention to the primacy of human values above everything else, and said that since Mr. Dodge concurred in this belief, he felt they would always have a basis for agreement.

Simultaneously, Huessy dispatched a letter to Davidson, urging the following action:

Dear Frank,

Council meeting suggested with the participation of Mr. Morrell for Friday night, January 3rd. Please make sure to get immediately the precise information as to Mr. Morrell's schedule. This Council meeting should be held together with the whole Tunbridge group, or with a considerable part of it. It is felt that at this meeting the rights of the Council, and the rights of the group should be clearly defined. The Council feels that without such a clear statement it would be impossible to carry on. The Chairman of the Council suggests that Council and (Tunbridge) group should have equal authority in the following: a) qualification of recruits, b) hiring superintendent, c) planning and working out projects, d) discharge of officials or recruits.

Please get as many members as possible up here on January 1st to prepare for the meeting with the Council and Mr. Morrell. The Council feels that a regular news sheet should be printed to keep everybody posted—for example, in the *Chelsea Herald*. Please require such a news sheet from Arnie (Childs) immediately.

The work project so far meets with little sympathy in the Council because Brocklebank Hill is thought to be poor soil. The Council would still prefer to put individual farms back into production directly. There is obviously a considerable gap between the strategical planning for the whole watershed, as understood by Mr. McKaye, and this approach which still thinks only of individual farms. There will have to be a lot of mutual enlightenment, and Mr. McKaye will have to be invited to the January 3rd meeting, too, if possible.

If an ordinary CCC director would be appointed, the Council would immediately disband. The reason given is that we would then have the CCC laziness, the CCC routine, the CCC tradition, the CCC working hours, the CCC viewpoint — and in short, it would be just a CCC camp.

Happy New Year,

Eugen[9]

Another note was sent along with the above letter asking for the appointment of Lawrence Bowen as acting foreman for three months, provided funds would be made available to pay the manager he would have to hire for his own farm. This official appointment of a local man would satisfy the Council, at least momentarily, and would help breach the clouds of antagonism which were beginning to gather over the opening of the Camp. Davidson was requested to elicit a speedy decision from Washington on the Bowen appointment.

* * * * *

The proposed joint meeting, which probably should have contributed significantly to the general harmony, was held during the first week in January. However, there is no detailed record available as to exactly what transpired. Morrell evidently showed a willingness to provide what was necessary for the physical welfare of the Camp, but there appeared to be no definite conclusions reached on the issues which Dodge had raised. The status of Lawrence Bowen remained undecided.

The rebuilding of the Camp itself had bogged down considerably, due to the lack of building supplies, the severity of the weather, and a general holiday lassitude on the part of the construction crew. The Tunbridge group began to trickle back after January 1st, and in a couple of days almost everyone had returned. The Washington mill had turned sufficiently to grant the transfer of regular enrollees from the various other camps to Sharon. The barracks were not completely renovated by the 3rd, but it was decided to bring the new men in as soon as possible. This move would speed construction by increasing manpower, and also give the recruits a sense of tangible participation in the preparation of the Camp.

* * * * *

The opening itself was not destined to go unnoticed by the outside world. Except for the local Vermont newspapers, there had not been much previous publicity in the press, except for the coverage of the Tunbridge rally by the *New York Times* and the *New York Herald Tribune,* and the Boston papers. There had also been a few references to the camp in the syndicated columns of Dorothy Thompson, and Mrs. Roosevelt. But now reporters on special assignment started to appear, looking for "angles," and before long the spotlight of national interest began to shine brightly on the Sharon hillside.

9. Sharon

Now that the experiment was gathering a full head of steam, several people, friendly and otherwise, began to voice their private fears and misgivings as to what shape the Camp would take. Among the friends were Dean Landis, who was on the Supervisory Committee, James Rowe, the Presidential assistant who was supposed to "watch over" the Camp, and Mrs. Roosevelt herself. A letter of Davidson's illustrates the point:

> Dear Mrs. Greene:
>
> I met friend Lanigan in Washington over the week-end. Please keep in touch with him and see that he doesn't go off the deep end in worrying about the practicality of our venture, Eugen's temperamentality, etc. There *are* problems to be sure, but Jim is in danger of yielding to the fears of Landis, Jim Rowe, etc. He should visit us soon and find out what is going on.
>
> The opposition, as well as our benevolent allies, permit various rumors to float around, some of which may (alas) be substantiated by coming events, but so far there've been surprisingly few hitches. On Sunday, though, Mrs. Roosevelt was sufficiently upset by current reports to give Jim (Lanigan) and me a gentle reminder about getting along with people (because we made the mistake of inducing her to suggest that the Agriculture Department be free of rules and regulations for this Camp. We should have cleared with Agriculture first.) Lanigan has invited Olmstead to stop off in Cambridge en route to Vermont. I rely on your steermanship here. Landis apparently feels that Eugen is going to try to run the Camp by high-pressure insistence on his own prerogatives.[1] Even if this belief were entirely true, it would not be possible in practice. Landis has not yet consented to visit Vermont, and until he does, we'll have no way of convincing him we're O.K. . . . . . .

Mrs. Roosevelt, Landis, etc. are terribly concerned lest we make a practical error (such as not having enough iodine on hand) that would mess up the whole venture. Well, Agriculture has an excellent man (Wolfe) here this week to get things going; the real problem is to find a permanent superintendent.

The very best regards to you and Mr. Greene.

Frank[2]

As Davidson requested, Mrs. Greene did communicate with Lanigan. He in turn visited Landis, seeking to allay his fears about the Camp. Landis thereupon wrote to Davidson in a reassured manner:

I am delighted to learn that you seem to be getting on as well as you are with the William James Camp. I talked with Jim Lanigan, suggesting to him that he urge you to try to get the recommendation of our report carried out, creating a special committee to supervise the Camp, and I am glad to see that a committee of that type has been appointed. A good committee of this nature will buttress the kind of efforts that you want to make, and may be of some value from an advisory standpoint. I hope some time in the near future to get a chance to come up there myself.

You can always be assured not only of my best wishes, but of my willingness to help make the Camp a success.

Sincerely yours,

J. M. Landis[3]

There was so much physical work to be done at the camp-site that little time was available for group discussions or political planning. The question of command, and the selection of a long-term work project were both shelved for the time being, although it was quite apparent that the day of reckoning on these matters could not be postponed much longer. True to its word, the Department of Agriculture had sent up one of its own men to take over temporary control of the Camp. He was Glen Wolfe, of the Forestry Service, and his choice proved to be a happy one. He had tact, patience, technical ability, and a sincere interest in getting things off to an auspicious start.

By January 11th, most of the transfers had arrived. In addition to the boys recruited from the Bellows Falls construction cadre, there were representatives from Ohio, Maryland, Massachusetts, and Vermont camps. There were also half a dozen local farm boys, including Neal and Stanley Flint, the two sons of Ed Flint, one of the Camp's staunchest Tunbridge supporters. The total assemblage of enrollees numbered 42.[4]

Lieutenant Tierney had remained on the scene to run the Camp administratively until the construction was completed. Tierney's position in the hierarchy was not clearly defined, especially with respect to discipline, although he did believe that he had the authority to enforce such CCC rules as he deemed necessary. He therefore strongly resented any attempts by the enrollees or the Department of Agriculture, in the person of Wolfe, to challenge his control by setting up an internal governing body.

In spite of this undisguised opposition, a group meeting of all Camp members was soon held in the foresters' house (which had finally been secured from State Forester Merrill) to form an overall Camp organization. The college men were particularly anxious to see how many of the non-college boys would participate in the discussions. The great danger was, of course, that due to timidity, strangeness, and a lack of initiative, they would make little or no contribution. To the pleasant surprise of everyone, there was lively debate by the newcomers on almost every issue.

Schlivek was appointed temporary secretary by Wolfe, and discussion was opened on choosing the method which should be employed in running the Camp. Hobbing started off by saying he favored one general Camp manager. Page Smith suggested a work chief, plus a committee of five to handle other functions. Bagby added that the governing committee should be small, so that decisions could be reached without too much discussion. It was voted unanimously that whatever organization was agreed upon should last only for a two-week trial period, and then be reconsidered. Hobbing made a motion that there be a Camp manager, and a committee of five, including men to take care of property, mess, social arrangements, the Camp schedule, plus an unattached (planning) member. This motion was amended to eliminate the specific functions of the committee, since these might vary from time to time. Bagby proposed that the manager be the only elected officer, and that he should pick his own committee, in the manner of a "cabinet." Allan Dupras, the first of the non-college enrollees to speak up, objected to Bagby's proposal on the ground that it made the Camp manager too much of a "dictator." Schlivek supported this stand. Hobbing voluntarily withdrew his motion, and Page Smith said that the committee should be elected, and then appoint a manager either from its own members or the Camp as a whole. Robert Dumas thought that the manager should be elected, with power to appoint a committee, since the new boys did not know enough fellows to select specialists. Schlivek then moved that a Camp manager be elected, to appoint a Council of not more then five members which must then be approved by the Camp as a whole. Smith said that final authority should be with the committee, not the manager, who should act as the committee's agent. Schlivek's motion was then carried unanimously.

Following this legislation, O'Brien, Smith, Chamberlin, and Gus Guyette, a transfer from Poultney, were nominated for manager. Another Poultneyite raised the question of how much CCC experience each nominee had, and it was found that Guyette had the most, including a good deal of farm work. Two other non-college boys then said that CCC experience was not important for this Camp, but local knowledge of the area and its people *was* important. After more discussion of qualifications, Page Smith was elected Camp manager for a two week period, with the authorization to pick his committee at once.

This ended the first inclusive meeting of the Camp as a whole, and, in spite of a noticeable lack of parliamentary procedure, it had been witness to a remarkably frank expression of views on all sides. People said what they thought, and did not shirk from mentioning names. Best of all, no one got angry.

The following day, a depressing letter was received from Arthur Root, who had been unable to return for the opening of the Camp. While in the NYA center at Waterbury, Vermont, he had contracted a heavy cold, which worsened during the two weeks stay at the foresters' house in December. This infection aggravated his chronic sinus condition, and he had spent a good portion of his Christmas holiday taking various treatments. Little relief had resulted, but he planned to return to Vermont anyway, so as to be present for the opening of the Camp. However, on the eve of his departure, he was involved in an automobile accident which injured his back and left arm, and precluded any possibility of physical labor for several months. In deep despondency at having to remain in New York, he wrote to Huessy:

> I am sentenced to several months of 'no physical exertion' with back or hand. What irony! What I need most is physical exertion. What can I do for the Camp? Shall I memorize the CCC act, study the politics behind it, investigate the history of the work service? What can I do *in* the Camp? You are an expert at turning liabilities into assets—here I am—a new liability. . . . .[5]

Because of his poor health, Root was not destined to ever join "Camp William James" as an enrollee, but he was an important participant in later events, which we shall describe later on.

* * * * *

During the last week in December, the Tunbridge group, in conjunction with the Council of the Eight Towns, had begun proceedings to form a private, non-profit corporation in the State of Vermont. This action grew out of a proposal originally made by Nathan Dodge. The purpose of the corporation was to enable land, and other real property, to be held for use by the Camp. If there were many Federal objections raised to working on private lands, and it seemed likely that there would be, the corporation might buy or take temporary title to such property, for educational and/or non-profit aims. As a result, there might be less opposition, legally and politically, to having the Camp work on lands held in such a manner. For example, the corporation could purchase the Brocklebank area, or a similar tract, in order to start a resettlement center and a sheep ranch. These holdings would be exempt from taxation as long as they were operated within the terms of the corporate charter. An additional benefit to the Camp would be that through joint representation on the corporation's board of directors, both the Camp and the Council would be drawn into the same orbit of thought and action. In fact, this collaboration was emphasized by the proposed name for the corporation—"Council and Camp, Inc." Each of the parties was to have one member among the directors, with the third member to be chosen from the many outside friends who might wish to be of assistance. With the help of ex-Governor Wilson, in Chelsea, the

Corporation did officially come into being in January, 1941. The incorporators were Nathan Dodge, from the Council, Robert O'Brien, representing the Camp, and Dorothy Canfield Fisher, as the "public" member for the people of Vermont. This corporate instrument was now ready for use whenever it should be called upon, and we shall discover shortly that its creation was a propitious bit of foresight.

* * * * *

On January 13th, Hendrickson sent his first memorandum to all the members of the Supervisory Committee.[6] He stated that Benton McKaye had announced definitely that he would be unable to accept the position of Camp superintendent. Therefore, Hendrickson was appointing Glen Amos, of the Forestry Service, as provisional superintendent. This move was necessitated by McKaye's refusal, and also by the fact that Glen Wolfe, first provisional superintendent, now found it necessary to return to his job in Washington. Amos was primarily a technical man, whose main interests were in timber and water conservation projects. Coming up to Sharon "cold," he could not visualize how the long-range purposes of the Camp, such as staff training and resettlement were to be achieved. He did not feel competent to take an active part in furthering these objectives, and preferred to maintain the unobtrusive position to which he had been accustomed in his regular work. So, for all practical purposes, the Camp was without an energetic leader, and the boys had to "carry Amos along" rather than follow his direction.

This persistent failure to acquire permanent leadership was having an adverse effect on everyone—from the enrollees to the members of the Supervisory Committee. The whole enterprise often seemed to be rudderless and temporary, as if the entire structure could collapse at any moment. Although intangible in itself, this gnawing feeling of insecurity became more prevalent with each passing day. Even the daily Camp routines, as performed by the self-governing organization which the boys themselves had selected, began to have a certain makeshift quality about them. But in spite of the need, there was no solution in sight.

* * * * *

Regardless of the nominal equality of all of the enrollees as far as status and rank were concerned, the college boys still felt they had an additional responsibility to the others. After all, they had done most of the talking and the "convincing," and they felt the obligation to produce results was primarily theirs. If the Camp was to progress, they would have to supply the incentive. Yet their own heterogeneity, coupled with the ever present problems of divided command, remote bureaucratic control from Washington, the thankless and never ending chore of trying to keep townspeople, Federal officials, enrollees happy and cooperative, plus the thousand and one unfamiliar details of just keeping the Camp functioning—all of these made the prospect of success a dim one. Frequently, the Camp became enmeshed in a net of aimlessness and despair.

The best description of this erratic camp life is contained in some diary notes kept by Hobbing and Page Smith, who recorded in vivid, although often fragmentary fashion, these daily experiences and their personal reactions to them:[7]

January 16th

George Phillips mentioned the problem of slackers. How can we make fellows work, or want to work? Can we divide ourselves between the 'rulers' and the 'ruled?' O. B. Stollard, from Ohio, said he would rather have a lieutenant giving orders. There has been some talk lately of guys being hungry.

January 17th

Bob O'Brien feels we're not in a 'war against war,' but in a reform school.

Lieutenant Tierney asserts his authority. Offers to grant leave at any time to anyone who has no work around Camp. Page asked if he could discuss the general medical situation with him and the doctor, and Tierney said it 'wouldn't be necessary.' All people have to sign for tools. Tierney is champing at the bit and is very huffy. He's in a hell of a spot. Wolfe could have checked him, but Amos *won't*.

Stanley Flint went home today, which is bad.

Bagby ran 100 degree fever, coughed up lunch.

Started making plans for dance. I felt dance was premature because we were not formed as a company, but of course, when these things come up we have to do our best to fit into the rhythm. Frank and others feel morale is low, but I think our group is over-sensitive to such things. Of course, there is no certainty in all this, no assurance of progress. We have to move slowly toward 'form.' We have to develop a discipline and a procedure of our own, with our own standards and pride.

There was bread-throwing at lunch today. It has been too hot in the barracks, especially at night.

Ralph Anderson's father is ill and he hasn't been in touch with his family for a month.

January 18th

Schlivek lost his temper with Lieutenant Tierney.

Last night, after the company meeting, which affected everybody very much, Fred Hall said that the whole thing would break down because the college fellows had the faith, but the others didn't. The college boys probably couldn't get ten others to feel the way they did, and so it would all crack. Bob Reardon asked, 'What's going to happen to this thing after you fellows leave?' Most fellows would feel more secure under a lieutenant. Jim Tierney, an enrollee from Massachusetts, said this was the most intelligent discussion he had been in since high school. As each idea came up you thought it was the best, but someone always seemed to come along with another answer which sounded better.

The square dance this evening was an almost incredible success. Ed Larkin, of Tunbridge, was one caller, and the other was the Rev. Fisk, from Hanover, who brought along records and an amplifying set. Girls came from Springfield, Vermont, as well as from Hanover, Norwich, Tunbridge, etc. The fellows were very reticent at first, but the Rev. Fisk used his whistle to good advantage, and the couples would break up and choose new partners. Everybody except Rullman and Leitch danced, and fellows like Tierney, Keefe, and Hall said they never had so much fun in their lives. They all wanted dances often. The girls had a grand time and will come again.

This whole affair is unprecedented in the CCC. For the first time since they enrolled, these fellows saw some real hearty fun and life. I felt, personally, that it was a little too early in Camp to do this. As yet we had done nothing, and so deserved nothing. But it was such a terrific success.

It will not help work habits, and should be saved for special occasions. Dances must not become routine.

January 20th

Bagby very ill. We called Dr. Smith from the village, and had arguments with the Lieutenant.

Terrible mess in the barracks this morning. Tierney counteracted our order to have people get up. Later in the morning, Herbert Agar, editor of the Louisville *Courier-Journal* came to visit, with the Bullocks, from Norwich, and Huessy. Agar looked around, but asked no questions.

Frank, Jack, Al and I drove to Four Wells. They felt very low, and got very silly, trying to buck up each other with jokes about serious things. We all agreed Mr. Amos is just a terribly small man. He always says 'I can't get this thing through my head.' He feels we are trying to escape from reality.

We had a talk with Huessy, who agreed on the need for bringing the new boys into the circle, so to speak. He is coming to Camp to live for a week. Needs a place to talk there, and hoped we could get the foresters' house cleaned up. We discussed the work project, which looked discouraging, because we found out that mere ownership by our corporation did not make the land 'public,' and we could not work on it as a Camp. We must contact farmers on work to do and try to figure something out *soon.* Eugen suggested corporation lease land to Camp. Doubt if this could be done.

We came back to Sharon dead tired, and worried about Phil's condition.

January 21st

Another mess before breakfast. But made great progress all day on building garage. Tried to teach Sam Gentille some carpentering. He is one of Page's recruits.

Jim Tierney dropped a remark that the Tunbridge group was too sensitive. Probably right. Bud Fisher went into kitchen to help George Flowers. Ralph Anderson went home to see his sick father. He got a phone call from his mother last week and she cried over the phone. We gave him train fare and he promised to be back in 6 days and repay us.

Preiss, O'Brien and Keefe went to Montpelier, where Secretary of State told them the corporation was not strictly educational, and therefore had to be taxed. We got in touch with Stanley Wilson, who said Secretary of State didn't know the law, and that he (Wilson) would fix things up tomorrow.

Got a package from home—tobacco and cake.

January 23rd

Bob Bourdelais, a new recruit, arrived Tuesday, after the Council meeting on Monday night had O.K.'d him. He took the train up to White River Jct. and hitch-hiked the rest of the way. Was very glad to get here, and appreciated the friendliness of everyone. Liked the idea of being able to smoke at meals. He is full of expectations, and Wednesday he worked overtime, remarking that this broke all precedents for him, but he didn't mind it at all. There was very little swearing in this Camp, he noted, and it appeared to be an intelligent bunch of fellows.

It seems to me that everything in Camp is 'opening up.' More and more communication is possible, as we get common experience. Sam Gentille even felt impelled to *ask* if anyone minded if he took time off to write a letter.

Eugen has been here since yesterday. He has a tremendous amount of spirit. Has been holding brief interviews with the new boys. They have given him various descriptive titles, such as 'nice little fellow,' 'a card,' 'chow-hog,' etc.

Royal Hill and Harold Parsley, farm boys from Vershire, arrived to enroll. They say there is a lot of good farm land in their town. 200-400 bushels of potatoes could be raised on an acre.

Fremont Smith, of Ohio, is wonderful with his colorful expressions. 'Scoot her up there,' when he wants a board to nail on the garage roof. 'How's that there end for being square, boy,' all this being said with a southern Ohio twang, which few of us have ever heard before.

* * * * *

Eugen and Mr. Amos went over to Brocklebank yesterday. O'Brien said he is now worried about the feasibility of the project since the land is weak and unproductive. It has value, but perhaps not as the first project. We shouldn't hurry it. Eugen said he knows that the second time you visit such a deserted place, it's discouraging. But if we don't bring back the most remote place and connect it up with the community again, we will never succeed. Many local people don't even know who owns Brocklebank.

Our work system of eight hours a day is absurd. I find myself fretting, and getting to work earlier in the morning, just because the time right after breakfast is not fit for *anything*. I hate this clamping down at 4 o'clock every day, and I shudder to hear the whistle. We should have experimental days when the hours are changed.

We need a flagpole and a library.[8]

* * * * *

While the Camp was thus grappling with its daily problems, there was further trouble brewing on the Washington front.

During the past few months, the Roosevelt administration had begun to develop the Lend-Lease program to aid those who were fighting the Nazis. In order to make headway, the President had to carry the majority of the country along with him. This was a formidable task, since the United States was still officially neutral, and there was a large bloc of vocal isolationists, both in and out of Congress. The methods by which the United States could supply Great Britain and her allies with material help, short of actual belligerency, became the chief concern of Roosevelt and his aides. Consequently, most major domestic issues receded in importance on their agenda.

This situation was advantageous to the enemies of the Camp for two reasons. In the first place, as long as the Administration was so pre-occupied with foreign affairs, it could not devote comparable time and attention to the activities of its numerous agencies and bureaus. Therefore, a piece of shrewd maneuvering or bargaining by any of these agencies and bureaus would be more likely to go unnoticed or unchallenged by the "higher-ups" because of its relative unimportance in the global scheme of things. A clever politician like McEntee could use such extra latitude to good personal advantage, and he realized this only too well. Secondly, the delicate balance of public opinion on neutrality had to be carefully maintained by Roosevelt. One false step in the realm of publicity and his entire plan could be ruined. The President felt that he could handle his opponents successfully on the Lend-Lease question, but only if there were no other squabbles to sap his strength and divert the attention of the nation to extraneous matters. After all, the Administration would have to exhibit its own unity to the country at large, and nothing could be tolerated which disturbed the appearance of harmony in the Democratic party. With full grasp of these two important considerations, McEntee was now fully aware of the potentialities which were open to him. He had patiently bided his time, waiting for the right moment to move.

This moment came on January 4th, the same day on which the Camp had officially come into being. On that date, Representative Albert J. Engel, Republican, of Michigan sent a letter to Secretary of Agriculture Wickard requesting information on the Sharon camp. Representative Engel stated that his first knowledge of the Camp had come from an article in the *New York Herald Tribune,* on December 29, 1940. This article, which was unsigned, purported to explain and interpret the aims of the new Camp in considerable detail, and had included several pictures of the campsite and personnel. Sensing that Engel might be hunting for an "issue" which would politically embarrass the Administration, Wickard took great care in preparing his reply. Such interrogation by the opposition was to be expected, and ordinarily would not have caused any anxiety. However, the timing was such that the Democrats wanted to minimize the risk of adverse newspaper headlines. The publicity might begin as a tempest in a teapot, and wind up a full-blown gale. Therefore, the Secretary of Agriculture took plenty of time in drafting his answer. He could not be sure what Engel's motives were, and he thought it best to give the most comprehensive explanation he could deliver. He said in part:

> The news story to which you refer seems to be a well-intentioned but somewhat over-enthusiastic, and hence inaccurate, description of this project. This Department was not consulted on the story, and it does not represent our views.
>
> The actual facts are that the Department of Agriculture has set aside at Sharon, Vermont a regular CCC side-camp for the purpose of trying various specific suggestions for the improvement of CCC administration. The Department has undertaken this project with the cooperation of the War Department and the Federal Security Agency.
>
> Establishment of such a Camp at this time is the result of a long process of discussion, involving many people and many groups. The discussion was crystallized in a recent report of a special committee appointed at the request of the President, and headed by W. W. Alexander, of the National Defense Commission. The Committee studied the present administration of the CCC camps, and recommended that one or more demonstration camps be established to test possible improvements, and to serve as a nucleus for a training program for future camp leaders. . .
>
> Suggested changes could be tried out in these camps, and their results carefully observed. Those which proved successful could then be carried over to the CCC generally, and those which did not work out in the demonstration camps could be abandoned with no great loss. Finally, the defense emergency has made necessary immediate action toward securing well-trained civilian commanders for the CCC camps.
>
> *Unified control by one Federal agency* - while the present set-up has worked reasonably well, it has suffered from the traditional difficulties of divided responsibility, and there has been some loss of efficiency. To determine the possibility of unified control, full

responsibility for the conduct of the Sharon camp has been given to this Department.

Unified command within the camp - The divided responsibility at the top has been reflected in the present organization of each camp. Each of the officials (commander, work foreman, educational adviser) has been reporting through a separate chain of command, and, naturally, there have been gaps and conflicts in authority. To remedy this situation, it is proposed to try out, in the Sharon camp, the idea of having one camp superintendent responsible for all phases of activity.

Non-military command - one of the objectives of the Sharon camp will be to give us experience with non-military command.

A cross-section of enrollment - One of the severest criticisms of the CCC is that, as presently organized, it has tended to develop an un-American sort of class system. Since all the boys were from relief, or near-relief families, there has been a strong tendency among the enrollees and the general public to regard the CCC as a sort of dumping-ground for youth of a special social 'class.' Certainly, it is not a tendency which should be encouraged by the government. It was our thought that if the CCC is valuable in building good citizens for democracy out of boys from relief families, it is equally valuable for other young men. . . . .

To this end, the Sharon camp will provide for the enrollment of about 14 or 15 unemployed young men from non-relief families college graduates and others, along with 35 or so CCC boys chosen in the regular way.

This aspect of the camp was probably the occasion for the reference to the 'moral equivalent of war' and the 'privileged youth' in the *Herald Tribune* article to which you referred in your letter.

Cooperation of local groups in project planning - One of the most important aspects of present CCC operations has been the lack of cooperation, and the occasional bad relations, between the camps and the local communities in which they are located. This is a phase in which this Department is particularly interested, since we feel that the camps can and should be making a real and permanent contribution to the community life. To work toward this ideal, it has been suggested that the local people should sponsor the camps and assist in the planning of the work they do. . . . .

In everything it does, this camp will be guided by the Civilian Conservation Corps Act, and will observe all standard CCC regulations, except for certain overhead expenditures made necessary by the demonstration nature of the camp.

The particular young men[9] mentioned in the newspaper article deserve credit for developing many of the suggestions for improvements listed above and for encouraging local interest in the project. Some of them will be included in the camp as regular enrollees.

Altogether, we look upon the Sharon camp as a sincere effort to improve CCC administration in a sound trial-and-error way.

I appreciate your interest in the project and would be happy to supply any further information you may desire, and to receive your suggestions for improvement in the proposed program.

Sincerely,

/s/ Claude Wickard
Secretary[10]

This was an extremely well-prepared letter, and was a lucid statement of the background and aims of the entire project. Precisely how Engel reacted is difficult to determine. Either he had already made up his mind to attack the Camp, regardless of any explanations which its proponents might have, or else he was not convinced that the experiment was sound and well-founded. He may have wondered why, if the entire CCC machinery needed overhaul, the Director of the Corps was not one of the prime movers of the new Camp. He may or may not have contacted McEntee on the matter, and if he did so, he certainly would have come away with a vastly different picture of the Camp than that conveyed by Wickard's letter. So, whether Engel and McEntee were in joint opposition to the Sharon project either by coincidence or by design, they served each other's purposes well. Republican Engel had found a "talking point" in Congress, and Democrat McEntee had found a mouthpiece. Again, politics had made a strange pair of bedfellows. Just prior to his receipt of Wickard's letter of explanation, Engel had told a press conference that the whole enterprise was a "columnists" camp, referring to its support by Mrs. Roosevelt, Dorothy Thompson, and Dorothy Canfield Fisher. Speaking of the college men, Engel scoffed, "I suppose Harvard may start a new course in straw-bossery."[11]

* * * * *

In sharp contrast to this political attack, came a letter from a Vermonter who, although of the same political affiliation as Mr. Engel, had the inestimable advantage of being a little closer to the scene of the Camp, and of having some contact with its personnel. This man, the Vermont District Superintendent of Schools for Orange County, wrote to Huessy:

> In my opinion, these proposals (aiding farmers and encouraging resettlement) are socially desirable and urgently needed; they are in conflict with no law or constitution; they embody what the local people regard as desirable in such an institution as a CCC camp; and they square perfectly with the social criterion that the highest good of the greatest number is served in a democracy.
>
> The boys at the Camp are a fine lot, and the splendid men from Washington who have visited them have given them no end of encouragement and enthusiasm. But unless they have something vital to do at once, something they can recognize as meeting a real and pressing human need, a wonderful opportunity to serve the present and future good of America will be lost. Some say that the venture is small and lacks importance. On the contrary, it is great. In all history, every great purpose or movement to meet a basic human need had a humble beginning. Let this one begin now, in a small way, by unemployed boys eager for this kind of experience and service while there may be yet time to do the whole job. We do not always need to learn our lessons through misery and suffering. Surely there is no excuse for such a method now—the radio and press make them all too vivid. I do not want to even think about the results that failure to begin this task at once may bring to our people.[12]

Would Mr. Engel have allowed his mind to be influenced by a wise and heartfelt letter such as this? The odds were against it. Yet the Congressman made the headlines, and the Vermonter did not.

* * * * *

On January 28th, Hendrickson sent a letter to Nathan Dodge, President of the Council of the Nine Towns (now including Vershire), remarking:

> Dear Mr. Dodge,
>
> Now that the Sharon CCC camp has opened and a company of young men are on the job, I want to tell you again how much we appreciate the part you and your neighbors have taken in this project.
>
> The interest shown by your Council of Nine Towns, which in fact led to the establishment of this camp, is certain to help get this project off to a good start. We are counting on you and your Council to keep in close touch with the project. As you know, Mr. Glen Amos has been

> named Acting Superintendent. I am sure he will welcome your advice and suggestions at any time.[13]

Hendrickson also wrote to Huessy:

> I am somewhat in doubt as to the advisability of following your suggestion that I prepare a definitive statement of the Department's objectives in the Sharon camp at this time. I feel that while the general objectives are clear in my mind, as they are in yours, any attempt to pin them down right now may be premature, as they are sure to be modified as we learn from our experience in operating the camp.
>
> I have no objection to the development of a mimeographed Camp (press) organ if the boys and Mr. Amos agree that it is desirable. However, I feel strongly that the contents and distribution of the paper should be examined very carefully, with due consideration being given to just how much, and what kind of publicity the Camp wants. As an old newspaper man, I know that things which are frequently intended only for internal consumption are picked up and misinterpreted. My suggestion, therefore, is that if you do start a paper, you should steer away, insofar as possible, from any statements which might possibly be interpreted as committing the Camp or the Department to particular policies which we may later wish to revise. . . . .
>
> I am enclosing, for your information, a clipping from the *Washington Post* of January 23rd which is an offshoot of the inquiry from Congressman Engel, our reply[14] to which I sent you recently. The clipping, and the letter I sent you, indicate pretty clearly the sort of unnecessary controversy which I believe we can avoid by watching our publicity policy closely.[15]

It was clear from this letter that Hendrickson was not anxious to put anything on the Camp in writing for public consumption. He hoped that Wickard's letter, which had probably been composed by several members of the Department, would satisfy Engel and that the storm would blow over. Therefore, he would have liked all publicity to be shut off for the time being, unless absolutely unavoidable. He knew that it was an easy thing for politicians to make purposeful " "misinterpretations" if it suited their interests to do so.

Meanwhile, when questioned by the press concerning Engel's outburst, McEntee feigned an attitude of surprise when such "experimental and illegal" projects as resettlement were mentioned as being considered by the Department of Agriculture for the Sharon camp. He also stated that the enlistment rule still required the applicant to show "need" before being allowed to enroll.

* * * * *

As the Washington pot began to boil again, stirred by newspaper articles and wild rumors, the boys at the Camp kept trying to get some order into their own lives. But the path was not becoming any smoother. There was considerable over-crowding in living quarters because the second barrack had not been completed on schedule, and about twenty enrollees were forced to sleep in the foresters' house until the new building was finished.

Here are some further revealing excerpts from diaries of Camp members. Although these excerpts may seem rather unconnected in thought and expression, it must be remembered that this is often how "on the spot" impressions appear to us. These notes are not part of a prepared article, or the product of careful editing and rewriting. On the contrary, they represent life as it was lived from moment to moment, with all the sharp and sudden oscillations between exuberance and despair. For this reason I have reproduced the notes just about as I found them. Here are people trying to understand and interpret what they were doing while they were doing it, without the benefit of hindsight or retrospect. It was a difficult and confusing thing to do, but this sort of "impressionistic" writing is probably more akin to what really goes on in the human mind than is a mere reporting of facts, no matter how grammatical the prose. These diaries are not lacking in quality or authenticity. Rather, they have an abundance of them. In after years, men can often rationalize their actions, and become well-supplied with reasons and excuses for things they have done But the spirit of the moment, as it was lived, can never be artificially manufactured at a later date. It is with such considerations in mind that these descriptions of the Camp's struggles should be read:

January 29th

Monday, boys drove to Plymouth camp for 'shots.' Bob Clark chilled his feet on the way back, and they stopped at Hotel Coolidge in White River Jct. to warm up. Some went for haircuts, and the Lieutenant came in and gave them hell.

Eugen said the other day that this is not a 'children's' camp. But look at the ages. Charley Davidson, from Ohio, figures to spend six months here, then he's going out west. Fremont Smith didn't make any serious choice to come here. . . . . he said he didn't figure he bettered himself or worsened himself. There is no serious purpose in these minds, no drive to fill the day. So, for the time being, it *is* a 'children's' camp. It's much too early to say anything to the boys about this. The words would not strike home, and they would be unrepeatable after the first failure.

Just what kind of a situation are we in? Our group (college men) is racked by disease, dispersion, varying approaches and intensities, emotional strain, uncertainty, inefficiency. The other fellows operate in their old ways. They read *True Confessions,* bull around, lounge on their cots, take it easy. Are we going to form the marching men of a new life here? Or is this just a regular camp where college men are in it, too?

* * * * *

February 1st

We simply do not get to work on time. We struggle in and out, and it all goes easy. The Camp is disorganized, ravaged by sickness, etc. No uniformities are observed—no common reading, no uniforms, no call to the whole group. We are all still individuals.

February 1st

Table waiters wore aprons tonight. Immediately the office was established and dignified. In the same way, barracks leaders must have whistles.

Foresters' house toilet is filthy—skis, and people sleeping downstairs mess it up. Dishes are unwashed; people don't sweep upstairs. However, we'll stay until the second barrack is painted. I was appointed barrack leader yesterday.

Ralph Anderson still overstaying his leave.

Mr. Kenlon, Chief Inspector of the CCC was here yesterday—a big, foolish figure. Subjected us to some very thorough, hell-bent questioning. He did not speak to any of the non-college enrollees.

Page spoke tonight of our being able to send 15 men out on a soil conservation project. The first part of the work may be to draw wood, etc. Then we need dump trucks, steam shovel, bulldozer, jackhammer, compressor, dynamite. This would be a good project. Perhaps Soil Conservation District could lease Brocklebank, and that would solve all problems, or many of them.

Page went to Chelsea last night to get examined for the draft.

We hope to be able to police at the Dartmouth Winter Carnival.

We have already spent a month to get the Camp in shape. We should understand that this is justified only in view of the anticipated long service of the Camp to this area. So far, this Camp life has been nothing special, but a lot of fellows like Red Winces, from Maryland, expect it to be different. These fellows are not crying for education, and the winter makes a start even more difficult, but it must begin soon.

Sunrise is beautiful here, and yet everyone seems to go it by.

February 2nd

Myer Berger here from *New York Times.*

Pay day.

Letter from Ralph Anderson, saying his father was very ill, and he (Ralph) was taking his old job again. Mr. Amos wrote and told him to get a statement from his employer. Ralph said he would pay the seven dollars he owed Page and Enno, and wrote to Lieutenant asking for his trunk.

Trip to dance at Norwich, and to movies at White River Jct. Dance very successful, movies not so. O. B. Stollard left the movies early, and was picked up by Fuchs and Winces, who were on their way home from taking doctor back to Plymouth. We lost 25 minutes hunting for Stollard.

February 3rd

With so many people ill, seven or eight leaving Camp for the week-end makes it impossible to have a continuous, all-out Camp. We must limit leaves to three or four per week-end.

Went to see Eugen. Arthur and Mrs. Greene were there, along with Phil Bagby, who was recuperating. Eugen would not get down to 'brass tacks' on the work project or the sheep ranch.

February 4th

Some work done in Camp, but the place was empty and scattered. People just sat down to lunch; few came to breakfast. Good skiing in the afternoon. Jim Lanigan arrived with Jim O'Donnell and Frank Walsh.

February 5th

Made work schedule for the week.

Spent most of the day figuring out the barracks arrangements. Johnny Rullmen made plans for coat hangers. He and Jones and I cut wood for pegs, and Johnny made a sample.

I made a barracks roster and moved O. B. Stollard. Made the mistake of asking his consent, and he objected. Al Eiseman made a much more thorough reshuffling, and this will be read as an order.

Lanigan much interested by the 'row' in Washington. Everyone there says we can't run an efficient Camp without the Army—Jim Rowe[16] says so too. Lanigan's only solution was for us to run a clean, disciplined Camp.

Neal Flint came back and took a dozen fellows to the ski tow in Tunbridge. Schlivek, Keefe, and Tierney went to see Nate Dodge and he agreed to get hold of farms where we can cut wood.

Amos said wood-cutting on private land is possible. If farmer supplied team and worked with us, he could keep some of the wood. This would be an ideal project. It digs into the existing economy and does much-needed work. It gives us contact with the farmers, and corresponds with work normally done in this season. It also gives experienced boys a chance to do work they like, and gives the other boys a chance to learn. It spreads us through the communities.

Must go over our budget. We have $4,000 for salaries, although $3000 would be enough. $700 used for construction. $2500 available for all else, including gas, oil, repair of staff car, etc. This is a greatly simplified set-up.

Paul Keefe is coming along much better. He realizes that by sending him to Montpelier, and others to see Nathan Dodge we are trying to get the new men on equal status with the rest of us and teach them the ropes. Jim Tierney, his closest friend, resents this, and thinks he knows it all already. They both told Al Eiseman that they thought our discipline as group members was dishonest and that the college men should do much more personal griping, and should not hide their feelings. They felt that in the first few days they were here, there was a patronizing, conscious 'bending down' by the college boys.

There has even been some difficulty about the very favorable *New York Times* story of Meyer Berger, because all the college men were listed by name, and the rest were just called 'other enrollees.' *The publicity has really created the college, non-college distinction in the Camp.* This has been the most harmful aspect of the publicity. No one in Camp has said anything about Eugen. Rullman said he hoped that the right people would read the *New York Times.*

The doctor was here Friday. Page and Roy were taken to the Hospital in Hanover in an ambulance. They have bad cases of flu.

February 6th

Had long talk last night with Rullman. He said his mind worked sort of slow. It worked on real things, not on general matters. He went with one girl for two years, and then they were separated. Said she never asked him to dance, because she probably figured he'd ask *her* if he wanted to dance. Says he can do without girls; some fellows can't think of anything else. Says he is like a hermit. Likes to be alone and to read.

Fremont Smith was up in arms this morning about the towns. He bawled out the woman in the Sharon store for the way people in the town were gossiping, and believing the newspaper stories, and not cooperating with the Camp. He wants to go to every one of the nine townships as soon as possible and explain to the people what we're aiming to do. He's wonderful.

Lloyd Roberts' feet bleeding from his 26 mile hike from White River Junction. He came back last night with Dumas; Gus Guyette also back. All got hearings for being AWOL. Amos asked Lloyd if he were looking for a soft job in the dispensary, and Lloyd almost wept.

O. B. Stollard loafed all day—chews tobacco, swears. A real problem. He must be deprived of the pick-up. Charley Myers is getting offensive and insolent about his job as supply clerk. He must be moved out. Herb Lamb suggests Clarence Leitch.

Amos wants to go out to pick farm for wood cutting. Wants to take two or three men off regular work to plan the long-range program, and says we don't want to plan it too hastily. He's making the map.

Had swell meeting with C. K. Webb, Chairman of the Board of the White River Soil Conservation District, and S. L. Tinsley, of Soil Conservation Service. Webb explained history of the District. It was an excellent meeting, and now the boys understand what they will be doing. Twenty or more attended. Where else in the CCC does this happen? There is a perfect feeling of equality between Tinsley and 'Camp William James.'

After last night's meeting the fellows defended the idea of college boys in the camps. And they see the fight on the outside to be a result of the publicity. Now they're all getting to be one. There are hold-outs, of course.

Eugen is already concerned about the next fifty, and how to recruit them.

Boys have agreed in meeting on new order in barracks. This is good, because this self-imposed order can now be enforced. Now the barrack leaders can make them keep up to the mark.

Arthur was here—he's going to Arizona.

February 10th

Plumbing is freezing in this weather.

Only ten men in Camp, 16 out working, 10 on overhead, 6 sick. This is a weak showing.

Camp won't be good unless we agree on our futures and point ahead. We need a lot more exercise and sport, loud laughter, and vigor. Farming doesn't appeal to boys today. It's not the long hours, but the loneliness and emptiness of the land that hurts. Only groups of people can settle an area. Isolation is ruinous. The smaller the unit, the more self-discipline it takes to keep going. For instance, our Camp is more difficult to operate than a unit of 200, where men could be lumped together more impersonally. In addition, we are constantly worrying about the survival of the Camp.

We need to find a place for quiet talks, where people can go in pairs and small groups. Life in the barracks is too public. John Rullman would never have told me in the barracks what he told me in the 'White House.'

February 18th

Stanley Flint and I saw a number of farmers in Tunbridge, Chelsea, and Vershire on the possibility of cutting wood on shares on their land. Farmers feel this is the best thing that the government had done yet. It enables the Camp to serve its real function in regard to the labor supply. Some fellows don't like the project because it smacks of charity to the farmers, who get all the benefit free. But there is no other project at the moment.

Frank told me of the brilliant job Mogan and Winces had done in trying to convince Jones[17] to stay in Camp, with an eye to resettlement. They told Jones that if he left he'd go back to being the hired hand that he hated to be. They agreed that a lot of Vermont farmers were dumb and lazy, and that Jones shouldn't have to work for them.

To Frank, this brought up the whole idea of resettlement, so that fellows would have something to look forward to after June. Question of how this resettlement could be accomplished. Frank thinks Farm Security might take whole thing over, but I think he is wrong. To me it suggests an experimental farm, although I once condemned the idea as not committing anybody, and as just being 'interesting.' But now I see that if we can make a go of it, it might be the beginning of a new pioneering. But where? Bob doesn't want Brocklebank anymore. The general feeling in Tunbridge is against it. I had gone along with Huessy's idea of starting in the toughest place first, and I held his position because I was sore at the townspeople for their gossip and weakness. I argued that we were morally obligated to do Brocklebank. But I see now that we must do something nearer at hand. Stanley Flint has given me hope by saying that the people are all 'for' the sheep project, only not on Brocklebank.

So we have two big objectives—the farm and the sheep ranch.

A fellow like Jones will not be reached by our talk, but by work. And not work that is theoretically for an ideal, but work that is hopeful in terms of his life and that of his friends. He can't see far, and of course the timber stand improvement, as work for the future, is a joke. Even cutting wood on shares, although it is good work, is not enough to mean much to Jones.

Winces observed that the SCS work wasn't helping the farmers who really needed it. The SCS waits for people to come to it, and it seems that only the relatively rich people come. By way of changing this situation, Al and Jack announced they had signed up three poorer farmers around Tunbridge for the SCS. But Tinsley may not approve the applications. We shall see.

Story going around Tunbridge that an FBI man told a salesman that he was going up to Camp to arrest Huessy and six students for holding a meeting under the swastika. But people in Tunbridge are getting used to the gossip themselves.

This evening a couple of us had a discussion on the problem of education in Camp. One can talk to the new fellows, of course, and they may absorb more than they let on. They won't take the lead but they must always be let in on what's happening. They won't do the thinking at first, either, but the point is to have them follow you. For instance, Winces doesn't love ideas, or burn for them, but he's unconsciously taking them up inside him. He doesn't value himself for his ideas, but they're there.

Communication between boys is still hard. We must work at it individually, get them all to say something, perhaps, on this wood-cutting idea. They will then feel they've been consulted, and they'll defend the idea. This is better than a whole group discussion, which looks too formal, and involves too much feeling of responsibility on their part, because they always think in terms of a few people.

Some of the fellows have voiced a desire to go to college. Should we encourage them? Jack says we have no right to steer them, nor the qualifications. But we can, we must.[18]

This kaleidoscope of inner Camp life was something which outsiders seldom saw, and it probably would have dismayed them to discover such a plenitude of emotional confusion. Although the boys often magnified their numerous personal difficulties out of proportion to their severity, these difficulties were not to be brushed aside or sublimated into rosy hopes for the future. The fundamental insecurity of the Camp was further heightened by the "false front" which was exhibited to the majority of visitors, who came to observe, criticize, and offer advice. These visitors were usually more interested in the Camp as a "unique idea" than they were in its actual form. They did not realize how much of a strain it was for a Camp member to talk about the larger aspects of resettlement in America, when he was, for the moment, more worried about whether there were enough potatoes on hand for lunch. Moreover, the constant barrage of publicity, intensified by Engel's attacks, caused the boys, especially the college group, to become irritable and self-conscious.

Unfortunately, the tempo of this publicity began to increase rather than subside.

10. The Battle Is Joined

On January 30th, a reporter[1] for the *Boston Globe* had written a particularly unfavorable article on the Camp. He ridiculed the ideas and the people involved in the experiment, and gave the impression that McEntee had been cleverly hoodwinked by some crafty fellows in the Department of Agriculture. His most irresponsible statement, however, was that behind their lip-service to William James, Dorothy Thompson and Professor Huessy were really admirers of Adolf Hitler, and were seeking to copy his youth training methods. This falsehood, printed without a single basis in fact, was most damaging. Besides, people were reading this report during wartime, and they needed very little convincing to believe that the Camp was a Nazi plot to infiltrate the lives of American youth.

This "lead" was all that Engel (and McEntee) had been waiting for, and he made the most of it. In a statement on January 31st, he flatly suggested that the Sharon Camp was the first part of a plan to institute Nazi-type work camps in this country, and that the presence of "over-privileged" youth in the Camp was to train them to be Hitlerite leaders. Engel also pointed out that Huessy was not an American citizen, and that he had been intimately associated with the German work camps from 1925 to 1933. The newspapers gave wide coverage to this statement, which was far more sensational than the fine article by Meyer Berger which later appeared in the *New York Times* on February 2nd. Berger, alone among the reporters, had thought enough of his assignment to spend a day and a half at the Camp before drawing any conclusions about it.

Following Engel's blast in his direction, Huessy replied through the press (although his reply was generally given much less coverage than the accusation) that he never had any connection with the Nazis, and that he had actually been forced to flee from them to escape persecution. He also stated that his work camps in Germany had been democratic in theory and operation, and had been supported by the German republican government while it was in power. Subsequently, the camps had been perverted by Hitler's youth movement, which Huessy had opposed. Other friends also came forward with strong defenses of the Camp, and of Huessy personally.

Not the least of these was the long and sincere declaration made by Senator Aiken of Vermont, whom Engel certainly could not have accused of harboring Nazi sympathies. Aiken said:

> Recent news dispatches and newspaper columns have indicated criticism of an experimental CCC camp at Sharon, Vermont, known as 'Camp William James.'
>
> I trust that such criticism is directed at this Camp because the critics are uninformed as to the facts. I am a Vermonter, and the good people of my state have asked me to make clear these facts.
>
> While I was Governor of Vermont, the young men who initiated this Camp talked with me more than once regarding their hopes and plans. They are a clean-cut group of college men, representing more than one racial group and more than one (religious) creed. No one could meet these boys without being impressed by their honesty and sincerity of purpose.
>
> (The Senator then quoted from 'A Request For A Hearing,' which the Tunbridge group had written prior to the September Rally to explain their coming to Tunbridge and what they hoped to do.)
>
> As a life-long Vermonter, I know what it was that seeped into the lives of these boys, and why they chose to give their time to this Camp rather than seek more lucrative positions in our economic world.
>
> They won the confidence of their hill town neighbors. They enlisted the advice and counsel of Professor Eugen Rosenstock-Huessy, of Dartmouth, a Vermont resident. A mis-informed columnist has stated that Professor Rosenstock-Huessy appears to be an admirer of the efficiency of the Hitler youth training methods. May I say that Professor Rosenstock-Huessy is about as great an admirer of Hitler or anything Hitlerian as is Franklin D. Roosevelt. In fact, it was Professor Huessy's attempts to build a self-reliant youth of Germany that

brought him afoul of Hitler, and resulted in his virtual expulsion from the country.

(He then reviewed the Tunbridge rally and the resultant petition to the President.)

The result of this petition was that the President gave the plan his approval. It was also supported by Mrs. Roosevelt. In this connection, let me say that as far as I know, not a single town within the range of Camp William James has ever voted the Democratic ticket.

This week I had a letter from Ed Flint, of Tunbridge. Ed is the local creamery manager and is known to a hundred thousand people as Manager of the Tunbridge World's Fair. I should like to quote from his letter to me in regard to 'Camp William James':

'I have been very interested, and a close student of the work; in fact, so much interested that my two sons have enrolled and are there now. The college boys tell me that they have gotten something from the work on our farms, that Yankee 'something' that Coolidge said Vermont had enough of to supply the whole nation if all the other states ran out. It is this Vermont individualism that they are willing to give a year's work for.

I attended a dance given there in the mess hall last Saturday night. There were 80 there—camp boys, men, women, girls, and boys from Tunbridge, Royalton, Sharon, Strafford, Wilder, Springfield, and Hanover, N. H.

I watched what went on. I saw not a boy or girl leave the hall until it was over. Neither did I see or smell liquor of any kind on anyone. I think it was as clean a dance as I ever attended. Two of my daughters attended. I am writing this in good faith, and I think it O.K. for Mr. Engel to investigate the project. I will be pleased to give you or anyone any information I can.'

'Camp William James' is experimental as yet. It should have the opportunity to prove itself; and if this Camp fulfills its purposes satisfactorily, America needs a thousand more camps like it. I hope to see the time when every boy in America, be he rich or poor, will have the opportunity to spend a full year working on our forests and our farms. By that means we can build men in mind and muscle; we can instill tolerance, understanding, self-reliance, and leadership into their character.[2]

In spite of this sterling and well-documented defense, neither the newspapers or Engel would let go of their choice publicity tidbit. On February 6th, a House appropriations sub-committee began what it quaintly called "a quiet study of an experimental Civilian Conservation Corps camp for college graduates which was started recently in Vermont." After the first day's hearings, at which McEntee was a witness, some committee members stated that they believed the CCC (meaning McEntee, who had just testified) was "not in favor of the idea underlying the camp." They also criticized the "German" aspect of the project. These criticisms again made the headlines, while the refutations continued to be little more than footnotes.

On February 11th, Engel carried his charges directly to the floor of the House of Representatives, and made particular note of the fact that Huessy was an alien. We recall that several months before, Huessy had attempted to accelerate the normal process of obtaining his citizenship so that he could take part in the Camp's activities officially, and also to forestall just such an attack as Engel was making. Engel had discovered this, but he accused Huessy and the Department of Agriculture of trying to speed up the citizenship procedure *after* he (Engel) had made his charges. This last was, of course, untrue, but Engel was not now interested in the validity of his remarks. His chief criterion was their news value.

* * * * *

While the controversy raged, the Department of Agriculture had withdrawn almost completely into a shell of silence. As Administration officials, already in an unenviable position from their own point of view, they did absolutely nothing to counteract Engel's irresponsible charges. All appeals from the Camp and from the Council of the Nine Towns were met with a tight-lipped "wait and see" response.

* * * * *

This mounting crescendo of Congressional criticism and breast-beating was having a calamitous effect inside the Camp. A quotation from a resume of the state of affairs by Huessy illustrates the situation:

> Mr. Barclay[3] reports from Washington, in the *New York Times* that it is the exclusion of the Army from the Sharon experiment that has produced the 'storm' over the Camp, and he says further that the whole purpose of the enterprise is that the Department of Agriculture

wishes to try out a 'small soil erosion experiment.' What could be further from the truth?

Other correspondents are told that 'straw bosses' are trained. This was a most unfortunate phrase, which has logically led go the attack against these boys on the ground that they wished to get positions (presumably as minor camp 'bosses') with salaries ranging from $1800 to $2800 a year. In reality, they could all secure much more lucrative jobs elsewhere.

The use of the term 'straw bosses' in an official utterance has had disastrous effects on the Camp morale. In this statement (Engel's), the college boys were clearly lined up against the rest of the Camp. Never before had such a distinction been made with reference to the group. In the ensuing confusion over this matter, five non-college boys left the Camp, out of a total of twenty-eight—a most serious loss.

I understand very well that such explanations as those quoted above have been given in order to minimize the importance of the Camp, and thereby mitigate the opposition to it. But appeasement does not work. If the Camp's aims are minimized and departmentalized, this will only result in Mr. McEntee's success. He will then have isolated the Department of Agriculture from all the innumerable friends of this project, in and outside the government. Ask any such friend how he reacts to the statements now being given out to the press. Herbert Agar came to Camp at our invitation, and he asked me to write about it in his magazine, 'Free America.' It is necessary for me to show him the significance of this Camp within his frame of reference, and in his vocabulary. The very use of the term 'straw boss' in my article could be enough to kill his interest completely.

This entire erroneous concept goes back to the time of enrollment in this Camp, when the boys had to put into writing that they were 'needy.' Yet our whole experiment is based on the fact that they were *not* needy. The Department of Agriculture had its chance here to insist that every boy fill out the form, under Reason for Enrollment — 'because I wish to serve my country.' This, after all, was and is the truth. Now if this answer had been given unanimously, neither Mr. McEntee nor Mr. Engel would have survived the ridicule they would have incurred if they had tried to dismiss the boys for this statement, or blamed the Department of Agriculture on its selection of a reason. However, the whole investigation, as it was actually handled, could not be understood by the majority of the enrollees, and it left in their mouths a sour taste of hypocrisy and confusion.

Further along these lines, we should note the strange vocabulary we allow to be used in public debate. For instance, the terms 'labor service' and 'work camps' are picture as opposed to the CCC. The Communists attack work camps, and Mr. Engel attacks labor service, as though the CCC were not a work camp *and* a labor service. The CCC *is* a work service, or I do not know what this term means. For most of the boys, whose families are on relief and who have nothing to fall back on, it is practically compulsory. It is not legal and physical compulsion, but it is, nevertheless, strict *economic* compulsion, which is no less overpowering than any other kind. But by allowing Mr. Engel or the *New Masses* to play up the labels 'work service' and 'labor camps' as something foreign and horrid, contrasted to the existing CCC, it is difficult to keep the record straight.

In the CCC we already have a work service based on temporary relief. The question is: will it develop into another mechanized machine, such as the Army or our factory system, by becoming compulsory, or will it save us from ossification by turning in the opposite direction, through releasing the creative energies of our youngsters and old people by the admixture of volunteers?

The issue is still open.[4]

It did not remain open for very long. On February 17th, without prior notice, McEntee advised the Department of Agriculture that he was ending his toleration of the experiment, which had been fully autonomous for only three weeks. McEntee's move was astute in its timing. He could count on little serious opposition in official Washington, since he was operating within his executive rights, and his superiors were engrossed in the problems of Lend-Lease. Moreover, the misleading press campaign of the preceding month, fostered by Engel's fictitious charges, gave him the assurance that "Camp William James" would not have any unified public support if it chose to battle for its survival. McEntee, in his letter of notification to Morrell, gave the following reasons for his decision to "modify" the agreement between himself and the Department of Agriculture:

I am requesting these changes (directing the War Department to assume command of the Camp) because I feel that they are to the best interest of the Corps as a whole, as well as the group now at Sharon, Vermont. . . . .

We recognize the value of experimentation, but feel that this experiment does not give the promise of success for which we had originally hoped.

If the work project at Sharon is not sufficiently developed to permit the effective use of the enrollees on such a project, I propose to detail this entire group of enrollees to the Bellows Falls, Vermont, camp, or other camps, until such time as a worthwhile project is available.[5]

The significance of the letter was clear. It ended the existence of the Sharon camp as an experimental enterprise, and consequently destroyed the effective and recognized connection between the Camp and the Council of the Nine Towns. Furthermore, the status of the enrollees, already made hazardous by the newspaper stories and the vituperation of Engel and his cohorts, was now more precarious than ever. There was a distinct probability that all personnel would soon be shipped to Bellows Falls and other camps, and that the unity of the group would be shattered forever.

This grim prospect had to be faced, and some decisions were required very soon as to future action. Immediately after McEntee's announcement, several days grace were necessary for everyone to collect their thoughts and to begin searching for counter measures. McEntee's move had been released to the press, and on February 20th, the news was printed nationally under a variety of captions, of which this one in the *New York World Telegram*[6] was typical: "Army to Take Over CCC Camp for 'Rich.'" This kind of headline naturally left its readers to draw their own further conclusions about the matter.

Even though the Camp had never approached the condition of complete unity of its members, these outside assaults, directed as they were against the Camp as a whole, had a considerable rallying effect on the boys. The almost instinctive resistance which most human beings show toward unjustified and underhanded attacks was now coming to the fore. There were, of course, many enrollees, especially non-college ones, who were forced to view the situation in ways other than their personal preference might dictate, and there were a few instances of actual estrangement. These boys had economic considerations and obligations to dependents which could not be ignored. For them, the choice of alternatives could not be made lightly.

The first local reaction to McEntee's order was the attempt by the Camp to marshal the power and influence of all of its friends in order to preserve its government status in some form. This status was of vital importance because only through such standing could the Camp's research and leadership training be translated into wide-scale action. If the Camp were totally reduced to private means of support, it could safely be ignored by the bureaucrats, and at best it could probably not spread out beyond the few towns that it served. Besides, loss of government sponsorship would deprive the Camp of the home it was so laboriously constructing; would increase its operating expenses enormously by cutting off food and essential services now supplied by CCC; and would strip it of the vast Federal sources of technical and material assistance on work projects. It all added up to a major disaster.

Spurred on by these dark thoughts, the boys filled the telephone lines to Washington with their hopes and fears. Calls were made to Lanigan, to James Rowe, to John Fox, to see if some way out of the pincers could be found. A suggestion was put forward to place the Camp under the Farm Security Administration, but a maze of legal considerations blocked this proposal, and there was no time to wade through them. Letters were hurriedly dispatched to Senator Aiken and Representative Plumley of Vermont by Nathan Dodge urging their intervention. Mrs. Greene sent a letter to Mrs. Roosevelt reviewing the deep ties between the Camp and the communities, and explaining what a severe blow the loss of Sharon would be, both materially and spiritually. Most of these appeals were spontaneous and unsolicited.

Many public officials, such as Senator Aiken, acted without delay:

> Dear Nate:
>
> Thank you very much for your letter of February 20th regarding Camp William James. I have contacted the CCC about this, and I intend to do all I can to see that the Camp is allowed to continue its experiment.[7]

While these unorganized, and at times frantic, efforts were being made to wriggle out of McEntee's grasp, the membership of the Camp held frequent "councils of war." The Department of Agriculture, having been relieved of its management responsibilities, could no longer be counted as an ally. Indeed, even the Supervisory Committee which had been set up to administer the Camp, and which had never become active, was now little more than a figurehead. The forty-two members of "Camp William James" shortly realized that they were facing their "Dunkirk" alone. The trend of the discussions was all in the direction of evacuation of both the Camp and the CCC before McEntee could bend them to his wishes. If McEntee's appointed commander were accepted unchallenged, no initiative or freedom of action would remain to the boys. They would become isolated individuals once more, to be inevitably separated from each other and dispersed to camps all over the country. More than this, the bond between the Camp and the communities, through the Council of the Nine Towns, would be irrevocably severed.

Thus, the primary choice to be made was whether the enrollees wished to stick together in as large a number as possible and try to make a fresh start on their own, or whether they should admit defeat and let events make their own destiny.

The news from Washington continued to be bad. Everyone, it seemed, was up in arms against McEntee, but only verbally and "in principle." It was reported that the CCC Director was attempting to get the publicity-hungry Dies committee to take a hand in investigating the Camp, in the event his present moves to destroy it were unsuccessful. This prospect of a long, distortion-laden battle over the Camp remained decidedly distasteful to the Roosevelt Administration, for reasons which have been previously mentioned. In addition to this, the Camp could not openly criticize and berate its sponsors for their lack of support at the very moment it was pleading for it. Such tactics would only anger and antagonize the Administration, and would gain no positive ends. Likewise, a heavy broadside against McEntee, personally, would be ineffective because the Camp had no power by itself to force the Director to rescind his order, or to resign. Only the Administration leaders had this prerogative, and they were most reluctant to use it. McEntee had parried every attempt by Senators, Congressmen, and supporters of the Camp to make him change his mind. His methodical answer to them was simply to quote the CCC statute regarding operation of the camps and to advise them of his "duty" to carry it out to the letter. To this discretionary use of his office there was no effective rebuttal.

Therefore, most signs seemed to point toward a mass withdrawal from Sharon at the earliest possible date. This procedure, direct though it was, posed tremendous difficulties. The boys had no money, no equipment, no place of retreat, and they were still under the jurisdiction of the CCC. Each of these primary difficulties had to be overcome before any movement was possible. The first step was to secure honorable CCC discharges for those who wished them. As has been pointed out above, several of the non-college enrollees felt they could not take the risk of losing their meager CCC income by trusting to the uncertainty of private endowment for the Camp. There were many excellent boys in this group, and the prospect of losing them for a few dollars of security was a heavy blow. They had come, as the others had, in good faith and full of high expectation. Now they were disillusioned by the turn of events, and were disconsolate at the course they had to pursue. Many were ashamed to ask to go back to their old companies, where they feared both reprisals by the command, and the derision of their old friends. Truly, the damage to the morale and the spirit of these young men was enormous. Many of them had never had much vigor and hope in their lives before they had come to Sharon. The Camp, in spite of its many cares and hardships, had at least provided the bedrock of real fellowship and the spark of future promise. And now, after a few brief weeks, all was again darkness and despair.

Since it was now within McEntee's power to give a dishonorable discharge to any enrollee who did not obey orders, the personal good record of every boy in Camp was endangered. Professor Huessy addressed himself to this matter, and asked Hendrickson to call a meeting of the Supervisory Committee so that honorable discharges could be guaranteed to those who sought them. At least this much was due to the boys. Hendrickson replied that he would direct Morrell to ask McEntee for such a guarantee, and that an answer would be forthcoming "within ten days." The assurance of individual freedom from the CCC was thus temporarily left in doubt.

A meeting of the Council for the Nine Towns was hastily convened to determine where the Council and the communities stood in this crisis. Although the Council members were not elected officers in a representative sense, and were not legally authorized to speak for their fellow-citizens, they were influential and vital ambassadors. Without the backing of the Council there would be slim chance of success if the Camp were to become a private institution. At the meeting, which was attended by some of the Camp members, the Council was given a report of the various happenings up to that moment, and their implications. The result of the meeting was the passage of two resolutions:

> 1.) It is the sentiment of the Council and the towns that if the Camp is to remain a (regular) CCC camp, we will withdraw our support from the members of the Camp unless they are able to carry out their original project.
>
> 2.) It is the sentiment of this meeting that we approve of the conduct of the boys and their work at the Sharon camp but, if the Camp is continued as a regular CCC camp, we would support the boys in seeking an honorable discharge at this time.[8]

Huessy was authorized to present these resolutions at a meeting of the Supervisory Committee which Hendrickson had called for March 10th, in Washington. At least the communities were now informed as to the facts, and were aware of the peril threatening the enrollees. Huessy also intended to find out at the Washington meeting whether the Sharon camp-site and buildings could be transferred to the guardianship of Council and Camp, Inc., the non-profit educational corporation which had recently been brought into being. The plan would be to have the Federal government lease the Sharon facilities either to the corporation directly, or to the State of Vermont, which would in turn make them available to the Camp. This scheme was not laid out in too great detail, but it represented one means of solving the question of housing for those who "seceded." At worst, there could be nothing more than a refusal, and this was not unexpected.

In all honesty, it must now be said that this open conflict between Camp William James and the CCC administration, which was climaxed by McEntee's order, did not rally all the Camp's friends in equal measure. Several members of the Supervisory Committee were wary of supporting the Camp too vehemently. One of them, Nat Sage of the Massachusetts Institute of Technology, actually recommended McEntee's appointee[9] for commander as an "efficient" man, and "easy to get along with." This conception, which only thought of individual personalities, completely missed the significance of what had happened. As Huessy commented, "They (the Supervisory Committee) want to kill the boys' ideas by keeping them quiet. They wish to accomplish this by keeping their bellies well-filled. This indolence on the part of the Department of Agriculture is more exasperating than McEntee's direct attack."[10]

Dean Landis, it appears, considered it somewhat "unfortunate" that Huessy had played such a major role in the formation and growth of the Camp. He believed that Huessy's vulnerability with respect to his lack of citizenship and his former connection with the German work camps had made the Camp equally vulnerable to attack. While this may have been politically true, and while the Camp may have suffered greatly through the publicity given these facts, no one in the Camp looked at the matter as simply a question of expediency and convenience. Had the Camp been a purely bureaucratic creation, Huessy could have been divorced from the project at the first sign of trouble. But it was not that kind of an organism. Huessy had been one of its guiding lights. His energy and his complete identification of his own fortunes with those of the boys were not gifts which are forgotten when the going gets rough. He was entitled to, and received, the same kind of loyalty from the Camp as he gave to it.

This is not to say that Huessy, like any other man with deep convictions, could avoid meeting resistance, or even making enemies. Such clashes were inevitable. Furthermore, his differences in temperament and nationality emphasized his often unorthodox intellect. Many people opposed him not only for his doctrines, but because of the way he expressed them. (We recall his exchanges with Hendrickson in December, and the dubious effect of his personality on Landis in January.) Yet it is important to state that those who criticized him most were invariably those who knew him least. In the course of time and contact, people often changed their minds about him. To illustrate this point, here is an example of how one man's feelings were altered as his friendship with Huessy grew:

> I came from Tunbridge—the most conservative town in Orange County. Orange County is the most conservative county in Vermont.

> Vermont is the most conservative state in the Union, and I suppose I'm the most conservative man in Tunbridge. But from the first, the Camp project appealed to me. On the other hand, there were all kinds of rumors, such as the boys being 'fifth columnists.' So I said, 'If they're so bad, let's get them off in the woods where they can't do any damage.' Then there was the rumor that it cost $500 to have Dorothy Thompson at the rally—why, there isn't that much money in Tunbridge.
>
> After the formation of the sponsors' committee, we didn't know what we were going to do. Things haven't moved as fast as I've wished, but I suppose that can't be helped. . . . .
>
> Now about the Camp. They have a leader I like to think of as a spiritual leader. I was not much impressed when I first met him, but I've come to appreciate him as a man of sterling qualities. I sympathize with his losses in coming to this country. Although he is of another nationality—a people with whom we are practically at war—I'd trust him as much as I'd trust a man I've known all my life.[11]

The point of this quotation is that an individual like Nathan Dodge, whose habits, speech, appearance, and education were as dissimilar to Huessy's as it is possible to imagine, could feel genuine friendship and respect for him. These feelings were reciprocated, and merely add proof to the contention that real human understanding is primarily the product of personal relationships, rather than hasty generalizations. There is no substitute for calling a man by his right name, and being able to shake his hand.

The purpose of the preceding few paragraphs is not to propagate or evaluate Huessy's theories and beliefs. Such matters are not within the scope or intent of this book. However, there has been considerable misinterpretation of his position and influence in "Camp William James," ranging from that of a Svengali to that of a Machiavelli, to name a few conceptions. Thus some explanatory statement was necessary. The Camp itself had often been judged solely on the basis of what the person making the judgment happened to think of Huessy personally. I mention this specifically because such judgments were frequently unfair, both to the Camp and to the man. Huessy was a chief figure in the evolution of the Camp; but so were a lot of other people. A reading of this history will hardly support the claim that he was the dominant and dictatorial figure.

* * * * *

By coincidence, Dorothy Thompson had been engaged by a student organization at Dartmouth College to give a major address in Hanover on March 3rd. She was scheduled to speak on the world crisis in general, and a large audience was in prospect. The day before her speech, she contacted the Camp and urged as many enrollees as possible to attend. She intimated that there would be some mention of the Camp in her talk, but she did not say how it would be related to the rest of her remarks. In response to this invitation, about thirty members of the Camp were able to make the trip. The meeting had been well publicized, and the hall was filled to capacity. In fact, a loud speaker system was set up in the College chapel to handle the large crowd. It had been a long time since two thousand people in Hanover had turned out to hear a public lecture. There was even a group of students who journeyed up from Harvard for the occasion

From the start, there was little doubt as to the temper of Dorothy Thompson's remarks, and where her sentiments lay. Using the camp as a concrete example of her thesis, she excoriated the frustration and emptiness of American life, which too often worshipped physical well-being as the highest human objective. There were, she felt, other instincts in life besides the desire for material pleasure, namely, the instinct of self-assertion, and the instinct of love. People nowadays were afraid of emotion, afraid of living, afraid of enthusiasm. A new creativity was needed, and she used the story of "Camp William James," its founding and its trials, as her illustration of what should be done. In conclusion, she said:

> Now what has happened? A great fear grips the bureaucracy. It is the fear that someone might do something under his own steam in a new way; might diverge from the pattern. The whole great structure totters with fear before forty or fifty boys who entered the CCC because they wanted to. That is dangerous to the bureaucracy. The boys even say they will run their Camp cheaper than the government could. But they musn't, because that will upset the system.
>
> For the first time in the history of the CCC a whole community welcomes a camp, wants to work with it, collaborate with it, plan with it. The mere fact is revolutionary. The bureaucracy says it is dangerous. The great inexorable wheels of the system start turning. 'We will move the Camp to another community and thus destroy the

> bloodstream connecting it with the people. The esprit de corps will be shattered. It is dangerous because it contains enthusiasts. The nucleus is a group of young men who don't want jobs in Washington. That in itself is weird and strange.'
>
> This 'Camp William James' and what happened to it at the hands of the bureaucracy throws light on the whole decadence of freedom and democracy. Power is passing from those who create to those who file catalogues.
>
> I came here to ask you to help us to awaken a new birth of democracy and freedom founded on common brotherhood. I want you to break down the Washington bureaucracy and help make Mr. McEntee take his stranglehold off the experimental work camp already agreed upon. Please, I would rather see a dozen young men who are willing to *do* something than two hundred who will just talk.[12]

There was no question but what Dorothy Thompson's appeal was dynamic and sincere. She had brought her meaning and her plea right home to the students themselves. Immediately following the prepared address, a smaller and more informal meeting was held in a campus building so that discussion could be carried on by those who wished to pursue the matter further. As Miss Thompson spoke to the small group, urging her listeners to come to grips with specific problems such as the Camp, the room's atmosphere began to change. Voices grew more intense, more assertive. Finally, one green-clad CCC boy, who had been taking it all in silently, rose and said, 'I don't believe writing petitions and all that sort of thing honestly counts for very much. We need you out there badly. I'd like to know how many would come—tomorrow." Three voices cried, "I'll come!" Other hands went up and voices called in a mixture of emotions, conditions, eagerness. Times and dates shot across the room. Then somebody rose and tried to institute parliamentary procedure. Through the confusion, a meeting time was set for the next day, and the gathering adjourned on a high plane of enthusiasm.

The immediate result of the evening's events was to arouse the audience, especially the student body, to a considerable emotional pitch. A comparable excitement had been generated by few speakers within the memory of those present. Dorothy Thompson had vehemently brought her case "to the people," and the impending fate of the Camp had been her chief talking point.

What would come of it?

The next day, a meeting was held at Dartmouth for those students who wished to take the kind of action which Miss Thompson had recommended. Several members of the Camp were present to tell what was needed and to talk to prospective recruits. It was made plain that any volunteers would have to give their full time as enrollees, whether it be for a week or a year. No one could be accepted who did not come on the basis of "all-out." It was clearly stated that the college boys were not to be donors and observers who were doing the "other half" a favor by living with them for a few months. Page Smith summed it up by saying that the Camp had given him an education at least as whole and complete as he had received in Dartmouth. After the discussion, some of the students voted to submit a petition to the President and Trustees of the College asking for a semester's leave of absence to serve in "Camp William James," and requesting permission to return to the college in good standing at the end of that period. The petition read:

> We are under no illusions about the gravity of the request we have to make of you. The present uncertainties surrounding our futures as young men in the world of 1941 have served to make us uncommonly aware of the opportunities and obligations we possess as college men. We love Dartmouth, and intend to finish our college education, but first we desire to lend our hands and backs for a while to the urgent tasks now before our country. Some of us have already determined to do this in any event. Others prefer, however, that Dartmouth College back us wholeheartedly in the move so that more of our fellow-students may see their way to accompany or follow us. We believe that the active and benevolent sanction of the Administration will set a profound example for other colleges and universities. Therefore, we ask that any students desirous of taking this action be given formal leave for at least one semester.
>
> A similar request is being submitted (by Harvard undergraduates) to the officers of Harvard University.
>
> /signed/
>
> William Uptegrove, '42 Clinton Gardner, '44
> Robbins Barstow, '41 Richard Miller, '43
> William Lowry, '41 Russell Hurlburt, '44
> Edward Little, '41 Edward Chalfont, '42

The effect of this petition was to stir up mixed opinions on the campus. Many people felt that these students had "gone off the deep end," and that if they would wait a week or so, reason and cooler heads would prevail. Conversely, there were those who felt that delay would only lead to vacillation and lack of positive action, and that high enthusiasm should be regarded as an asset rather than a liability.

The Administration of the College was in a difficult position. They had no way of knowing exactly how determined the petitioners were. If the petition were granted, it might set off a mass exodus from Hanover, and disrupt the entire program of the College, at least momentarily. If the petition were denied, some students might defy the College, and leave anyway. Disciplinary action of a drastic nature would then have to be undertaken which might put the College in an extremely uncomfortable position, such as being accused of "autocratically suppressing the patriotism of the students." Either choice was fraught with possible dangers, and no immediate decision on the petition was rendered.

* * * * *

Following the Dartmouth activities, a Camp meeting was held at Sharon, with Dorothy Thompson, to see what the next steps should be. Miss Thompson gave a resume of her talk of the previous evening, and urged the Camp personnel not to become discouraged. She felt that new recruits would come from Dartmouth, and that the outside friends of the Camp could be counted on to help save it. Page Smith, acting Camp manager, thanked Miss Thompson for her support in a difficult hour, and said that the boys appreciated her strenuous efforts in their behalf.

The urgent question still to be answered was whether the enrollees should stick together, or else break up and call it quits. Huessy urged that the little "nutshell" be kept going at Sharon for at least a couple of weeks to see what developed on the Washington scene. A suggestion was also made that a part of the group leave the CCC and set up privately in Tunbridge, allowing the others to remain in camp and preserve connections with the government. There were many objections to this latter scheme, since it really amounted to abandoning the men in the CCC to their fate. The consensus of opinion was that it would have to be all one thing or all the other—either stay in the Corps, and see what happened, or collect as large a group as possible and leave together. Those who remained in the CCC would then do so as individuals, for their own good reasons, and would have no responsibility or obligation to those who had left.

The risks of the private camp were such that many of the non-college enrollees could not assume them, and they frankly admitted their inability to take the step. On the other hand, many of the college boys felt a strong obligation to the local farmers and communities. If the Camp remained a regular CCC outfit, they believed that continuing on as enrollees would be a breach of faith with the local people. The original purposes of the Camp, including help to farmers and the promotion of resettlement, had to be carried out and worked for, regardless of the auspices. If the government would not help, then they would have to go on alone. It was obvious that these two views could not be held simultaneously, and that each would claim a certain number of adherents. Most of the boys realized that a choice had to be made at once, and the pleas for delay by Dorothy Thompson and Huessy could not dissuade those who wished to leave.

Directly after this meeting, at which an evacuation vote was passed, arrangements were begun to prepare for the exodus. The pressing needs were housing, some interior furnishings, and limited funds for an initial purchase of food. On their own initiative, three of the non-college enrollees, who had not even met many of the Vermonters personally, set off in search of a house. Presenting the facts squarely to such people as Lawrence Bowen and Nathan Dodge, they called upon them to make good their past pledges to aid the boys, whether in the Camp or out of it. This bold campaign achieved prompt results. Through the generosity of Marian Mentzer, of Tunbridge, an abandoned farm was donated to the group as temporary quarters. The irony of this whole excursion was that after triumphantly returning with news of their victory, these three boys, led by Fremont Smith, cryptically announced they were staying in the CCC. No amount of persuasion could move them.

"Jes wanted you to know we could get things done, too," Fremont said. "We went up to Bowen and give 'im hell. 'Looka here,' we said, 'we're leavin' Camp and we need a place to stay. You people want us here, so what are ya goin' to do about it?' Boy, he did somethin' alright. We stayed right with 'im all the way.

"Well, you got your house, by Jesus. Now go live in it."

So saying, he lay down on his bed and picked up his *Wild West* magazine. Most of those who heard Fremont Smith make his farewell speech found themselves swallowing hard a few times when he had finished. There were too many like him who were going to be left behind.

The next two days saw further progress made. Jack Preiss and Bill Lowry once more secured bedding on a rental basis from Dartmouth College, and trucked it up to the Mentzer farm. Local people contributed various articles of furniture, such as chairs, boards and saw horses to serve as a dining room table, a few carpenter's hand tools, and some burlap to fill in the chinks in the walls. Mrs. Greene again donated some money to buy food and a few other essentials. At this moment, word arrived from Hendrickson that an honorable discharge from the CCC would be granted to anyone in the Sharon camp who wished one. The notification had come with perfect timing, and on March 6th, twenty-four boys went to Bellows Falls, Vermont to sever their connection with the government. The reason they gave? "To help establish 'Camp William James.' "

11. Interim Camp

Thus began an entirely new phase of the struggle. The tremendous efforts and energies of the past year and a half were now to be written off—forgotten. The painstaking groundwork which had been laid in Washington, the hundreds of talks made and letters written to convince the skeptics, the countless hours of labor represented by the plumbing, trenches, the new barrack, the garage, built at Sharon in the dead of winter, the eighteen CCC boys who had come a long way to become part of this new and hopeful project—all of these left behind, simply by writing one's name on a discharge form.

For many good and obvious reasons, it can be argued that the whole enterprise should have ended then and there. Surely there could now be little hope of bringing about any reforms in the CCC, much less to begin a national voluntary work service movement. Almost half of the camp personnel had been lost through secession. In addition to this, the inroads of the draft were now a reality. Arnold Childs was first to go, early in March, and Page Smith was to be called up before the end of the month. There were still no long-range projects in operation, or even worked out on paper, and if there had been, there were no tools or equipment to carry them out. How long could twenty-four men eke out an existence on such prospects in a rickety old dwelling which, in its prime, should only have housed eight people? The "interim camp" calculated it had between two and three weeks' resources, and that a more permanent plan would have to be formulated within that time.

After making their "move," the new Tunbridge group, for such it was once again, sent a message to the Dartmouth students who were offering to leave school to join them. The events of the past seventy-two hours had occurred so rapidly and had altered the picture so drastically, that it would have been asking too much of these men to desert their college careers at this time. The farmhouse was already overcrowded, and the fate of the group was very much in doubt. Much sobered by their own precarious position, the Tunbridge boys wrote, "Allow us to enlist you with prudence and circumspection. We ask you to remain in college to await our call for help and assistance." This almost pious statement contrasted sharply with the high waves of emotion which had surged up a few days before.

* * * * *

It would be worthwhile here to try to analyze the underlying causes and effects of this rather dramatic evacuation of the Sharon camp.

Among the causes were the fairly obvious ones which have already been mentioned. But more impelling than these professions of obligation to the Vermont people and the pursuit of worthwhile work programs was the feeling of frustration and despair which the Sharon Camp represented. If the boys remained in the Corps, they would have shown admission of defeat on all fronts, and the eventual dispersion of Camp personnel would have signified complete surrender. Most of the boys, especially the college group, being fully aware of the issues and principles involved, could not stomach this kind of passive defeat. They had to keep on fighting, no matter how grim the future or insuperable the odds. It might be said they were resisting more by instinct than by logic, for their logic had surely told them to stop. This was one of those curious but elevating moments in people's lives when they keep on fighting simply because they *have to.* There is something in the mind and heart that will not give in of its own volition. This was the thing which really made the boys keep going, and it was that feeling which William James would have recognized at once as a moral equivalent of war. Out of the misery of the rundown Mentzer farm it was shining as bright as a beacon on a hilltop. By this one act of lone defiance, the boys had paid their "blood tax"—without knowing it. This was why they had come back to Tunbridge.

What choices were left for tomorrow? The whole shape and scope of the movement had been transformed. Physical assets were nil and funds could now be procured only from private organizations and individuals, plus what the boys could earn themselves by daily labor for the farmers. One effect of this situation was to lay new emphasis on the camp as an economic unit. The Camp henceforth had to "make" money in order to survive, and this in itself was an innovation. The communities now had to absorb the Camp into the local economy. The Camp members were no longer government employees who were "loaned" to the citizens to do various jobs. They were now private individuals, trying to earn their way on the same footing as anyone else. This change of status was very important, since it cut the prop of financial security from under the entire structure. The boys now had to compete for jobs with older, more experienced people, and were therefore at a considerable disadvantage. Only by hiring themselves out as a group, for very low wages, could they compensate for their lack of skill.

Another effect of the decision to keep operating, was the increased desire to find some new means of group expression. The Camp could not be allowed to degenerate into an employment bureau, living on a day to day basis. Some definite form had to be found which would be larger and more enduring than the present group itself.

This problem was at least partially solved by a lucky accident. It will be remembered that the non-profit educational corporation, Council and Camp, Inc., had been formed in January for the primary purpose of acquiring and holding real estate and other properties on which "Camp William James" might wish to work. This would have circumvented the difficulties in the path of Federal acquisition of private lands. When it became evident that the government could not, or would not, erect a building at Sharon to serve as a reception center for the resettlement project, some other avenue had to be found. Mrs. Greene had suggested that the corporation should act as agent for the Camp in trying to raise funds from private individuals and foundations. She specifically recommended the "Edward Filene Good Will Fund," which had headquarters in Boston and whose Director, Mr. Percy Brown, was a friend of hers. The principal work of the Fund was to assist worthy projects with grants of money which would enable them to achieve their goals. Robert O'Brien, the representative of the Camp on the board of directors of the corporation had spoken to Brown early in February and had outlined the proposal for the reception center. Brown was interested, and asked that a formal request for money, along with an explanation of its intended use, be made in writing to the Good Will Fund. He said that he would see to it that the Board of Directors took prompt action, one way or the other. He, personally, felt hopeful of success. Accordingly, O'Brien had dispatched a letter in which he said:

> Dear Mr. Brown,
>
> Following our conversation, I herewith submit, on behalf of Council and Camp, Inc., of which Mr. Nathan Dodge, Tunbridge, Dorothy Canfield Fisher, Arlington, and myself are the incorporators, and which has been set up by an act of the Secretary of State of Vermont, our request for a gift of $3,000 dollars for our immediate task of erecting a reception center.
>
> The trouble with resettlement in Vermont has been that previous attempts were made by individuals who expected immediate returns, and who used depleted soil and abandoned farms without instituting a thorough-going change in economy, without taking time to establish local contacts and to learn the character and climate of the region.
>
> It is our intention to base resettlement on a long-range program. We will take the time out to form living groups first, and only second to this shall we dare to establish individual settlers. The old farmers are not an integrated group, nor would any newcomers be capable of constituting one by themselves. However, when properly introduced to each other, and when helped by a third group (Camp William James) devoted almost exclusively to their integration, these two elements can cooperatively plan and build the kind of mixed economy which is so badly needed. In this process, the farmers 'old' and the farmers 'new' would come to know each other and to consider each other as full partners in the future of their community.[1]

This letter had been written while the Sharon CCC Camp was still a going concern, and although the events of the subsequent three weeks had altered the appearance of "Camp William James," it had not changed its goals. It was now problematical whether the new private structure of the Camp would add to or detract from its chances of receiving this aid. Yet a grant from the Fund was the only concrete step which would be in time to salvage the human assets which had migrated to Tunbridge.

While awaiting the decision of the Goodwill Fund, the boys got along as best they could. It was the tail end of winter, but the snow and cold gave them no respite. The floor of the farmhouse began to sag dangerously under the unaccustomed number of occupants, and had to be "shored up" with green posts cut in the nearby woods. With many of the second story shingles and clapboards gone, along with numerous panes of glass, sleeping was like retiring in a wind tunnel. The position of night guard (tending the fire in the pot burner heater) was the most coveted job in the Camp, despite the fact that it meant being up most of the night. Sanitation was rudimentary, since all water had to be carried up in milk cans from a spring a quarter of a mile away. A one-hole privy, located in the drafty wood shed, served the entire group. Meals were delegated to cooking crews of two men each, with two others assigned to dishwashing and some primitive house cleaning. The basic diet consisted of hot cereals, bread with jam and peanut butter, an occasional soupy stew, and oceans of coffee.

On the working level, the largest group was engaged in tree cutting and hurricane timber clearance on the farm of Phillip Whitney in Tunbridge. Other boys went out singly, and several hired out by the week. But most of them returned to Camp each night (usually *after* supper, if they could manage it). Whatever was earned from any source was put into a common pool to help defray operating expenses.

Frank Davidson had made one more trip to Washington to determine whether something could be salvaged from the political wreckage of the Sharon site. A faint flicker of Federal assistance might yet be preserved. The idea was this. The Sharon site was to be shut down, so that it would not become a regular CCC camp, and thereby exert a negative influence in the community. Then the Farm Security Administration would be asked to hire about a dozen of the boys in Tunbridge to work part-time on some of its "special area" projects in the vicinity. There would be considerable opportunity for planning new long-range projects which might later be Federally approved. The twelve boys would each be paid about $30 a month for their assistance. Thus, through their appointment, the door would always be left open for more active government participation. At first, Davidson found Olmstead and the Farm Security people rather favorable to this scheme, although they were all sensitive about further conflicts which it might engender. At the same time, he contacted Vermont's Senators Austin and Aiken, Representative Plumley, Henry Wallace, Supreme Court Justice Stone and Frankfurter, and Mrs. Roosevelt. He made appointments for Professor Huessy to see all of these, except Mrs. Roosevelt who would be out of town, during his trip to Washington to attend the final meeting of the Supervisory Committee.

This meeting was held on March 12th, and it was not rich in positive accomplishment. Hendrickson, as Chairman, disclosed that a grand total of thirty-six of the original forty-two members of the Camp had eventually received honorable CCC discharges. The rest had remained in the Corps. Huessy presented the resolutions of the Council of the Nine Towns supporting the boys, as well as opinions from Dorothy Thompson and others that some means should be found to have the government support the Camp independently for at least six months. These possibilities were discussed, and the only feasible plan seemed to be the part-time Farm Security jobs, mentioned above. Appleby said the Department had no legally approved means of supporting the new group in Tunbridge, and Nat Sage re-expressed his opinion that the boys should have stayed in the original CCC camp. Hendrickson, who clearly wished to wind up the entire matter, objected to the Farm Security scheme as placing an unwarranted obligation upon the Department of Agriculture, and possibly inviting more damaging criticism and publicity. Appleby said that if the twelve men were hired, those remaining in Tunbridge would have to disband so that these twelve would not appear to be supporting the entire group. The rest of the Department representatives concurred. Mr. Sage agreed that the group should break up, or at least contract to a self-supporting size. Huessy countered that any real breaking up would certainly destroy the spirit of the boys who were left.

The questions of the future use of the Sharon camp site and the needs of the White River District of the Soil Conservation Service were considered. The needs of the SCS were in doubt, and Morrell thought the CCC camp facilities would probably be closed down entirely, unless there was an urgent job to be done. Appleby recommended that Morrell try to get McEntee to leave the campsite physically intact for a while so that the plan to turn it over to the State of Vermont, which would then lease or give it to Council and Camp, Inc., could be thoroughly examined.

Professor Huessy summarized the needs of the Tunbridge group over a four month period until private support could be developed and new recruits found. He figured that between three and four thousand dollars would be needed to keep things going. Appleby pointed out that it was not a matter of cost, but rather of the legal capacity and administrative wisdom of the Department contributing to the Camp as it was now constituted. Furthermore, he did not see much future ahead for the group. The other members of the Committee then questioned the desirability of making any contribution. A Mr. Hudgens, of the Farm Security Administration, was called in and asked about the possibility of hiring the twelve boys. He said it could be done, but was reluctant to take part in such a move. The matter was held in abeyance pending further consideration by Farm Security.

Finally, it was proposed that the Supervisory Committee be relieved of further responsibility for the Camp and that the Committee should be dissolved forthwith. This was agreed to, and the Committee voted itself out of existence a few months later.

The result of this meeting, and the subsequent failure of the Farm Security Administration to supply any assistance, marked the final severance of relations between "Camp William James" and the Federal government. But the Camp had little inclination to moan over this final break, for a few bright spots were appearing in the clouds. First, Henry James, the third son of William James, had sent a check to help pay for Camp running expenses. Second, within a week after the first exodus from Sharon, six more enrollees had resigned from the CCC and had joined the group in Tunbridge. This raised the total number to thirty, and meant that there was still a considerable nucleus of boys with which to build anew.

On March 26th, Nathan Dodge, as chairman of the Council of the Nine Towns, received a letter from Paul Appleby giving official notice of the withdrawal of the Department of Agriculture from the project. This was in response to a last-minute telegram from Dodge asking that the Camp be saved:

Dear Mr. Dodge,

Your telegram asks us to make a grant to Council and Camp, Inc., to help it run 'Camp William James'. . . . . The fact is that no matter how much we might like to, there is no way whatever in which this Department can make such a grant or otherwise assume any responsibility for the continuation of the Camp.

I realize that from your point of view, and that of the boys, this position may well seem to be deliberately unsympathetic, but it is not. It is simply a recognition of the facts as they stand.

This does not detract from the fact that the Sharon program is, in most of its aspects, a good program, and one that should be pursued. It is just, as I have said, that it is not, in its present stage, the sort of program that this Department is authorized to carry out.

Please believe me when I say that we in the Department are grateful to the people in the Nine Towns, the Tunbridge boys, Dr. Huessy, and yourself for the excellent work you have all done. Whatever happens, 'Camp William James' stands as an outstanding example of the kind of citizen interest in improving their government which is of the highest value. Its lessons will not be lost. We learned things from our brief experience with the Camp which, I can assure you, will be carried into many aspects of the work of the Department and will result in widespread benefits.

Please keep me posted on developments on this matter because you know that I am very much interested.

Sincerely,

/s/P. H. Appleby
Under Secretary[2]

And so the Vermonters, in their turn, were told that the door leading to government aid was irrevocably, though reluctantly, closed. From now on, no one on the Council or in the Camp harbored the illusion that some Federal "miracle" would occur to eliminate all their troubles.

McEntee had won the day.

* * * * *

At about this time, the boys in Tunbridge received what proved to be their last major visit from a representative of the nation's press. Mr. Bill Cunningham, a Dartmouth man, and one of the chief columnists of the *Boston Herald,* came up to the Mentzer farm to get the true story of the past few months. He spent almost two days talking to the boys, meeting local people, and trying to discover precisely what was being done—and why. His feature article was entitled, "College Idealists Face Losing Battle," and in it he pointed out that in spite of high purposes and earnest effort, the Camp was in a bad spot. He also found the members somewhat inarticulate when asked to describe their movement. This, of course, was not a new failing, and we have seen evidences of it before. On the other hand, despite the stresses and strains of the political battles, the constant shifting of personnel and locale, and the pre-occupation with the details of living from day to day, the general ideas were there, and had been stated over and over again. The democratization of the CCC, the training of leaders for it, the aid to the local farmers in their work, the inauguration of a reception center to encourage resettlement—all of these things were well-known in principle. But there was admittedly not much to show for the almost two years of work and sacrifice which had been given to the attempt to translate them into reality. Cunningham managed to catch the atmosphere of resignation which now prevailed around the Camp, and to express it in his article. He sympathized with the boys' plight, and considerably admired their quiet but firm determination to continue their work. His summary and evaluation of the Camp turned out to be one of the best articles about the boys ever published, but it had come too late to do much good.

* * * * *

The key to securing private financial backing lay squarely in the hands of the directors of the Goodwill Fund, and they had promised to give a prompt answer to the formal request made by Council and Camp, Inc., via O'Brien's letter. In anticipation of a possible grant-in-aid, the boys had begun looking around the vicinity for a satisfactory farm which could be purchased for a reasonable sum. Guided by Nathan Dodge, Ed Flint, and others, they finally located a place which seemed ideal. This farm was several miles off the main road, on Tunbridge East Hill, and was owned by Ed Rivers, who had lately been unwell, and therefore desired to unload his responsibilities. The farm was basically a good one, although the house and barn were in some disrepair, and the land needed rejuvenation. There was plenty of marketable lumber and pulpwood, along with a substantial "sugar bush" of maple trees. These trees would be ready for tapping about the first week in April. All in all, there did not seem to be any major deficiency on the farm which could not be easily remedied.

Above all, there would be plenty of willing hands to do whatever was necessary. For instead of losing its precious manpower, the Camp was gaining new adherents, who more than replaced those who were lost to the Army. The great blasts of unfavorable publicity which had attended the Congressional uproar did attract some persons who were interested in finding out what lay beneath the surface. During January and February, a thin but steady stream of young men, motivated by more than mere curiosity, had sandwiched themselves in among a host of more voluble, but less purposeful, guests. Several of these young men, such as Daniel Goldsmith and Daniel Bernstein of New York, David Mellor, a Dartmouth graduate from Stockbridge, Mass., and others quietly joined the fellowship of the Camp and went out to serve their apprenticeship on local farms, just as the original Tunbridge boys had done. This background of farm work and living with the Vermonters was a prerequisite for each volunteer, in order to prove his fortitude and sincerity, and to help him discover for himself the essential spirit which had led to the founding of the Camp. After this "initiation" he could then join the rest of the group on equal terms and feel "at home" with them all.

On April 6th, after two more weeks of expectation, following a personal visit by Percy Brown to Tunbridge for a conference with the boys and a survey of the local scene, the good news came. The Goodwill Fund had voted to grant "Camp William James" three thousand dollars to purchase the Rivers farm as its permanent home. At the same time, Mr. and Mrs. Greene, whose past generosity to the Camp had not been surpassed by anyone, came forward with another magnificent gift of one thousand dollars to purchase the reception center (i.e. the farmhouse on the Rivers property). Finally, the Goodwill Fund also contributed enough money to pay the running expenses of the new Camp for about six weeks, so that the tasks of moving, cleaning up the grounds, and planning the spring's work could be accomplished without undue privation.

At Camp William James in Tunbridge in the summer of 1941. *Above:* The tractor described on page 174, with the farmhouse and sugar house in background.

Below: Nancy Blaine, a founder of the Camp's "female division," feeding the pigs.

12. Rebirth In Tunbridge

This sudden onrush of good fortune worked wonders for the morale of the entire group. Amid the shouts and cheers which greeted the telegram from Percy Brown, the Camp began to prepare for its second movement within a month. Only this one was much the more pleasant of the two. The terms of the agreement between the Goodwill Fund and Council and Camp, Inc. were most generous for the latter. The Fund placed the entire responsibility for planning and developing the property in the hands of the boys in the Camp, with the corporation acting as legal owner. The Fund demanded no representation on the board of directors of the corporation, nor were any requirements made concerning policies to be pursued. The mortgage simply stated that if the Camp were to run the farm satisfactorily, and in accordance with its stated objectives, for a period of five years, then Council and Camp, Inc. would become sole owners of the property, free and clear. If operations ceased, or were drastically curtailed before the five year period was over, the farm would revert back to the Fund, to be disposed of at its discretion. The Greene's gift, given in memory of a young French friend, Roger Faure, who had been killed in the Battle of France, was presented with the same general stipulations, although not similarly expressed in a mortgage. The major part of the Fund gift, along with that of the Greene's in its entirety, was put into capital investment, with the farmhouse on the Rivers' place now becoming a real "hearth where the young of all nations may meet."[1]

The Camp was rapidly organized for its new role. After Page Smith's departure, Robert O'Brien had been elected Camp manager, and Jack Preiss was put in charge of getting the farm work under way. Alfred Eiseman took over direction of house and barn repairs, and supervised the kitchen. Spirits were indeed high once again. The house foundations were repaired, the roofs shingled, the barn and stable thoroughly cleaned, and wood gathered for "sugaring." The increasingly warm days, coupled with crisp nights, had started the maple sap flowing during the period of moving, and although the boys had not had much experience in making maple syrup on their own, they tackled the job eagerly. Carrying the brimming five gallon sap pails through the hip-deep snow slowed them down after the first few days, but they never stopped, and there were plenty of replacements for those who became worn out. The product was not what might be classified as "Vermont Grade A," but it was passable enough, and was retail marketed in New York and Boston by various parents and friends. This operation brought about $500 into the treasury, and was evidence that the Camp did not intend to rely solely on the gifts of others for its material support.

In spite of the fact that this sugaring operation had been begun and completed before the end of April, with profits accruing to the Camp, the formal purchase of the farm and the buildings had not yet been consummated. The by-laws of Council and Camp, Inc. had just been drawn up by ex-governor Wilson, and were awaiting approval by the incorporators. After this approval, a board of directors would have to be elected to formally conduct such corporate dealings as handling funds and acquiring property.

O'Brien therefore wrote to Dorothy Canfield Fisher, who was recovering from a serious illness, requesting that a meeting of the incorporators be convened at her home in Arlington, Vermont to accept the by-laws and elect the directors. Mrs. Fisher agreed to have the meeting, although it meant taxing her limited strength, and she urged that a replacement be found for her position. She felt that she was too far from the scene to contribute much help, and also that a person with specific agricultural knowledge would be more valuable. O'Brien then persuaded Ed Flint to fill the gap left by Mrs. Fisher's impending resignation. On the 17th of April, O'Brien, Dodge, Flint, and George Phillips, who was to act as temporary secretary, journeyed to Mrs. Fisher's for this first meeting of the corporation. Mrs. Fisher's interesting, on-the-spot report of this meeting illustrates the kind of personal strain and mixed emotions with which all of these people entered upon their task:

About one o'clock, after lunch, we settled down to our meeting, and my four guests didn't leave the house till about five. And every one of those four hours was occupied in the most earnest, conscientious, heart-rending, attentive effort to do the right thing in this matter of the organization of the Camp.

Bob and Mr. Dodge had brought along a set of by-laws which had been worked out with Mr. Stanley Wilson, ex-governor of the state, and a very able lawyer. We read them carefully, and voted to accept them. Then the question of directors came up. Bob nominated me, formally, and I, formally, declined the nomination because I live too far away, and have not the special knowledge now needed. Mr. Flint was nominated and elected. Then Mr. Flint took the chair temporarily (all this was done with the utmost correctness in parliamentary fashion, you see) while Mr. Dodge was nominated and elected. Then Mr. Dodge took back the chairmanship, and Bob was nominated and elected. All this went through in record time. The question of (adding) two more directors came up. Mr. Dodge thought it much better to have that (added) number, if for nothing else than as a margin in case of illness. Mr. Dodge is, as you know, not at all sure of his own health.

But Bob had a strong feeling against having more than three. He seemed a little reluctant to say exactly why, and divining that he might not think it courteous to give his real reason, frankly, I urged him to let us know what was really in his mind. It came out that he feared that if there were five directors, the number would be too largely weighted with older people. It was pointed out that if there were, as Mr. Dodge wished, two young directors and two older people, that would make an equal representation on both sides, with Mr. Dodge, as chairman, not voting except in the case of a tie. Bob was very unwilling to agree to this, and said that if three of the five could be from the Camp, he would have no objection to having five directors. Mr. Dodge said that if Bob objected to leaving in his hands the responsibility of breaking a tie, he (Dodge) would resign.

Bob said, and I agreed with this, that Mr. Dodge's resignation would be tantamount to saying he did not approve of the Camp. Hence it would be very undesirable at this time to have Mr. Dodge resign.

Bob then said that if enough confidence was not felt in the boys, after all the sacrifices they had made, to allow them really to have the final authority on all matters connected with the Camp, he felt their sacrifices had not been appreciated. George Phillips then said that it wasn't a question of sacrifice on the boys' part, or confidence or lack of it in Mr. Dodge, but rather of trying to find an organization which might be a sound pattern for other such communal undertakings in the future.

All this discussion was not, as you can imagine, conducted as briefly as I have summarized it here. Every effort was made on all sides to be entirely open, and to withhold none of the reasons felt to be cogent. Mr. Dodge repeatedly said, with real feeling, with his usual dignity, and with the selfless wish only to do what was best for the Camp, that he would be willing to resign. Bob, evidently under considerable tension, repeated that he *felt* that if there were five directors, three of them should be from the Camp. We could not understand Bob's objection, since *he* had planned the three-director organization with a two-to-one representation of older people.

Seeing that Mr. Dodge was growing paler and paler, and finally that a little trickle of sweat began to run down his face, although we had no fire in the room and it was cool, I suggested that the best thing to do was to adjourn to another time, allowing Bob a chance to talk the situation over with Mrs. Greene and Professor Huessy. This recess was agreed to.

I then asked Mr. Dodge, who looked so pale and exhausted that I was quite concerned, if he wouldn't like a cup of tea and something to eat before taking the long trip back. He accepted with some eagerness, saying that his doctor directed him to eat five small meals a day rather than the usual three larger ones. So I hurried out to the kitchen, made tea and sandwiches for us all, for we were extremely tired. This was the first time I had taken on any such activity since my operation (and it was exactly the kind of thing the doctor had told me not to do.) I was deeply sympathetic both with Mr. Dodge and with Bob, and greatly admired both of them in their sincere and disinterested attempt to get the right thing done.

But after tea, with their hats in their hands, and Mr. Dodge's hand on the latch of the door, Bob suggested that we should reconvene the meeting, and that he would vote for the five directors—two from the Camp, two from the local people, and Mr. Dodge to break the tie. I had no idea in what spirit he made this suggestion. That is, whether he was really convinced of the wisdom of it, or that he simply thought something had to be done. The meeting had lasted so long, and Mr. Dodge was so tired, that I thought it best not to make any objection. So we sat down, hastily reconvened, and voted the measure. . . . .

It is difficult to remember afterwards precisely what were the words said during four hours of earnest talk. But I am sure of the spirit, which was admirable. I kept saying to myself, 'This is reality. The reason we are having these differences of opinion, this long discussion, is because the enterprise we are trying to forward is no longer a project being talked about, but is entering the field of actuality.' It is always a grave matter to leave theoretical discussion and come to grips with actual material facts. How many human undertakings have fallen by the wayside at the first breath of reality! It seemed to me that the 'Camp William James' project stood up sturdily as we tried to transplant it from hope and idealistic theory, into the real earth under the open sky of life.

/s/Dorothy Canfield Fisher[2]

Subsequent to this lengthy meeting, which had sorely tried the relations between the Camp, represented by O'Brien, and the Council of the Nine Towns, in the person of Mr. Dodge, the other two directors were chosen. They were Lyman Burbank, a farmer of Chelsea, and George Phillips, who became permanent secretary and clerk. A full directors' meeting was then held, on April 28th, and the corporation, using the grant made by the Goodwill Fund, was authorized to purchase the Rivers' farm as a permanent home for "Camp William James." It was also voted to accept various other cash gifts, including the $1000 from the Greene's, with the total amounting to $1250.

Thus, by rather painful but necessary labors, the Council and Camp, Inc. organization was established, and thereby became the legal and economic arm of the Camp project.

* * * * *

Around the end of April, after the snow had melted and the ground was ready for productive use, the problem of working the land came to the fore. Two fairly ancient horses had been purchased with the farm, but these did not seem "up" to coping with the large amount of work to be undertaken. The local Farm Security agent was engaged to make a farm plan, and to indicate the best utilization of the tillable acreage. Government-supplied lime and phosphate were to be provided free if the work was mapped out in detail and if the agent's recommendations were followed. However, the old team of horses was plainly inadequate for the job, especially when guided by inexperienced hands. This stumbling block could have been most formidable if it had not been for another rare streak of good fortune.

Early in May, Miss Katherine Taylor, director of the Shady Hill School in Cambridge, and a good friend of the Greene's, visited the Camp with Nancy Blaine of Chicago, who was attending art school in New York. Miss Blaine was dissatisfied with her work, however, and had come to Vermont with Miss Taylor to see what "Camp William James" was trying to do. She was immediately and profoundly impressed, and vociferously demanded to be allowed to help in any way she could. Having heard in conversation around the farm that there was no means of doing plowing and seeding, she offered, point-blank, to give the Camp a new tractor. Aside from its magnitude, this offer was remarkable for the sincerity with which it was made, and for the faith which a complete outsider had shown in the Camp after only a few hours' contact. The boys scraped enough of their own money together, using most of the proceeds of the sale of the maple syrup, to get a fairly complete set of implements to go along with the tractor. So, within almost a matter of minutes, the order was placed with a local dealer, and the problem of "mechanical power" had evaporated. Truly, the wonders had not ceased. Indeed, Nancy Blaine was so taken with the aims and purposes of the project, that she decided to leave school in New York in order to help inaugurate the first "female division" of "Camp William James."

* * * * *

At this juncture, an unexpected episode took place which shook the new Camp profoundly. To examine this episode in true perspective, we must go back a little, and pick up the story of Arthur Root, whom we left in New York nursing an injured back and infected sinuses. Root's objective, as he had written Huessy, was to become an "asset" to the Camp instead of a "liability." He was also compelled to find some means of regaining his health. He had discussed his dilemma, in January, with Waldo Frank, well-known author and traveler, who had suggested that he go to Mexico as soon as he was physically able to make the trip. Frank pointed out that there was much rehabilitation work to be done there, and that the climate in certain provinces was beneficial for allergy sufferers. Acting on this advice, Root sent a letter to Ramon Beteta, Mexican Under Secretary of the Treasury, who was a friend of Frank's, and a key figure in the Mexican government. In his letter he explained the philosophy and practical aims of "Camp

William James," and asked for permission to establish a similar Camp, in one of the provinces, for both Mexicans and Americans. Beteta's reply was encouraging, and showed him to be a man of depth and understanding:

My dear Mr. Root:

I am answering your letter of January 23rd, that came to me with a note from our mutual friend, Waldo Frank.

I have always held the cynic opinion that war is the most interesting and thrilling occupation that mankind has ever found. Nothing like war to bring out what is best, and what is worst, in us. Sports, debating, missionary activities are pale substitutes for war, psychologically speaking.

In the Mexican violent uprising, I have had the personal experience of witnessing to what an extent fighting constitutes the most powerful form of stimulant the masses can find. For Mexican peons, for people who live the uneventful life of the rural communities, the revolution has often afforded the one great break in their insipid existences. I have often wondered, in the presence of the readiness with which people take up fighting, if war is not, after all, a natural occupation, and if back of the economic, political, and social causes of the Mexican Revolution, one could not also find a hidden urge which is deeper and more fundamental than any other stimulant.

I am advancing these doubts, not to discourage your project, but rather to express my great appreciation for it, because I feel that unless we find a constructive function which would be a good substitute for war, people will keep on fighting. Moral disarmaments, aimed at creating friendship and good-will, and destroying hatred, are alright, but they are not sufficient. Let us hope that work, constructive work, cooperative work, work in which people will put all their might and all their minds, work which would require heroisms and sacrifices, work which would be an end in itself, and not a means of making a living, work that would put boys of various nationalities in close contact with each other, will take the place of fighting in the minds of youth.

I agree with you about the necessity of having some official connection for the kind of project about which you have been thinking. My suggestion would be the National University of Mexico as the proper organization which could, and certainly would, be interested in such a project. I would advise you to write to the President of the University, Licenciado Mario de la Cueva.

I have told you sincerely how I feel about this project, and hope that you will find practical ways and means to carry it out.

Sincerely yours,

/s/ Ramon Beteta[3]

Before receiving this letter, Root had left New York for Tucson, Arizona, hoping to get some relief there from his headaches. Several weeks of inactivity convinced him that he could not endure for long the city's deadened atmosphere, which seemed to accentuate rather than relieve his own ailment. While taking Spanish lessons from a Mexican family he had met, he cajoled the Mexican consul into giving him a tourist visa, and subsequently set off on a hitch-hiking trip down the west coast of Mexico. After almost being sent back by the Mexican border guards because he was a hitch-hiker with "only $50," he managed to get a ride to Hermisillo, which lay almost at the end of the main highway. There he finally received Beteta's letter, which had been forwarded, and on the strength of it, he determined to go south to Guadalajara. Using his friendship with Waldo Frank, who was widely known in the country, to good advantage, he met numerous government and educational officials, with whom he discussed his ideas for a Mexican-American work camp. Practically all of these people seemed enthusiastic, and, like Beteta, they grasped remarkably well the moral, as well as the physical, aspects of the plan.

Not long after Root's arrival, one of the worst earthquakes in the history of Mexico brought sudden devastation and misery to a large area of the country. About 45 towns were affected, and some were completely destroyed. The most widespread damage was in Colima province. The city of Colima was totally wrecked, with only a handful of walls left standing. Most of the people had no shelter at all, and their exposure was made even more perilous by the rapid approach of the annual rainy season. When transportation to the area was re-established, Root hurried there to see if he could be of some assistance in the emergency. He became acquainted with Dr. Gustav Baz, Minister of Public Assistance, who was in over-all charge of the relief of the district. The government officials (who at first thought that Root was an engineer) hardly knew where to begin their task. They were even considering moving the entire city to a new location so as not to waste time and money cleaning up the masses of rubble on the present site. Root found there was little actual work he could do at the moment, but he became convinced that he could render some kind of practical help in the near future.

Money alone was not enough—new hearts and hands were needed to build houses and give the dazed inhabitants a spiritual life. So Root went back to Dr. Baz in Mexico City to find out whether some young Mexicans from the University could return with him to Colima as a working group. Baz was extremely busy, and it was difficult to secure an interview. After several days of waiting, Root did manage to see him and was urged to remain in the capital so that some meetings with Mexican students could be arranged. However, Root's funds were now running low, and in view of the great confusion which prevailed everywhere, he was not hopeful of getting a group together for at least a month. He decided, therefore, to return to the United States while he still had enough money for train fare to the border.

While all this had been happening, he had sent numerous letters back to Huessy and to the Camp, describing his experiences and his reactions to the country at large. These letters, as well as the whole concept of his adventure and the motives which led him to Mexico in the first place, had a marked effect on several members of the Camp in Tunbridge. At the end of April, O'Brien suddenly called all the members in from the farms for an "important meeting." To almost everyone's surprise, Frank Davidson spoke at considerable length, and with great emotion, about the material contained in Root's letters. He said that the Camp would have little real significance if its work were confined to Tunbridge. To him, the call for help from foreign lands was just as important as the needs of his own home town. He felt that some definite act was needed to establish the universal and international character of "Camp William James." At the conclusion of Davidson's remarks, O'Brien, along with James Tierney and Paul Keefe, volunteered to supply that act by joining Root in Mexico. To some members of the Camp, notably Eiseman, Preiss, and Schlivek, this scheme, besides coming as a distinct shock, did not seem wise. The pre-arranged "act," about which they had heard nothing prior to the meeting, was also galling because it had been worked out in secret, and had been sprung without warning, thinly disguised as a "spontaneous" move. Preiss asserted that while he felt that Davidson's expression was noble, and essentially true in the long run, that this was not the time for such an expedition. The Camp, he went on, was just emerging from a period of agonizing weakness and frustration, and the Mexican proposal would divide it again and dissipate its resources. One crisis could not be overcome by rushing headlong into another. The Camp, he concluded, had solemnly pledged in March that it had a duty and a desire to become secure in Tunbridge before fanning out, and that nothing could be gained at this time by sending "token" representatives to foreign lands.

With this beginning, the temper of the meeting increased in fervor, with each point of view gaining some adherents. In the end, after several hours of debate, the Camp voted to send the three volunteers to Mexico and to supply them with sufficient funds and "moral backing" to sustain their journey. The three chief opponents of this move, although accepting their parliamentary defeat, could not subscribe to the undertaking, and felt that it would pave the way for the dissolution of the Camp's structure. Furthermore, they could not comprehend O'Brien's action, in view of the fact that he had always been one of the staunchest advocates of making Tunbridge the center of the project above all other considerations. He was, even now, concerned with the details and functions of Council and Camp, Inc., which had so recently begun to assume its powers. Now, in a reversal of form, he had unaccountably decided to leave the country for a destination four thousand miles away.

Preiss, Eiseman, and Schlivek believed that it was not healthy for the Camp to continue on with such a fundamental rift in thought and action. As we have seen many times before, there had been numerous personal differences between individuals on a variety of issues, but these had always been reconciled with the main unity of Camp policy. Now the policy itself was a subject of disagreement, and there seemed to be no ground for compromise. Either the expedition would be sent or it would be abandoned. The three dissidents therefore decided that it would be better for all concerned if they withdrew from the Camp entirely. They felt that the question at hand was fundamental as far as the future of the whole enterprise was concerned, and that they could not abide by the decision which had been reached. When Root's letter, describing the Colima earthquake, came on the following day, the volunteers were more determined than ever to carry out their mission.

They left for Colima on May 5th, not knowing that Root had left Mexico City on the same day, on his way back to the United States.

* * * * *

Preiss, who was farm manager, Eiseman, who served as house manager, and Schlivek remained in Camp most of the month of May in order to get a good start on the spring work, and to show their eventual successors what had to be done in the coming season. The new tractor was now in use, and the farm work went along smoothly. After these boys resigned, George Phillips was elected interim Camp Manager until O'Brien should return.

Meanwhile, Root had reached New York, and had there received $500 which the Camp had voted for the Mexican enterprise, plus $200 contributed by Nancy Blaine, who was now in Tunbridge preparing a campaign to enlist a group of girls for the summer. However, he had not heard from or about O'Brien, Keefe, and Tierney, and was amazed to learn that he had passed them en route. He met Preiss and Schlivek in New York, and was much distressed that they had withdrawn from the Camp, since he felt that the break had been precipitated by his letters. He was assured that this was not the whole story, and that the issues had been deeper. Root remarked that he regarded it as serious that not one of the original six boys in the Tunbridge group was now in Camp. William Uptegrove, the sixth member, who was still an undergraduate at Dartmouth, had made up his mind not to join the Camp for the summer because he did not agree with the decision to sponsor the Mexican expedition. Likewise, Root had heard that Nate Dodge and Ed Flint, fresh from their recent differences with O'Brien over the structure of the corporation, were perplexed and disturbed by this open cleavage in the Camp. In many respects, then, the Mexican affair had caused extensive repercussions in Tunbridge.

Root returned to Mexico on June 15th, and finally made connections with O'Brien, Tierney, and Keefe. Plans were now afoot to bring several Mexican youths to the United States after the work in Colima had been completed. This would demonstrate to the Mexicans that the work service idea was not a "one way street." However, misfortune struck the American volunteers early, when O'Brien became ill with dysentery a few days after his arrival. The weather was unbearably hot and damp, which added to his discomfort, and further sapped his strength. His condition became so bad that it was imperative for him to return to the United States at once for proper medical attention. On his way north, he was obstinately detained at the border by Mexican guards, who suspected some irregularity in the sale of his car, which he had disposed of in order to obtain money for living expenses. When he protested vigorously that everything was in order, and mentioned the fact that he was ill, he was summarily clapped in jail, pending "investigation." Realizing that these delays could lengthen into days, or possibly weeks, O'Brien knew that his health could be permanently undermined if he waited too long. Even death from his disease was not out of the question. Therefore, he abruptly took matters into his own hands, and despite the risk of being shot by the Mexicans, he managed to escape onto American soil.

Undaunted by this sudden and dramatic exit by their companion, Keefe and Tierney continued on alone, and at last met Root in Colima. Efforts were begun at once to get a group of Mexicans together to send up to Vermont. The American Ambassador, Josephus Daniels, told Root that he would do his best to get visas for those who wished to enter the United States for a six months' period. This was soon to prove a lot easier said than done.

* * * * *

From June onward, the Camp in Tunbridge assumed a different social and economic role from that which it previously had performed. The amount of sheer activity increased enormously. There were so many comings and goings that it was difficult to keep track of them, and the quantity of personnel was very fluid. In place of unity of the membership, there was now diversity. Boys and girls arrived daily from schools and other jobs to work on the Camp farm or be despatched to farmers who had applied for help.

Orientation and the molding of group solidarity necessarily suffered from the needs of the coming haying season, and agricultural demands took precedence over the integration of the new recruits into the life of the Camp.

Recruiting expeditions increased in number and scope, and contributed to this atomistic condition. Hobbing and Davidson travelled to Harvard and Yale, where three men, Jack Bronston, Winslow Smith, and Norris Tibbets definitely committed themselves for the summer. Roy Chamberlin, who was finishing a term at Yale Divinity School in New Haven, also planned to come back, bringing with him Albert DeVivo, whom he had met at the local YMCA. DeVivo had ambitions to be a cook, and Chamberlin, recalling how difficult it had always been to find a man so inclined, persuaded him to give up his job in the city and gain his experience at the Camp. Charles Dell and Russell Hurlburt came from Dartmouth for the summer, and Clinton Gardner, a freshman, announced he was leaving college altogether, and would join "Camp William James" for "the duration." Chamberlin and Davidson then joined Nancy Blaine in a trip to Chicago, where they persuaded Jake Fox to give up his job in a filling station and come back to Vermont with them. Lee Knowles, who had visited the Camp early in May, left his position with a publishing firm in New York, and returned to Camp, bringing Charles Townley and Robert O'Dell, from Bronxville, New York. Hobbing went to Phillips Exeter Academy, and returned with the pledges of David Wales and Louis Churchill.

As a sort of climax, the girls' group was finally formed. Nancy Blaine joined Mary Bingham, Enno Hobbing's fiancee, in recruiting Cynthia Harris, who was studying at Wellesley. George Phillips, on a visit to Skidmore College, invited Eleanor Miltimore to join the Camp. Jobs were found for all of these girls immediately, since many of the farmer's wives were in just as much need of help as their menfolk.

This intensive campaign, reaching into many states, had a rich yield in manpower. A large number of farmers had sent in applications for assistance during the summer, and the Camp had no difficulty in putting as many as twenty-five recruits into the field simultaneously.

On the Fourth of July, a giant celebration was held to commemorate the first anniversary of the conception of the Camp. Ninety people were present at the initial flag-raising exercises on the Camp grounds. With his customary eloquence, Nathan Dodge reviewed the history of the first turbulent year, and his remarks were followed by group singing and a picnic lunch. At this meeting, many friends and members of the Camp, who had often been in contact with each other over the months only by letter and by telephone, were now meeting one another in the flesh for the first time. The cohesion and fellowship of the whole group was noticeably increased by these personal interchanges on the site of the Camp itself. For here was symbolized the Camp's survival in its new form, plus the challenge to make it grow from year to year.

13. The Downward Path

As the Camp embarked upon its second year, its composition had changed markedly. Of the original twenty-eight non-college CCC boys who had been part of the group at Sharon in January, barely a handful remained. They had dribbled away, singly and in pairs, almost unnoticed in the gyrations of membership figures, which fluctuated erratically from day to day. The shift of the Camp from public to private sponsorship had removed most of the vestiges of discipline from the daily routine, and many of the boys succumbed to the attraction of doing as they pleased, without much regard for the group. The first rush of eagerness brought about by moving to the Rivers' farm had soon subsided, and there was even more hard physical work to be done than had been required at Sharon. To boys who had not had much of a background in self-applied discipline, the relative anarchy of the private Camp provided them with a great temptation to pick up and leave if something was not to their liking. A few left without even a word of explanation or a goodbye—just walked down the road one day and never came back. Perhaps such losses were not preventable at this crucial period, but they did point up the signal failure of the Camp to provide an effective substitute for the very CCC rules and regulations which it had lately sought to abolish in its own sphere of operation. As a result of these defections, the replacements for the regular CCC boys were high school students and college undergraduates, whose service in the Camp was definitely limited to the vacation period of three months or less. This substitution of short-term recruits for the long-term regulars was most significant, since it foretold the time in September when the number of enrollees in the Camp would take a precipitous drop. In a larger sense, this change was also a negation of the pledge of the original founders of the Camp to give a year's service to it. Such a pledge was not exacted from any of the new members, who generally had the feeling that they were not so much joining a Camp as they were spending a summer on individual farms. This loose confederation of farm hands was something quite different from the dogged, earnest band which had convened at Sharon six months before.

Another unfavorable omen of the past few months was the almost total eclipse of the Council of the Nine Towns. This organization, which had given rise to so many furrowed brows among its members, had never fulfilled its potentialities, and had subsequently been little more than a "front" which could be represented in Washington as speaking for a large segment of the local Vermont population. But now that the Federal government had retired from the scene, the loose bonds between the Camp and the Council did not take up the slack. Furthermore, the formation of Council and Camp, Inc., had superseded the Council proper, and removed it from the field of physical relationship with the Camp. It must be said that most of the Council members retreated eagerly into their obscurity, and that they were glad to have done with their semi-official functions. Nathan Dodge and Ed Flint, by virtue of their membership on the board of directors of the corporation, were now almost the sole contacts which the Camp as a whole had with the communities. Although the boys did not realize it at the time, this was a long-standing and mortal defect, and one which would have to be remedied if the Camp were to continue in its purposes of resettlement and local participation in the formulation of work projects. For only by revitalizing and encouraging community participation in its daily life could the Camp find any justification for its existence as other than a summer idyll.

* * * * *

Shortly after the July celebration, Roy Chamberlin proclaimed his plans for founding a work camp in Alaska similar to the one which was being attempted in Mexico. Frank Davidson also made known his determination to leave immediately to join the Mexican group. However, although the Camp voted them its full support, both boys changed their plans within the week.

O'Brien, now recovered from his illness, returned to Tunbridge on July 16th, and re-assumed the post of Camp manager. Root announced from Mexico, by letter, that he was planning to return to the United States for good, due to the fact that the rebuilding of Colima was being delayed interminably by materials shortages. However, much good work had been accomplished there, and the Mexican officials and the residents of the city were grateful for the help they had received from the Americans. More than this, several young Mexicans had become interested in "Camp William James," and expressed their desire to spend a year in Vermont. The problem of securing permission to enter the United States appeared to be the only stumbling block as far as this was concerned. Ambassador Daniels had not been able to procure the visas which he had mentioned when the boys originally arrived in Mexico, and the growing military restrictions on foreign travel in the United States were making State Department approval increasingly difficult to obtain.

Upon Root's return, he was stricken with another sinus attack, and was forced to retire to a pollen-free area in the White Mountains of New Hampshire to "ride out" the hay fever season. While there, he made up his mind to enter Columbia Graduate School for the coming September term. This decision completed the divorce of the original Tunbridge group from the Camp, with the lone exception of O'Brien.

* * * * *

On the positive side, the first mark of permanence which grew out of all the summer's labors was the purchase of a farm by Dan Goldsmith. He had found his work on the land so satisfying, and he was so taken with the possibilities of agriculture as a way of life, that he resolved to be the first new Vermont settler from the Camp. This was indeed an historic decision, and it was an abiding expression of faith in the original ideals of the Camp. Even more unusual was the fact that in just six months of work in Tunbridge,

Goldsmith had been transformed from a New Yorker, who was at somewhat loose ends with life, into a purposeful and hard-muscled Yankee. Except for a slight difference in accent, his Vermont conversion was practically complete. Grant Corwin, the farmer for whom Goldsmith had last worked, and Nathan Dodge helped Goldsmith select his farm, and both of them were greatly impressed by his act. To them it represented concrete evidence that the Camp and the communities, working together, could produce excellent results.

* * * * *

In August, two outstanding events occurred. First, Mrs. Roosevelt came up to the Camp to see for herself what had caused all the political furor in Washington six months before. She had been cordially invited to Tunbridge by Davidson and Hobbing, who had visited with her at Hyde Park, in June, to supply information for an article she was writing about work camps. In conversation, they had told her of the progress "Camp William James" had made on its own resources. She made a note of their visit in one of her subsequent "My Day" columns:

> Two Harvard boys, sent by Mrs. Dorothy Canfield Fisher, came to see me at lunchtime. In order to obtain some practical experience, they have spent six months in CCC Camps, and have come out with a definite idea that a CCC camp should not be run as a relief organization, but should be open to boys of various income groups. I was interested to see that these young men had gone far in the realization that democracy which really functions must receive service from all its citizens. There must be no distinctions on the service plane. Everyone must give what he has to give, and must receive the same compensation, opportunity for training, and consideration when his service is needed by his country.
>
> I have always objected to compulsory military training by itself. I believe that, given the character and the discipline, it does not take long to become a soldier—but training for the qualities that *fit* you to become a soldier takes time.
>
> I feel that universal service should not be a question of military service alone. It should be a time when all boys and girls know they are giving a year of their lives to fit themselves better to serve their country.
>
> In return, they receive training in manual skills, some additional academic training when necessary, and some absolutely vital character training and discipline which can only come with group living.[1]

Mrs. Roosevelt drove up to Vermont in her own car, and spent the night at the home of Robert Slater of South Royalton, who was a former member of the defunct Council of the Nine Towns. She spent most of the following day at the Camp, talking to the boys and townspeople, and sampling some of cook Joe DeVivo's "cornbread special." There was no doubt that the whole countryside was thrilled by her visit, and the sincere personal interest she had shown in the work of the Camp.

* * * * *

Several days after Mrs. Roosevelt had left, the idea of an Alaskan expedition was brought up anew at a general Camp meeting. Several of the boys believed that with the Camp membership now at its highest level, their absence from Tunbridge would not adversely affect the work which was being done. Therefore, George Phillips, Russell Greenlaw, a former Poultney CCC enrollee, and Charles Davidson, who had come from an Ohio CCC camp, constituted themselves the advance contingent for establishing an outpost in Alaska. They had heard and read of the extensive military installations which were being erected throughout the territory, and decided to go to the booming city of Anchorage to help in the work. The entire north country was suffering from an acute labor shortage brought about by the feverish military activity in building roads and fortifications, and the boys felt their labors would be of real value to the defense program. Further than this, they wished to see, at first hand, what opportunities there were for development and settlement in this great, untapped province. Plans were made for them to leave at once.

This decision made it necessary to hold elections for new officers. Moreover, O'Brien, after his short term as manager, was now considering the possibility of becoming Professor Huessy's assistant at Dartmouth. With this prospect in mind, he resigned his position in mid-August.

The result of the elections placed Lee Knowles in the post of Camp manager, and Jake Fox, the all-around mechanic from Chicago, took over the duties as farm manager. Clint Gardner replaced George Phillips as treasurer. Now, for the first time, not a single one of the officers of the Camp was drawn from the old Harvard and Dartmouth groups. However, it is well to point out that this "succession" of command was not carried out in any purposeful manner, with the old leaders resuming their positions in the ranks. This would have been the proper way, and would have preserved the continuity of the various offices. But the reins of control were handed over to the new men without adequate preparation on their part for their tasks. They had too little experience, both historically and vocationally, in the Camp's work to properly direct the destinies of the Camp as people had come to know them. Yet the dissolution of the "first generation" of the Camp before the "second generation" was prepared to take over made no other course possible. The officers simply had to be chosen from those who were available on the spot, and no recruit was present who had been in the Camp more than a couple of months. For at this juncture, Frank Davidson decided to enlist in the Canadian Army. He was due to be drafted shortly, and he found himself less able to think of the work in Vermont in terms of the great war which was raging. This normal reaction to the war was merely a symptom of the times, and it was certainly not confined to the Camp in Tunbridge, but it found its outlet more and more in voluntary enlistments such as Davidson was making. The trouble was, from the Camp's point of view, that the demands of the armies and the navies were inexorably drowning out, with urgency and power, the more nebulous and long-range aims of the Camp. The war was fast becoming the ever-present monster which could not be denied. There is no disputing the fact that most of the remaining members of the Camp were also either expecting to be called for service soon, or were prepared to return to school in September. By October 1st, the shortage of persons at the farm would certainly be acute, as the great brigade of fifty, which had toiled through the summer, rapidly melted away. There appeared to be no remedy for this state of affairs, since it would have been ludicrous to ask youths of draft age for commitments to the Camp. No one could be sure where he would be even a week hence, and to have drawn a long-term pledge from a boy would have made a mockery of his good faith.

The impending disaster to the personnel structure of the Camp did not reach the three who were Alaska-bound. Distance, and the eagerness with which they embarked upon their new adventure had insulated them from the problem. On August 10th, the advance-guard had reported on their progress to date:

Dear Men of 'William James:'

Here we are, about to go. We are full of energy, of expectations, of anxiety, but as yet there is nothing to tell. In fact, it is only our own memory of consistently empty mail boxes at Tunbridge which prompts us to write at all.

At any rate, here we are in Seattle. That in itself is something.

Last Wednesday, we had set 'Knute's' radiator cap into the setting sun in Vermont, and stepped on the gas. In Columbus, the draft board detained us overnight, and so Charlie drove home to bid good-bye to Rutland (Ohio). Heading west again, our troubles really began. Charlie took over the bookkeeping and it taxed the ingenuity of all of us to keep the books anywhere near the equilibrium point. Russ kept the 'log,' but when it was lost, he never seemed to be able to catch up again. And it got hot, and 'Knute' blew a tire, and somebody taught Russ to sing 'Hutsut rawlston on the rilera' over and over and over.

But we struggled along until one night we stayed in a cabin in Missouri and made the mistake of taking showers. Result—6 athlete's feet. We itched clear across Missouri, Iowa, and well into Nebraska before that purple stuff began to help at all. Even then the cure was not complete until we hit Wyoming and saw a coyote, a prarie dog, and a real cowboy. Then to Yellowstone, where Charlie brought about a recurrence by soaking one foot in a geyser.

And so we came to Seattle, moved our sailing date up one date, sold 'Knute,' and had a night's sleep.

But here we are, and apparently none too soon. Things have been moving fast in Alaska. There is a great deal of construction work going on, about which we hadn't heard. New projects are being started even now. There is regular air service between Seattle and Fairbanks. Everyone in the country who operates a gas station or a cheapish restaurant knows people in Alaska. Many of them have been there. One even floated down the Yukon in a rowboat from White Horse.

We're off to do a job.

George, Russ, 'Red'[2]

In Vermont, however, there was more uneasiness than optimism. A rare bright note in this steadily darkening picture was the marriage of Enno Hobbing to Mary Bingham, who had spent part of the summer in the girls' division of the Camp. This event was held in Boston, and was witnessed by all those friends and members of the Camp who could possibly attend. The Hobbings' immediate plans were to set out for Alaska to reinforce Phillips and his friends, and perhaps to settle there permanently. Just before their departure, another letter arrived from Anchorage:

> Well, things have begun to move for us. And a recreation center for the Army, of all things, was the beginning. About a month ago, the U. S. O. came in, and went into action. Their first act was to arrange a luxurious, permanent recreation center for both soldier and civilian, complete with all sorts of equipment. But of course it won't be finished until 1943. In the meantime, there must be a program and a temporary building. The building is all arranged for, and the work is to begin tomorrow.
>
> Our job is to work with the U. S. O., and everyone else in Anchorage and Fort Richardson, finding jobs to do, and people to do them. That is not easy, when the Army has assumed full responsibility for the building, and when most of our potential volunteers are working a seven-day week on the air base crews or in the Anchorage shops. But we are hard at it.
>
> Meanwhile, old 'Red' is in Palmer, working for the cooperative dairy. Russ is still in the bakery. The boss there likes him and usually doesn't keep him working more than nine or ten hours—and besides, he has a daughter.
>
> As for George, he is piling brake shoes for the railroad at present (80¢ an hour), although he may quit that and get into something a little more personal, if he gets the chance.[3]

It is quite evident that the letters from Phillips, up to this point, showed that the boys in Alaska had not yet found a means for group expression which would tie them to the aims of "Camp William James." They were living in a war atmosphere, and it was very unlikely that much could be accomplished, except as some proposal might fit into the military scheme of things. As Phillips mentioned, the main avenue for his efforts was in the area of recreation, and even in this field, dear to the heart of every soldier, he could not count on very much help. The three boys were themselves separated by their different jobs and by having living quarters in separate towns. It was hard for each individual to avoid being swallowed up in the mass and confusion of the military establishment.

* * * * *

While these Alaskan hegiras were taking place, Arthur Root returned to New York, and continued to press forward his attempts to get Federal sponsorship for the Mexicans. He was in touch with the Office of the Coordinator of Inter-American Affairs, and had applied for funds to take care of the expenses of four Mexicans for a year in the United States. Mrs. Roosevelt was also enlisted to try to accelerate the granting of visas, through the State Department. In spite of these efforts, no definite answer was received from Washington for weeks.

Then, on September 10th, John Clark, of the Coordinator of Inter-American Affairs Office, wrote to Root and suggested that he contact Joseph Lash, head of the International Student Service with a view to joining forces. Lash had been in youth work for several years, and had frequently been sponsored and encouraged by Mrs. Roosevelt. However, his approach to work service had been primarily on the intellectual and college level, and had been similar to that followed by the American Youth Commission. Root discussed Clark's suggestion with Lash, in order to leave no stone unturned in his drive to secure funds. He found that Lash desired to conduct a "study" of all Latin-American youth groups, as a preliminary step in organizing Latin-American work camps. This was a herculean task, and would have consumed months. Root was more interested in getting the group of Mexicans to Vermont immediately than he was in such a lengthy proposition. It was decided not to join forces at the present time, due to this divergence of objective. Root, therefore, wrote Clark that he wished to keep his application separate from that of Lash's group, and that he still wanted funds of his own. Clark's answer, a week later, was disheartening, indeed. The request was denied on the grounds that the proposal Root had submitted did not provide for the kind of work which the Mexicans really needed. The American official felt that "the money could be better invested in projects which might provide techniques and information through which community undertakings might be insured a surer yield."[4] Root was bitterly disappointed at this reply, and sent another long letter to Clark emphasizing that "Camp William James" could give the Mexicans all the experience and practical techniques which had been suggested. He also sent a copy of Clark's refusal to Mrs. Roosevelt, reminding her of the interest she expressed, during her visit to the Camp, in bringing the Mexicans to Tunbridge.

Meanwhile, Hobbing and his wife were making their way to the West Coast, to join the Alaskan group. Paul Keefe and James Tierney, who had been languishing in Mexico for more than four months, during the fruitless negotiations to get visas for the Mexicans, now indicated that they wished to either go to Alaska, or return to Vermont. Hobbing wrote to them from Seattle, and advised that a return to Vermont was probably the best choice, since the Camp in Tunbridge was very short of manpower, and the Alaskan expedition did not as yet have any real program.

Then, unexpectedly, on October 10th, Tierney and Keefe sent a letter to Root announcing what they believed to be the fruition of the months of waiting:

> Well, we have finally completed a little bit of something. Last week we tried again for an appointment with Dr. Baz. We were halfway between joy and indifference when his secretary promised us an audience at twelve the next day. These promises were heard so often that by now they had begun to mean less than nothing. Tuesday at twelve, surprising to say, we were ushered into the audience chamber of Dr. Baz. We told him of our (unsuccessful) attempts to see Beteta, and he appeared interested. Well, he called up Beteta, and *told,* not asked, him to order tickets for us to bring the boys with us.
>
> Immediately, we rushed to where we might find Hector, to have him tell us definitely whether or not he was going. Hector said, 'With all the pleasure in the world.' With that, we set out for Beteta's office, and by six o'clock that afternoon we had put an order through to Colima demanding free passage for Hector Duenas, Alfredo Isais, and Roberto Vasquiz. The same night, we set out for Colima, with Hector in tow.
>
> Here again, in Colima, we ran into difficulties. Two of the fellows who had definitely promised Jim that they could and would go, now, for some reason or another, refused to accept. Roberto offered an out-and-out apologetic refusal. Alfredo could go, but with many reservations. But now the line-up has added Porfirio Guzman (you remember him, a tall, silent fellow) and we are all ready and willing. We had no trouble with letters of recommendation for the boys. We believe that now we have fulfilled all the requirements of the (American) consul in Mexico City, and we are prepared to leave Colima this coming Sunday morning.
>
> Jim and I would like to hitch-hike up to the States. This would save

the Camp over a hundred dollars, and would be a great experience for us. But since none of the boys can speak English, and have never done any travelling, we figure that it is best to go with them.

They are coming to you full of hope for the future. The three of them intend to study English, and whatever else is available. Nobody knows how much they will do, but their intentions are of the best sort. I hope that the Professor's (Huessy) plan for high school classes is not just so much more 'dream talk.'

Hasta la vista,

Jim and Paul[5]

This letter had two tragic sequels. First, the American State Department did not issue an approval for the admittance of the Mexicans. Mrs. Roosevelt had personally written to Sumner Welles, as a result of Root's plea to her, and had inquired about the status of the boys. Welles replied that the Mexicans could not be admitted as students because "Camp William James" was not officially listed as a school authorized to accept foreign students. Special application, and a subsequent inspection of the Camp, would have to be made to the Federal Office of Education to secure such approval. This, naturally, would mean further delays, and was certain to crush the spirit of both the Mexicans and Americans who were poised to cross the frontier at this very moment. When they heard this news, Tierney and Keefe were completely disillusioned, and concluded that they could wait no longer. Reluctantly, they abandoned their friends, whom they had brought so far and with so much urging, placating them as best they could, and promising to return as soon as matters were straightened out.

They now decided to "ride the rails" and hitch-hike, according to their original intention. No sooner had they entered the United States, when disaster struck again, this time physically. While attempting to climb aboard a moving freight car in Texas, Tierney slipped and fell under the wheels. His legs were badly injured, and he was rushed to a local hospital. The doctors quickly saw that one of his legs would have to be amputated in order to save his life. This was done at once. Keefe then telegraphed these grim happenings to the Camp and to Tierney's parents. The instantaneous response of the Camp and its friends was heartfelt and generous. The Tierney family was in modest circumstances and was quite unable to assume the medical expenses involved. However, they had no cause for anxiety on that score, since ample funds were contributed by the Camp, Mrs. Greene, Nancy Blaine, Norman Lazare, and others.

This tragedy finally brought the ill-fated Mexican episode to a close. It had been crushed, as we have seen, not only by the endless delays, red tape, and poor communications which had frustrated all efforts to achieve concrete results, but also by the personal injuries to O'Brien, and now Tierney. In the whole history of the Camp, seldom had so much been spent, in blood and resources, for so little. One might speculate that, in peace-time the immigration bars would not have proved to be impassable, and that the Mexicans would have been able to come to Tunbridge without much difficulty. But there, as elsewhere, the existence of the war ruled otherwise.

* * * * *

Here we must pick up again the story of the Camp in Tunbridge, because it was, supposedly, the trunk of the tree to which the Mexican and Alaskan branches were attached.

If the events recounted on the preceding few pages have often seemed unrelated, then the reader will have, paradoxically, a true image of the way they happened. For the two foreign expeditions, inspired though they were by similar sentiments and purposes, were widely separated from Vermont and from each other. Each had sprung from an impulse to "do something," to break out of the confines of Tunbridge into new and unknown modes of life. Other reasons were also given, of a more rational and practical nature, but these latter were not more important than those which stemmed from emotional drives rather than from the intellect. As we have previously noted, these impulses had created a deep rift in the Camp membership. They had resulted in the resignations of three of the original Tunbridge group, as well as the loss of several prospective recruits from Dartmouth.

But in spite of these defections, the foreign enterprises were both launched with earnest resolves and high spirit. The boys who left for these distant outposts felt secure in the belief that those who remained at Camp were backing them to the limit, both financially and morally. The steadfastness of this belief was probably the chief prop which sustained both expeditions. The three months of interminable waiting and shattered hopes which Tierney and Keefe endured in Mexico City while waiting to see harried government officials would have been unbearable if these two boys had thought they were alone. Likewise, the gropings and fumblings of Phillips, Davidson, and Greenlaw in the turmoil of Alaskan boom towns would have become altogether meaningless the moment their tenuous life-line to "Camp William James" was broken. Communications, restricted primarily to letter-writing because of the tremendous distances involved, were usually inadequate, even though the boys desperately needed each other's company by mail in order to overcome their individual loneliness and to feel that they still "belonged." Strangely enough, the longer they were away from Tunbridge, the stronger and more perfect their vision of it became. The remembrance of daily troubles on the farm, which they had all so lately known, quickly faded into oblivion, or became a matter of minor importance. The Camp became a symbol rather than an actuality. This was understandable, since most of us can attest that the memory of something believed in and worked for will usually tend to become exalted with the passage of time and distance.

The longer Phillips, Tierney, and the rest were away from "Camp William James," trying to represent it in their own ways, the more they believed in its permanence and continuity. True, the lack of letters from the Camp was annoying, but this alone did not dampen their ardor. These men did not know it at the time, but theirs was destined to be the last flowering of the faith and determination which had characterized the Camp since its inception.

* * * * *

Back in Tunbridge, a pall of gloom had descended upon all. The reservoir of manpower which the Camp had lived on during the summer was almost empty. By the end of September, almost all of the college and high school students had left for home, or had been drafted. The girls' "division," which had been so laboriously organized, was transported, en masse, to Framingham,

Massachusetts to find work in defense plants. The only members of Camp left in Tunbridge were Lee Knowles, manager; John Goldsmith, a cousin of Dan Goldsmith, who was now busy on his own farm; Albert DeVivo, the ubiquitous cook; Clint Gardner; Jake Fox; and Robert Young, who had arrived late in the summer. These six were all that remained of the summer high of fifty.

The chief problem, however, was not one of numbers. Rather, as we have said before, the continuity of membership had been broken. There had been no orderly succession of command, no intermingling of the new men with the old, no organized social and recreational activities. And worst of all, there was almost no tangible relationship with the townspeople. These conditions had existed at the time of Knowles' election as manager, but they had been minimized, and their effect postponed, by the feverish activity of the summer. Now, in the comparative peacefulness of October, they stood out in ominous relief. The bitter truth was beginning to dawn on some people that "Camp William James" had undergone a complete transformation ideologically from the days of the Tunbridge rally and the dramatic exodus from Sharon. Perhaps it had gone down the inevitable road to disorganization, starting on that tenth of March when it had defied the government and had proudly asserted its integrity. But here it was, a scant six months later, a small, skeleton group, without direction, or initiative. Some idea of the situation, and the feelings of those who were left can be gleaned from the following letter from Gardner to Frank Davidson:

Dear Frank,

This week-end we held a series of meetings, large and small. Their result will, we hope, solve some pressing and discouraging problems. Out of two days of talk and fellowship came clarification of the Camp's aims, some stimulating ideas, interesting plans for the future, and a definite psychological lift.

But let me start at the beginning.

Camp morale, as you probably know, has been slipping for at least a month—maybe more. The spirit so evident when I visited Tunbridge last Spring is lacking. Enmeshed in farm tasks, and quibbling among ourselves, we have been losing sight of the entire purpose of the Camp. And until Mr. Dodge came to supper the other evening, our contacts with the community were almost non-existent. This was a bad situation.

Following several preliminary discussions in Tunbridge and Hanover, we met Saturday afternoon on the hill overlooking the Strafford road. Speakers were Eugen, Mr. Dodge, Mrs. Greene, Katherine Taylor, Lee, Bob O'Brien, Nancy, and Arthur. Among those present were Al Eiseman, Jack Preiss, and Bud Schlivek. So, whether you like it or not, there were some qualities of a college 'homecoming.'

Here are things that were said:

Mr. Dodge—emphasized need for three-fold program—work, education, and recreation. Claimed we work too hard (I think he erred on that score. We just worry too hard.)

Mrs. Greene—urged us to keep in mind the world-wide significance of the Camp. From a different angle, she actually seconded what Dodge had said.

K. Taylor—giving examples, she pointed to importance of cooperatives, said they might offer a field for us.

Bob—welcomed everybody, but got little chance to push his pet scheme—eventual development of the Township College.

Eugen—chairmaned the meeting, and linked the words of the speakers, as a good chairman should. Stressed importance of rhythm in life, again the Dodge idea of balancing work, education, and recreation.

Sunday afternoon we met again. We went into greater detail on the work, education, recreation theme, agreeing that we must not be swallowed up by farm duties. Also, I think there was finally general accord that we are not farming merely for farming's sake.

This morning, the present Tunbridge group, those of us living there now, acted on the Camp agreement to curtail farm activities by reducing land in cultivation, selling stock, etc. We'll slaughter, and sell two cows, two pigs, and a couple of calves. No killing will be done, however, until we receive final advice from some local man—Dodge, Flint or others.

In trying to restore contacts with the community, we plan to ask the advice of farmers more than in the past. After all, there's some saying about making a friend of a man by letting him do you a favor.[6]

It was during the above series of week-end talks that several friends of the Camp, principally Mrs. Greene and Katherine Taylor, were struck by the changes, both physical and mental, which had occurred in Tunbridge. For them, the old drive and enthusiasm had disappeared, and since they had known the Camp and its founders from the very beginning, the contrast between "then" and "now" was enormous. They felt that, at the very least, a renewal of faith and enterprise would be necessary without delay if the Camp were to justify its name and heritage. Mrs. Greene's feelings are here expressed in a letter to O'Brien.

> Dear Bob:
>
> Let me correct at once what may be a false impression—i.e., that I think the Camp should be closed now. For I certainly do not advocate this, and I said all I had to say (at the meetings just held) only so that we might face the extreme price that might have to be paid unless a rebirth were possible. It would betray Lee in his present effort if he were made to feel that his allies did not completely back his leadership today.
>
> There would be another very grave aspect about closing 'Camp William James' now. In Percy Brown's letter to you, dated April 4, 1941, the terms of the gift of the farm to Council and Camp, Inc. included the provision that the real estate should return to the Filene Fund if it were not operated in the spirit of the original gift. Since Lee is now leader, would it not be appropriate for you to take Lee to call on Mr. Brown, introducing him, and reporting with Lee on the last six months. The obvious (Camp) difficulties of the present moment might not be wholly glossed over, either.
>
> It seems to me that if your visits to the Camp, perhaps for two or three days toward the end of the week, took place at regular intervals, it would be precious to those in Tunbridge.
>
> Do you mind these suggestions? I know how easily one may be in error at a distance about any point of detail. But Katherine Taylor felt as strongly as I did that the habit of convoking friends for concentrating decisions only in moments of crisis might now be superseded by a more flowing habit of life.
>
> Hoping to see you again.
>
> Affectionately yours,
>
> Rosalind Greene[7]

Obviously, deep-seated doubts had rooted in Mrs. Greene's mind, but her inherent loyalty to the Camp would not permit her to desert or oppose it at this time.

Throughout the fall, the Vermonters themselves had gradually lost all connection with the boys as a group. They knew some of them as individuals, and as farm hands. Many of the boys, for their part, had never really known Dodge, Flint, and the rest of the early-day stalwarts. As we have just noted, some of the Camp members were aware of this deficiency, and would have liked to remedy it. But the Council of the Nine Towns had ceased to exist, functionally, and there was no other organized medium through which any remedies could be applied. The corporation was not representative enough to replace it. Except for one shining achievement—Dan Goldsmith's purchase of his own farm—the settlement program was barren, either of results or of hope. The great plans of a year ago were now seldom talked about, and had given way to the problems of the moment. The Camp had become almost entirely introverted, and could not seem to encompass any work or ideas outside of its own physical being. The outer shell was there, but the living, growing pith had dried up and withered away.

From this explanation, it is now easy to see why the Alaskan and Mexican groups had indulged in their long-distance misconceptions. They saw and dreamed only of the shell, and were unable to know that there was very little left inside it.

* * * * *

A month later, things had changed little, as we can see from a second Gardner letter to Davidson, who was still in training as a member of the Canadian tank corps:

> This week I am boss at Dan's place, while he takes a trip out West to see his girl. He has been 'breaking me in' for the past few days, and is now on the train. As my chores etc. take me only five hours a day, I have brought with me all my notes, scribblings, records, bills, and unfinished business in general.
>
> The hour of opportunity is indeed passing quickly. Until recently, I have felt that I could not say anything until I had seen a group established at Tunbridge. I see now that this was a foolish attitude.
>
> Since you left Camp, I would say that we have been through several distinct phases:
>
> 1.) After 'devolution week' (a series of meetings designed to integrate the new members of the Camp into the spirit of the founders), a sort of beginners' anarchy prevailed. This was to be expected, because of the small carry-over of early members.
>
> 2.) Hunting for an allegiance, we fastened on the farm. The ideal was to run the farm well. We had unity for about a week.
>
> 3.) This brought on trouble between members, all on the plane of who 'griped' most, and how poor a worker so-and-so was. At this time some new members joined, all getting off to a miserable start.

> 4.) Finally, a 'council of war' was held at Eugen's. Greatest noise was made over the fact that we had lost touch with the community by struggling over our own farm.
>
> 5.) Then came the week-end meeting with the Greenes, K. Taylor, Nate and the 'old' boys. This seemed like a dream—it was so sharply divided from existing conditions. A lasting boost in morale did result, but the boost wasn't very great. The ideal then became 'do anything to get close to the community.' Farmers, like Grant Corwin, almost became deities.
>
> 6.) Things then ran alright for a while at Camp, with good efficiency, and a neutral feeling among the members. Very encouraging were the Thursday night musical sessions here at Dan's, Eugen's Monday morning lectures, and the attendance of at least one or two of us at town basketball practice. Still, any discussion of Camp's larger implications was impossible.
>
> 7.) Recently had two good business meetings, in which we all struggled over mutual problems. I am almost able to talk to Lee, and John Goldsmith and I get along very well. The philosophy right now is to serve Tunbridge well.
>
> Jake Fox would like to work out, and it will be marvelous if that can be arranged. The change for the better in Jake is noticeable, but he is not the right man to wield executive authority.
>
> We have no money (hurrah!) except a guarantee of 100 dollars a month for six months. We do need to scare up some outside money shortly, but the situation is not at all serious, and we all expect to work out for fair wages.[8]

This letter clearly reveals that very little progress had been made since the October meetings. Not one of the men at the Camp knew what they wanted to do, or how to go about finding out. There was a feeling that the Camp needed men, but how to get them, and from where they would come, no-one could say.

This slow, depressing period of ossification was mercifully brought to an end by the happenings of December 7th. The world had long been sure that the United States would become a belligerent. The only points of speculation were "when" and "by what means." Now all had been answered by the Japanese attack on Pearl Harbor.

* * * * *

The reaction of the Camp to the national war crisis was relatively decisive. Here was a situation in which the group could expire with honor, since its few remaining members would now certainly be called by, or enlist in, the armed forces. At a final meeting, therefore, it was voted to close the Camp, pending its disposal to the Goodwill Fund under the terms of the mortgage.

After a couple of weeks of concentrated effort, trying to get some order out of the chaos of the Camp's financial affairs, Lee Knowles telegraphed Mrs. Greene, on December 21st:

> Farm closed. O'Brien and two Dartmouth boys living there after Christmas on own budget. Everyone well. Finishing accounts. Will keep you informed in Norwich. Regards.
>
> Lee[9]

Presumably, with this cryptic telegram, "Camp William James" had come to its end.

14. Obituary Refused

But there was yet one more bubble of life which had not been pricked. Four thousand miles away in Alaska, the belated news of the Camp's demise had shocked and angered Hobbing, Phillips, and the others. Without warning, and without (to them) apparent reason, their own efforts had become completely isolated. True, they had never received much moral or material aid from Tunbridge after they had left it—and yet, they felt themselves part of it. The closing of the Camp appeared to be a rank desertion of the cause, and it had been undertaken without even a cursory discussion by mail.

Therefore, the Hobbings decided to return to Vermont for the express purpose of re-establishing the Camp. They arrived in mid-winter, and set up housekeeping at the farm. All of the friends of the Camp had urged them not to do this, since the task of revival would be almost a superhuman one, and would only result in further discouragements and unfulfilled hopes. However, these appeals fell on deaf ears, and the Hobbings could not be dissuaded from playing their luck as long as it would hold out.

The outlook was assuredly bleak. Lee Knowles' action in closing the Camp had already been accepted as the last word by everyone except the Alaskans. Mr. Dodge, although bitterly disappointed, consoled himself with the thought that the war was chiefly responsible for what Knowles had done. Others, like Mrs. Greene and Katherine Taylor, had been genuinely relieved. They were convinced that their premonitions of disintegration were now facts, and they could not bear to see some of the boys suffering under the delusion that everything could be saved.

Perhaps the saddest of all were the members of the Camp who were forced to pick up their belongings and depart. Some of them, like Jake Fox, Joe DeVivo, and even Knowles himself, felt that the bottom had dropped out of their existence. Most of their petty bickerings and personal difficulties had not stemmed from their basic incompatibility as people, but rather because they were caught up in a shapeless enterprise whose demands they had never really grasped. As one of them said in later years:

> I never could understand much about the purposes of the Camp, as Huessy used to tell them. I suppose the fellows who were there before us had it all worked out. All I could see was that we were helping farmers, and that was a good thing. Maybe we could have done more—I don't know.
>
> As far as the Camp was concerned, it wasn't bad. I didn't do much in the meetings because I never knew what to say. I wasn't 'in' on the plans, you might say, so I kept my mouth shut. I never knew where the money came from to keep going. Just angels, I guess.
>
> Of course, I missed a regular day off, and guests were always coming up when you didn't expect them. But you got used to it. I sure could have used a few extra dollars, though.
>
> But don't get me wrong on this thing. Although we had to close up, even though I didn't think we were giving it a fair chance, it was still important in my life. The main things I got out of the Camp were patience, and a tolerance of the other fellow's way of doing things. A fellow had to learn these two things or he wouldn't have lasted a day under all the troubles and arguments we had. I learned something about farming, too, although I wish it had been a lot more.
>
> Afterwards, I used to wonder what made me stay at all. I suppose you get attached to things, even a Camp which seems to be falling apart. I guess the spirit of the place held us together. I don't see now what else would have made me stay for 30 bucks a month.
>
> Everything considered, I think it was worth it. If I had a chance to do things over, I don't know but what I'd do it again.[1]

Clearly, these non-college recruits of the "second generation" had gotten the aroma of "Camp William James" if not the substance. A great opportunity to aid these boys, who were ripe for learning, and for doing, had been missed. But, as we have just illustrated, some of them did not go away completely empty-handed.

* * * * *

It would be pertinent at this time to again follow Arthur Root's story, as it has a direct bearing on the last phase of the Camp.

Root had entered Columbia Graduate School in September, but within a few weeks his sinus and hay fever caused him so much discomfort that he was forced to resign from the University, and go back under the doctor's care.

At about the same time, Dorothy Thompson, who had not forgotten her relationship with "Camp William James," conceived an idea for a so-called "land army," as an aid to agriculture. Enlistments and the draft had made deep inroads on the farm labor supply during the preceding year, and it was evident that high agricultural production would be seriously threatened unless some remedies were found before the next harvest. Miss Thompson wished to organize college, high-school, and other pre-draft age youth for summer service on New England farms. If operations were successful for the first season, they could be expanded into a national system in the following years. Places for the volunteers were to be found on farms recommended by the United States Employment Service, and these young people could then engage in a healthy and vitally needed summer's work. A corps of assistants and counsellors would administer the program in the field, with one of these being assigned to each county. At a chance meeting on an airplane trip, Miss Thompson told Root of her new plans, and he was very much interested. Learning that he was leaving school, she invited him to help get the program under way, and offered him the post of Director. He accepted, and assumed the responsibility of gathering a group of sponsors, and mapping out an organization. One of his first acts was to convince her that all efforts for the initial year should be concentrated on Vermont, so that a really thorough job could be done in a limited area.

Around the first of November, the legal and structural details of the "Volunteer Land Corps," as it was officially named, were ironed out, and a corporation was formed. In Washington Senator Aiken, an old friend of the Camp, advised that he would marshal the county agents and prominent farmers of his state to render assistance to the "Land Corps" wherever possible. Dorothy Thompson was beginning to round up financial aid in order to set up a central office in New York and to provide money for recruiting students in colleges and high schools throughout the East.

With this fairly rapid development of the "Land Corps" came Root's feeling that in some way it must be linked with "Camp William James." As soon as the Corps had become established, with its own officers and budget, the matter came to the fore. In January, a few weeks after the Hobbings had returned to Tunbridge to keep the Camp alive, Root addressed himself to this problem in a letter to Huessy:

> Dear Eugen,
>
> I am very glad that Lee (Knowles) came to New York. None of us had to go through the strain that he bore as manager of the Camp during the past month. He has helped me see, even though I do not agree with everything he said, the necessity of a two-in-one relationship between 'Camp William James' and the 'Volunteer Land Corps.' I accept the fact that for authority, management, direction, and ownership, Camp must be completely separated from the V.L.C., with Council and Camp, Inc. remaining solely in the hands of the original spirits of the Camp. With Enno and Mary back, this is expecially important.
>
> The structure of the Land Corps is right, if carried out in the manner we have wished ever since my meeting with Dorothy Thompson on that plane trip to Washington. You and I have always felt that the Land Corps and the Camp could nourish each other. The Camp would be the concentrated center for thought, strategy, and depth, from which leadership and firmness could permeate the larger Land Corps structure.
>
> With these thoughts always uppermost, I have proceeded the best way I could with the Land Corps. During the past week I have been working in the hope that Camp and the Land Corps would mutually embrace one another. This is certainly the faith that has won Dorothy Thompson to our whole-hearted sponsorship and support in these last months.
>
> It is practically the middle of January now. We had hoped to assemble at least twelve people by February 1st for a training period.[2]

This hope of Root's did not come to fruition. Technical and administrative work, as well as finance, absorbed much of his energy, and the task of choosing the supervisory personnel was more difficult than he had expected. The proposed training period for the field staff was therefore postponed indefinitely. Nevertheless Root went to Tunbridge alone to talk with Nate Dodge and others. By coincidence, his visit came on February 8th, which was the day on which Council and Camp, Inc., held its annual meeting. This year, the future of the Camp was the primary business to be discussed, and it was thought that Root's presence might help the directors to arrive at a decision. The following are the minutes of the meeting, as recorded by Hobbing:

> Mr. Dodge called the meeting to order, and especially welcomed Arthur Root. Mr. Dodge then went on to review the activities of 'Camp William James' in its first year of operation in connection with Council and Camp, Inc. While the Camp had not been as successful as it had been hoped, the time in which it could prove itself had been short. One purpose of the Camp, Mr. Dodge said, was to unite city and country, and in that capacity, the Camp had not been a failure. The times have been black, but, as in all wars, defeats were to be expected. Ultimate victory was likewise to be expected for the Camp as well as the nation.
>
> The meeting then accepted the resignations of Bob O'Brien and Lee Knowles, who had replaced George Phillips in August, as directors of Council and Camp, Inc. The following directors were elected for 1942: Nathan Dodge, Edward Flint, Dan Goldsmith, Enno Hobbing, Katherine Taylor. . . .
>
> Miss Taylor then reported on the wishes of Mr. Percy Brown, Executive Director of the Goodwill Fund, with respect to the Farm. Mr. Brown had felt that the value of the efforts of 'Camp William James,' which used the farm as its center, had already amply justified the gift of the Fund. Furthermore, the national emergency made all planning difficult. This led Mr. Brown to expect that 'Camp William James,' as such, would enter a latent period, and that the farm might best be operated on a minimum basis. He asked that he be notified as soon as the details of the farm arrangements were worked out.
>
> Mr. Flint remarked that Mr. Brown's suggestions tallied quite closely with his own views.
>
> Enno Hobbing explained his plans for operating the farm as a tenant of Council and Camp, Inc. He planned to run the place to support a staff of three. No more subsidies would be granted for the farm, and in turn, guests who came there would be charged a nominal sum for their board. The income and outgo of the farm should be balanced within short time spans.
>
> Arthur Root then explained the aims and activities of the 'Volunteer Land Corps,' of which he is the Executive Officer.
>
> Miss Taylor suggested that in view of the times, the directors should be ready to re-shape plans and arrangements whenever necessary. . . .[3]

Significantly, nothing was mentioned at the meeting about a

liaison between the Land Corps and the Camp. Evidently, Root was either unable or unwilling to make any concrete offer of cooperation at the moment.

* * * * *

The next three months did not produce any workable plans for revitalizing the Camp, or even for continuing the farm as a private enterprise, as Hobbing had outlined. Neither was Mr. Brown's request for details fulfilled. Consequently, early in May, Katherine Taylor wrote to Nathan Dodge and advocated the permanent closing of the Camp. This would mean reversion of the farm to the Goodwill Fund, and the liquidation of whatever assets the Camp might possess. In addition, the farmhouse, purchased largely by the gift of Mr. and Mrs. Greene, would also revert to the Fund for disposal along with the land. When all was sold, the Greenes would receive a proportionate share of the proceeds as a return of their donation. Accordingly, Hobbing made a complete listing of everything the Camp owned, and sent it to Miss Taylor, along with the following note:

> It has been arranged that Dan Goldsmith is to use, store, and maintain the tractor this summer. It ought to be sold in the fall, and should fetch about $800.
>
> Much of the furniture belongs to private individuals, who will want to call for things. Mrs. Greene, Eugen, and Clint Gardner have considerable amounts of personal property which they will no doubt want to regain.
>
> I will try to calculate how much value has been added to the place, and will send those figures to you soon.[4]

Hobbing was convinced that it would be impossible for him to keep on as tenant. The strain of applying his limited knowledge of farming to try to eke out a bare livelihood for his wife and himself was beginning to tell on him. Added to this, the many frustrations and disappointments he had experienced as one of the original members of the Camp weighed upon his mind and sapped his vitality. Finally, his impatience to become active in the country's war program found no outlet in the lonely routine of chores and wood chopping during the winter and early spring. He acceeded to the arguments of Miss Taylor, and had made plans to wind up the farm's affairs by June 1st. This time, it appeared that nothing could prevent the end.

* * * * *

But suddenly, toward the end of May, up popped Phillips and Greenlaw, just returned from Alaska. They had been advised of the Council and Camp directors' meeting in February, and had sensed that all was certainly not well in Tunbridge. Now they protested Hobbing's action, and argued that they would be willing to continue the farm as long as they were physically able to do so. But Hobbing had made up his mind that the project must be ended, and pointed out that the consensus of opinion among the directors of the corporation was that the farm no longer represented "Camp William James," and that the terms of the mortgage to the Goodwill Fund were not being met. Any further operation of the farm by the corporation would unjustifiably endanger the investment of the Fund, as well as the Greene's gift.

When Hobbing left the farm for good, he was under the impression that Phillips and Greenlaw had been converted to the idea that the Camp must be closed, and he believed that they could remain in Tunbridge only long enough to clear up the last details.

However, these two were determined not to give up yet.

In mid-June, they were joined by Richard Reid, a Dartmouth student, and the three of them decided to stay, at least for the summer. They were also encouraged by Dan Goldsmith, who offered to help with the farm work, and to exchange labor with the boys. Thus strengthened, they began their attempts to get the approval of Council and Camp, Inc. for their active residence at the farm. Their defiance of the stated wishes of several of the directors of the corporation posed a delicate problem. In fairness to the three men, the corporation could not bodily evict them, since such action would have been repugnant to all concerned, and would have callously repudiated all the sacrifices and good faith which every one of the Camp members had shown in the past two years. The situation was awkward, but these last hold-outs had to be convinced that they should leave voluntarily. Every opportunity, no matter how painful and distasteful to those who granted it, must be allowed to the boys to work out their own salvation. There was no other way.

* * * * *

Professor Huessy had remained somewhat in the background during the preceding six months, because there was little he could have done to change the course of events. But he did seek ways to transform the myriad reverses which the Camp was suffering into at least one constructive channel which might survive the war. The following letter is his summation of the trials of the Camp since Pearl Harbor, and a report of his concomitant efforts to save it:

Four Wells
Norwich, Vermont

Miss Katherine Taylor
41 Hawthorn Street
Cambridge, Massachusetts

Dear Katherine,

After our conversations, between you and Mrs. Greene and myself, my correspondence with Dick Reid and George Phillips, and my visits to Camp, I owe you a statement of my opinion of the situation.

For, in trying hard to explore the tiniest bit of opportunity for a preservation of the Tunbridge place, I have moved in various directions, and you might feel that my course has been far from clear.

You yourself have seen clearly that there was no 'Camp William James,' with a non-local purpose of a significance worthy of the name 'William James.' Mrs. Greene realizes, perhaps more deeply than anyone else, that the great name 'William James' can only be used if, and as long as, the undertaking expresses his vision unmistakably. Mr. and Mrs. Greene expressed this so eloquently in their letter to the Corporation of March 1941[5] that any member of Council and Camp who reads this letter again must be struck forcibly by the wide gap which separates the purpose of their donation to 'Camp William James' from the Rivers place in Tunbridge as of today.

The original Camp responded to a nation-wide, aye international, challenge. It opened itself to a government task. Since March 1941, we had to wait for some corresponding nation-wide movement which would take the place of the CCC connection. The Volunteer Land Corps seemed to be the possible successor to the governmental side of the task, and in this hope we waited from August 1941 to December 1941 for the growth of this new agency.

In this process of anxious waiting, however, the Camp itself lost its vitality, and on December 7, the day of Pearl Harbor, no yeomanry was left to man the Camp adequately, either in numbers, in intellectual strength, or in the capacity of leadership. So, Camp was closed. The war destroyed the remnants of the original CCC, and reduced the Volunteer Land Corps to an agency for high school children. In other words: the war ended the possibility that 'Camp William James could be the local partner and the personal counterpart to any nation-wide material organization or movement. Every step taken after December 7, 1941 must be envisaged in the light of the war and its impact on all pre-war plans or expectations for 'Camp William James.'

I need not go into the various details of the story of the last six months. I note that Enno and Mary took over the place as tenants; that they were so busy on the place that community relations could not be renewed. When I came to Camp at the beginning of June, I found, for example, that Russ Greenlaw had not had time to see his former boss on his farm, although Mr. White was now rather sick and without help on his place. Obviously, the farm took every ounce of energy from its inhabitants, and they became more and more isolated.

In order to remedy this result of the war pressure, several schemes were discussed. My own idea was to tie up the Camp with the army, to throw it open to men on furlough, and thereby to create some expectations among the soldiers for the potentialities of a post-war effort. Quite apart from Tunbridge, it seems reasonable to think that most men in the army feel definitely that their service to their country will not end with the war. Furthermore, a hasty demobilization may spell ruin economically. It might become highly desirable to instill into as many army men as possible the confiction that they should proceed, after the war, with great patience. Hence, it would seem that these men should be put in a situation in which they could anticipate this post-war task in an invigorating and convincing manner. Places like Tunbridge would then serve for the army as moral 'power stations' which could add significance to the war effort, in the hearts of the soldiers.

This, however, is a very general consideration, and it is not at all clear that the Rivers place would be a good place for beginning such 'Sunday work' for soldiers. Nevertheless, I tried to meet the hopes of Council and Camp for the preservation of the Rivers place by taking up the matter of an endowment 'for the duration.' I realized that for the time being the Camp only represented a residue of pre-war conditions, but I thought it possible to convert it into a place where post-war life might be anticipated for army men. The reception of soldiers there is, of course, impossible as long as members of the first crew still remain, because the latter are primarily challenged to enter the war themselves

Accordingly, we hoped that Mr. Flint might be found willing to participate in the management. My own viewpoint was: if we can now find one man *outside* our group who can be won over to the post-war role of the place, and who will sponsor its endowment for the duration, or at least for a longer period than just one year, I would trust our own plans again. Otherwise, it seemed evident to me that we could not be judges in our own cause. Obviously, our own group is apt to be carried away by its initial momentum and to be deaf to the realities of the present day. To me, the capacity of finding a new sponsor became the test for the soundness of our obstinacy. I have not met with success in this search, although it was made under favorable circumstances.

I have exhausted my means for securing a post-war significance of Tunbridge, or a connection with the efforts of the soldiers. Also, any pre-war condition for the existence of Camp has vanished. We no longer have any right to carry the name 'William James.'

When the corporation was founded, its charter read that Council and Camp should cooperate with 'Camp William James.' At this present moment—it is the day of the fall of Tobruk—the only thing left is the Corporation. No 'Camp William James' exists. This Camp ended as a reality on December 7, because then Lee Knowles, the last Camp manager who had been elected by a representative group of Camp members, resigned.

Between December 7 and today, all the people who went back to Camp did so as individuals. This was clear in Enno's case. He took over as tenant against the advice of a strong group of the original Camp members.

However, although no 'Camp William James,' properly speaking, existed after December 7, 1941, I myself hoped that there remained the potentiality of *re-founding* it once more. In this conviction, I took the steps mentioned herein. In this hope, I helped prepare the publicity of the last months. The shell was still there. A completely new start did not seem absolutely impossible.

I no longer can envisage such a rebirth of 'Camp William James' on the Rivers place. The Corporation is not backing a 'Camp William James' there, neither in present-day reality, nor as a germinal potentiality. The property is there which is, under the terms of the gift, owned by the Good Will Fund. Since the Good Will Fund is established for the promotion of cooperatives, it may well be that the Corporation can get together with the Good Will Fund, and find a public usefulness for the Rivers place. In this case, the Corporation might function as a local outpost of the Good Will Fund in the future, and this, it would seem, is not without its merits. But the original dualism, 'Camp William James' and Council and Camp, would then have been succeeded by a new dualism, Council and Camp and Good Will Fund. And I do not feel that these two corporations could annex the name 'William James' for their new purposes.

The founders and name-givers of 'Camp William James' have been:

Mrs. Henry Copley Greene

Frank Davidson

William and Alexander James, by authorizing Enno Hobbing and Robert O'Brien to accept their father's name for the Camp

Myself and the group at the foresters' house, including Mr. Dodge, Mr. McKenzie and Mr. Flint.

The government, by recognizing this name as the right name for their experimental leadership training camp.

Their trust is not invested now in any of the group at Camp. George and Russ were left there by Enno in order to *close* Camp. Simply by staying on the place, these two men can hardly feel authorized to be 'Camp William James' indefinitely, against the explicit intentions of their predecessors.

I now fully understand why you insisted ever since December 7 that Percy Brown should be asked to deal with the property and to determine future policies. I may be forgiven for having tried for another six months to fan the ashes of the first and second and third fires into a new flame. The new fire has not developed. The immensity of the war explains why nobody should insist indefinitely on pre-war schemes of things.

I do hope that Mr. Percy Brown will find ways of using the good work that has gone into the land in a satisfactory manner, and for the benefit of Tunbridge. But I don't feel free, from now on, to use the name 'William James' in connection with the Rivers Place.

We owe this to the name of William James, to the people of Tunbridge, to the members of Camp who wished to be soldiers and not vacationists.

You may make use of this letter in any way you deem helpful.

Very sincerely yours,

(Signed) Eugen Rosenstock-Huessy

Without doubt, Huessy made this statement with a heavy heart, for he had given the Camp as much of himself and of his resources as any other individual. Admitting defeat was all the more bitter when he knew that in more propitious times success could just as well have been attained. It was not easy to survey the wreckage of so taxing an enterprise, and still to honestly believe that all had not been in vain. Somewhere, perhaps only in the minds and souls of the boys themselves, would the real value of this experience be found. But in those tumultuous days, no one could tell for sure.

* * * * *

Several weeks after Huessy had announced his position, Phillips wrote to Katherine Taylor concerning a forthcoming meeting of the directors of the corporation which would conclusively settle the fate of the Camp. For with each passing day, the tortured extension of life on the farm was preying upon the thoughts of all involved. Here Phillips attempts to give a complete statement of his position:

Camp William James
Tunbridge, Vermont
July 5, 1942

Miss Katherine Taylor
41 Hawthorn St.
Cambridge, Mass.

Dear Miss Taylor:

We were very glad indeed to hear from you, at such length. We have wanted a clear picture of your thoughts at this time. But much better, of course, is the news that you and Mr. Brown will be with us this weekend for a good talk.

At this meeting we want to come to an understanding. After all, we are pretty much the same people we were a year ago, and still wish to work with you in the closest way. But we do evaluate the present situation in very different ways, right now. And so, in preparation for our gathering, it might be well for us to clear up a few of the many misconceptions that have grown up about our activities and our hopes for the future.

First of all, about the legality of our being here at all! You have never mentioned this point, but I know that it has been a bothersome one for several of our friends, and perhaps for you, too. The meeting of Council and Camp at which Enno resigned decided two things. First, they decided to make every attempt to assure a permanent operating basis for the camp by some arrangement with the Land Corps. Second, in case of complete failure, the directors voted to petition Percy Brown for one year's leeway in which to work out in some fashion a significant plan for the continued operation of the place. Our staying here was in no way a slap at Enno and Mary. It developed from the sincere belief that the corporation's plan could and would meet with success. The fact that Dick (Reid) saw fit to throw in his lot with us was significant in the sustaining of this belief. But from the legal point of view, our being here is in full concordance with the expressed desires of Council and Camp.

Now, as to the place of the Land Corps in any permanent settlement. I don't think that a solution to our problem *depends* on the Land Corps - at all - but I do think that the Land Corps is by no means out of the picture. I say this with full knowledge of their formal meeting, too. I say it for two reasons. First, there have been many shifts in policy already, as first one and then another group in the organization swayed the rest. We can expect more of the same, especially now, when plans are becoming realities. Second, we have met Land Corps kids. Dick talked with them in New York, in Boston, at Barnard the other day. There was a group over here for lunch, two weeks ago. Today eight of the nearest boys and girls came, with Jack Preiss, and we did a good deal of talking about the serious side of their work. There are real possibilities to many of these young people. Their interest mustn't end with this summer, I don't think they will permit it. That is where Camp must come in.

Next, there is this assumption that we are an isolated group on a farm, working all day and all night with our noses to the grindstone. This, believe me, is not at all true. We have been shorthanded, and we have been busy, certainly, but all the while there has gone on a great deal of what passes technically for 'community relations.' On two occasions within the last month there were large gatherings of local folks here, complete down to the square dancing in the kitchen. We have been active in the church, and our new choir, as Eugen could tell you, is flourishing with quite unprecedented activity. Dick, especially, has been tireless in his efforts. He is a leader with the 'Three M' group in South Tunbridge, and only this week was asked to serve as minister for the Union church service. Among us he has led a much-needed drive to cease thinking of Vermonters as 'these people,' and to put relations on a more human basis, for good. In this respect he reminds one of Bob O'Brien, without the wonder, but with a deal more consistency, and a capacity for sustained effort. This is one of the reasons why Dick will continue to be an important guy around here.

Now, as to the question of whether or not we are 'Camp William James,' I shan't attempt to answer that in this letter. We are not arrogant enough to assume that we here, and only we, are the Camp. We accept gladly the fact that 'Camp William James' is lots of places and people. But that should not preclude the continuation of work here. One might justifiably feel, for instance, that our concessions to the war should include the ceding of more mature members to the army, but that as many of the good things as possible should continue here, *if they can.* The truths we discovered together still hold. So while we fight the short-term battles on the firing line, the long-term war should go on being waged, by Dan and by others.

Do you want this to happen? We certainly do, and you agree, as your hopes for the Land Corps indicated. The thing should happen. What are the obstacles? Transportation. A tough one, but bound to be so anywhere off the main line. We'll have to swallow it. Next, the manager, Mr. Flint is, great good luck, a 'natural.' Funds. Another tough one, but we can meet it. Finally, the real 'Camp William James' elements. For the present, there are the three of us, (not to mention Dan). Until Fall, at least, Dick, just the man for some such new setup.

There are no guarantees of success. There never have been, but that hasn't stopped us yet, and we shan't allow it to now. We may fail to answer any one of these vital questions, but for the sake of all that's gone before, and all that may happen after, let's give this opportunity every ounce of energy that it deserves. That's what we are determined to do. That is what we want to tell you when you come.

How about lunch here Sunday? I've written to ask Mr. Brown. It would be a fine chance to talk things through, off the record, and a very pleasant occasion as well. Come if you can. And in any case, we shall all meet at Nate's. We look forward to it.

Sincerely,

George

The meeting took place, as scheduled, and after much pro and con discussion, the boys were given one final month to develop a long-term plan. It was voted unanimously that the absence of such a plan would result in universal agreement to cease operations at the farm. At long last, there was 100% acquiescence by the three Camp members to the placing of a time limit on their endeavors.

Soon after the meeting, came a last minute consultation with Root and the "Land Corps." In spite of a previous "Land Corps" dictum which said that the Corps could not assume any commitments with regard to the farm, Root still privately wished, somehow, to make use of the Camp. But the gulf between the two organizations was growing wider instead of narrower. Richard Reid, in particular, did not wish to be swallowed up in the "Land Corps" body, and he insisted that the Camp retain its identity in any cooperative arrangement. Root fundamentally disagreed with this thesis, and felt that the "Land Corps" could not obligate itself to support the Camp without retaining its own complete freedom of movement. These differences could not be reconciled, and they spelled the end of any possibility of uniting the two groups.

Reluctantly, Phillips then wrote to Percy Brown:

Dear Mr. Brown,

The time has now come for a definitive report. We have not been able to conclude a long-term plan of the sort which would be necessary to justify the operation of this place as the Camp. The 'Land Corps' has decided not to cooperate to the necessary extent, and we shall not attempt to do the entire job ourselves. The farm is, therefore, yours.

But in fairness to the land, to our place in the community, and to our own consciences, we would like to work here until the crops are in. This is the one request we make of you.

Since you have been such a genuine friend, I should like to add a word about the affairs of the past few weeks. At one point it looked as though there was every chance of success. Arthur Root came here and talked enthusiastically about the job we could share with the 'Land Corps.' And Dan Goldsmith volunteered to leave his farm in South Royalton and stay here for the duration. But the 'Land Corps,' as a whole, has been unwilling to make a positive move, and they refuse to take any initiative here, at least for the present. The 'Land Corps' has been officially notified of our position, so there should be no misunderstanding.

We as a group, farm or no farm, intend to do all we can. The need is as great, or greater, than ever. And so, during the months that are left to us, we shall do all we can to ensure the continuance and development of something important right here in Tunbridge. The details, of course, will have to be worked out, but we don't interpret the loss of this place as a failure. The world still offers challenge aplenty, for all of us.[6]

Katherine Taylor received a copy of this letter, and got in touch with Phillips once more, reiterating her arguments:

Dear George,

The weeks since we talked together in Tunbridge have gone by with incredible speed.

With the impact, day by day, of the terrific news from all over the world, I have found it impossible in the month since I have seen you, to believe in the rightness of an investment of time and money and energy in the Tunbridge place. It seems to me that everyone now, young and old, must be ready to work in the place and in the way in which he is most needed for the winning of this war. I agree with you that the need in rural communities is as great as ever, or greater. I agree with Arthur that the work of the 'Volunteer Land Corps' must continue in some form or other. I still hold to my opinion that 'Camp William James' is now an entity separate from the Tunbridge farm. Its work must go on in various parts of the world through the lives of the individuals who have that tremendous initial growing experience, and who can live it out wherever they are. . . . .

I know this is hard for you and the others, George. I feel terribly sorry. In good faith, however, I must give you my own sincere thought in this matter, and have done so as well as I can in a brief letter.

With every good wish and affection,

Katherine Taylor[7]

There now remained only the formalities of liquidation. After completing the summer's work, Phillips gave full power to act in behalf of the Camp to Nathan Dodge and Ed Flint, as trustees:

Know all men by these presents that I, George Wendell Phillips, do as representative of 'Camp William James,' late of Tunbridge, Vermont, appoint Nathan P. Dodge and Edward R. Flint, of Tunbridge, as trustees. They are hereby empowered to hold the assets of the aforementioned 'Camp William James' in the form of United States war bonds and stamps until such time as these assets can be put to use in some way worthy of the aims of 'Camp William James,' as determined by the trustees in agreement with any former member or members of 'Camp William James.'

/s/ George W. Phillips

Tunbridge, Vt., Sept. 8, 1942

By virtue of these quiet, legal sounding phrases, "Camp William James" officially ceased to exist. "Late of Tunbridge," indeed!

* * * * *

Council and Camp, Inc. began to act at once to turn the assets of the Camp into cash, and to hand the property over to the Goodwill Fund. The Greenes were to be given $350 of the money realized from the sale of tools and equipment, and they would be reimbursed further when the Goodwill Fund determined what should be done with the farm. The quit-claim deed to the real estate and buildings was duly executed by the directors of the corporation on October 1st, and ownership passed to the Fund on that date.

Since it was impossible, because of the war, to elect five new directors of Council and Camp, Inc. who would be definitely available to attend future meetings and transact business, the present directors voted to disband and to have the charter of the corporation stricken from the record books of the State of Vermont.

The obliteration was now complete.

15. Postscript, 1945

In view of all that we have described, it is not surprising that a great majority of the members of "Camp William James" should have attached special private importance to their identity with it. For many of them, it had been one of the biggest adventures of their lives. In early 1945, almost two and a half years after the Camp's demise, the reactions of these individuals were, in many instances, still fluid and inarticulate. Most of them did believe that their time spent in Tunbridge and Sharon had been of great personal benefit. A few thought otherwise.

In spite of the overwhelming pressure of the war, and the diversified functions in it to which the former Camp members were assigned, it was only natural that some general accounting should eventually be made of why the Camp had closed. Many of the reasons were already well-known. Yet where they fitted in the whole picture, and what, if anything, could be salvaged from the remains of the Camp were still unanswered questions.

These thoughts revolved in many minds, and particularly in the mind of Dan Goldsmith, whose story had epitomized the power which was latent in the idea of a "moral equivalent of war." For he, more than anyone else, had found his life transformed by his Camp experience. His settlement in Vermont was the zenith of the more than three years of intensive effort which had bred the phenomenon of the Camp's existence. His singular achievement had proved that the goals of the Camp were not wraiths, but rather that once accepted, they were principles by which human beings could live useful and satisfying lives.

It was particularly fitting, therefore, that the most fluent request for an explanation of what "Camp William James" really meant should come from Goldsmith himself. This request did not emanate from his farm in Vermont, nor was it sent to Percy Brown, or to the directors of Council and Camp, Inc. who had presided over the physical liquidation of the Camp.

It came from a hospital in France where, as an infantryman, Goldsmith was recovering from wounds sustained in action. It was sent to Rosenstock-Huessy, whose faith and tenacity had often stood between the Camp and utter despair, and to whom the entire enterprise meant considerably more than an "experiment in soil erosion control."

The exchange of letters follows:

Dear Eugen,

With ample conveniences at hand, the soldier in a rear area hospital should by all means use such opportunities for writing some good letters. I find my one-sided correspondence rather hopeless, but some day some mail may catch up with me.

Am convalescing well from the results of a slight wound, and will be soon joining my outfit again. It would be hard to say I look forward to this, and yet any difficult task is easiest taken by being with it continuously. Once one leaves the (front) lines, the longer away from them, the harder to go back.

It would certainly be hard for me, when I do go back, to believe that the hardships are a privilege to bear. I know well enough that we are paying the price for errors made by many peoples. It also seems to me that the majority of men who feel that complete sacrifice is a privilege are our enemies, the followers of their living, fanatical leaders. If a man is to be a good soldier and a good Christian, he is bound to meet with inner conflict. The fact remains, though, that when one is up on the lines, God becomes closer than ever . . . . . .

No, I am not really sorry to be here, and if luck is with me, I'll come out a better man. At least it is my desire to turn these experiences into all the good they are capable of giving.

After exchanging words with my different companions here in the ward, a common statement directed my way is, 'You're lucky to have something to go back to that you like.' What more could a man ask for than I've got, thanks to the boys who started Camp!

Eugen, I never really understood what caused the abandon of "Camp William James." I don't see how anybody can deny the basic worth of Camp as it was. Yes, there were many errors, and undoubtedly we narrowed down to concern over mere farm operation, but there is yet to be an equal or a substitute for its worth. *What we experienced cannot be denied—or should not be—our younger brothers.*

Now that there are larger numbers of veterans returning home, I hopefully look forward to hearing some good rehabilitation plans.

Sincerely

Dan

* * * * * * *

Four Wells
March 4, 1945

Dear Dan,

Your letter from a field hospital made me pause. Although you are overseas, you still could not refrain from asking about the place which 'Camp William James' should hold in our assessment of the future. As a farmer of Tunbridge, you are the only member of Camp who will return to the town in which the second part of its story was lived. Nathan Dodge has died. Mr. Flint has moved away. The Rivers place, on whose land such good work was done that the neighbors all compete for the right to use the fields now, is sold.

You are not the only one who asks for an explanation. Mr. Flint wrote me that he was still convinced of the soundness of our approach. No other agency, he said, not even the 'Volunteer Land Corps,' had surmounted the real obstacle—the collaboration with the community. Others have been very critical. Nancy Blaine wrote that a week with the C.I.O. could teach her more about the state of the country than a whole year in Tunbridge. Enno Hobbing seems to be bitter about his experience when he returned from Alaska and found Camp on the way out. Of greatest concern to me is the fact that we have lost touch with Russell Greenlaw, the faithful of the faithful. I do not know why nobody seems to be in contact with him. Captain Robert Young, somewhere in France, still is devoted to the cause which brought him to Brocklebank Hill; but we had to report to him, Cynthia Harris, Margrit, and myself, that on our last excursion to the top of Brocklebank we did not see anything but the past, the bygone past.

The history of Camp has never been written. And I am sure that there are as many histories of it as there are individual members. I do not claim that my history is the correct one. It is barely possible that the following few remarks may unite a relatively large number of members in common agreement on some of the essentials. I shall try to establish some sense of perspective, or of proportion. I hold no brief for interpreting the whole story more correctly than the others. But I shall try to connect the various phases since I feel that some of you look too much at certain separate phases. The whole sweep of our venture should be kept clearly in our minds. This will have two advantages. First, it will make those who have been in it only part of the time, like Page Smith, Nancy, Bob Young, conceive of the whole of it as one action. And second, as a consequence of such unified vision, our little 'Camp William James' may acquire its proper place in the midst of such gigantic struggles as these two world wars, the Russian revolution, and the Nazi counterrevolution.

As long as the Camp is seen in its fragments only, either the summer in Tunbridge, or the December in the foresters' house in Sharon, or the January in the barracks, or the winter of 1941-42, it looks tumultuary. And it also looks so short-lived that only a fool could mention it today, beside the exertions of two thousand million people all over the globe during the last few years. However, if it has a curve, a rhythm, a dramatic plot, then its meaning need not be lost, and any bitter feeling of disappointment at its closing would be quite unjustified.

I, myself shall not be a judge of this. But I wish to put two and two together.

The story of 'Camp William James' began in June, 1939 and ended in the fall of 1942. The story is part of World War Number Two.

It is not the story of some private fools, or the story of an idea alone. It is linked up with certain political and social facts of a public character. Point one of my plea is that any member of Camp who forgets this, misjudges his and the Camp's actual function.

In 1939, some 300,000 unemployed young Americans were segregated in CCC camps. Their educational advisers, in a meeting in Hanover, N. H., expressed their conviction that to be a citizen, with reference to these youngsters, meant—and I quote literally from the record of this official conference—'to be profitably employed.' Mind you, this country of pioneers proclaimed, in a defeatest mood, that 'to be a citizen was to be profitably employed.' It was a complete renunciation of every value for which the United States has ever stood. For to be a citizen really means to be able to found your city or your civilization *yourself* if you have to. In the CCC boys and in the playboys on our college campuses, this pioneer faith in creating new realms was withering.

And this clash between two irreconcilable conceptions of citizenship made and unmade Camp William James. It made it. For against the passive, civilian, hopeless definition of a man as 'playing with ideas' in college, or as 'being employed' via the CCC, 'Camp William James' stood for the experience of the soldier, that it is he, after all, who guarantees and remakes his country. Woodrow Wilson said, before the First World War, that if people would live in peace-time as though it were war, wars would become unnecessary. This same thought was in William James' mind when he wrote: 'As long as we have not found means of living during peace as though we were at war, wars must have their way.'

This present war is proof that Wilson and James were right. 'Camp William James' came too late to make a dent in the lives of nations, and to avert a war. Had it been on a world-wide scale, a war could conceivably have been avoided. But it is much more important to state this: that war became unavoidable and indispensable because no 'moral equivalent' for war had been created on this colossal scale. The economies of the Western powers did not readjust themselves in the depression between 1929 and 1940. It took a war to revitalize American capitalism, under the spur of Russian and Nazi and British armaments. We owe this war great benefits—the very benefits ascribed to the martial spirit and the soldier's faith by William James.

The essence of all this is that there can be no lasting peace by the treaties of the lawyers or by the bayonets of the soldiers, but only by some soldier-like attitude among the civilians, from now on, in peacetime.

Admittedly, 'Camp William James' came too late—thirty years too late—to prevent the war. It was an attempt in the last minute. And it was crushed by this fact. The war unmade it. It was really closed on the day on which Lend-Lease was signed by the President of the United States. I was in Washington on this day, March 10, 1941, and can testify to this fact. There was an immediate connection between the two acts. To inaugurate Lend-Lease, the President had, of course, to sacrifice all smaller plans. He needed the votes of the unions. And since Director McEntee had the confidence of the unions,[1] his way of running the CCC could not be corrected by the President at this juncture. This was all frankly stated at the Supervisory Committee meeting which took place in the offices of the Department of Agriculture a few days later.

The President still approved of us. The Department of Agriculture still approved of us. But the war made itself felt. And thus ended the official support of 'Camp William James.'

I think it is comforting to know of, and to keep in mind, this relation between war and the 'moral equivalent' of war. We did not fail either by our own mistakes, or by any disappointment or change of heart on the part of those who built up Camp. We failed because the President, who felt that his definition of citizenship was momentarily *challenged* by ours, had to choose his definition *over* ours.

But every principle for which Camp's definition of citizenship stood then, is now realized in the war effort. A war can only be fought if these principles are recognized. The war has not refuted our principles, but rather the principles of the men who thought of the unemployed as outcasts of our economic system. We, in Camp, thought of these unemployed as assets in the rebuilding of America's communities, and potentially, the communities of the earth. Everybody, since Pearl Harbor, seems to agree with us now on this count, since these same unemployed are now helping to fight the war.

Point two of my plea is that Camp never was conceived as a private enterprise. For the girls' group, and for those men who joined Camp after March 10th, 1941, this is not self-evident. But we were asked by the government to train leaders for a nationwide service during a nation-wide, aye, world-wide depression. Our contribution to the fulfillment of this task, which will recur with intensified vehemence to the whole of mankind, was fourfold:

a. The unemployed must not be segregated. The curse of unemployment is that a man loses his social contacts. The curse can be turned into a blessing only when, during his public employment in a work service, his social contacts are restored and strengthened.

b. The whole community, not a material piece of land, must be served by a 'moral equivalent' of war. This is necessary because the true martial spirit is not mobilized unless 'enemies,' as in war, are conquered by the work service army. Water may have to be drained, woods cleared, fires combatted. Besides these material jobs, all of our indifference, pettiness, sloth, lack of vision, are the true 'enemies' of any plan which can come near to an equivalent of war. The true experience of the work service must be in how to rebuild a community. And a community is not represented by a soldiers' barracks or a logging camp, but by a long-range society of all age groups, both sexes, and all classes. We implied, under (a.), that the unemployed individual, in the work camp, must find comrades from all walks of life because he cannot survive his segregation outside of it. We now add the second rule—that the camps cannot be set out anywhere in the country, as in a vacuum. Unfortunately, this is the very link by which our educational system has been broken out of the chain of each community. In the work service, the harm done by the isolation of our high school and college system is to be repaired. For under our present educational system, youth dreams its dreams of the future *outside of and against the home community.* But somebody has to re-vitalize the vision of the local community by lending his enthusiasm, his faith, his expectations to the folks back home. In Nathan Dodge, we found an advocate of this very combination of youth and age. And Mr. Flint, to this day, sees this quality of Camp to be our outstanding contribution. So far, no other agency, or plan, or discussion, has taken it into consideration.

c. Because the work service cannot be rendered to dead things, but only to real people, it must be protected from being merely a national or state agency. Life will come to such service when it is conceived as either bigger or infinitely smaller than the boundary of any one nation or state. The service can have life simultaneously on a global and a local scale. The need for this wide range lies in the fact that all social groups smaller than the nation—families, villages, counties, sections—have been sucked dry by the nation. Furthermore, the churches, and all other international ways of life, have become nothing but 'international.' Their local roots are drying up. And that is not creative.

d. Camp was certainly not meant as a course in social information about the state of the country. The learning of social facts has to be protected against the snobbery and childishness of the learners. He who has not served his country, and has not made himself responsible for starting or restoring society, even in microcosm, has no means of understanding a society. He may know millions of facts, but they all remain natural facts. And the definite difference between a natural and a social fact is that we know how to evaluate a social fact. *A natural one has no value.*

These four points will come up time and again after this war. They are all very inconvenient and are difficult to translate into any abstract legislation and administration. They defy purely bureaucratic solution. They may well not be solved; perhaps they will not be tackled. And there will be another war.

But these facts were mentioned here to explain to you why, after March 10th, 1941, it was impossible to fold up. We had told the government that our members were at its disposal for at least a year, and that we could prove our point in no shorter period than eighteen months. These two points seem to be forgotten among you now. They are, however, of the greatest significance. When the government brusquely said: 'Thank you and goodbye,' the year and the eighteen months could not be stopped from running. When our group made this investment of its time, it was one undivided and indivisible whole. To have cut the year into tidbits would have been like taking a pair of scissors and cutting up a hundred dollar bill, as a means of creating something new.

And for this reason a lost cause had to be carried on. This is no contradiction in terms. It is true that after March 10th, 1941, we could not possibly succeed because we no longer were an agency of the public law of the land. And it is equally true that we could not desert the cause before we had made sure that the quite extraordinary constellation of our group had become visible, and had gone on record for its real faith.

In the May, 1942 issue of *Survey Graphic,* Stuart Chase wrote us up. He went up to the Camp as late as January, 1942, and he was able, at that late date, to still find the old spirit aglow. Now don't misunderstand me. We did not work for this article, or for any such publicity. The article is not more than a little symptom. For, in human affairs, some degree of extension in time is a condition of having existed at all. As an illustration, the three months during which General Wainwright held out on Bataan were futile. And you should search your heart to make sure that you realize the meaning of his defense. In a way, I feel that his hopeless resistance was a greater act than the reconquest. And, in our humble way, we may claim that our carrying on in Camp was in the manner of such a slow retreat. I would also claim that our retreat achieved its purpose. I do think that I have a right to say that since I had no illusions about the ultimate outcome, I found it often very difficult to keep going. On the other hand, the rhythm of the Camp was determined by the faith of its various members, and each member had a different approach to this problem of timing. Page Smith was spared all qualms by leaving in March, 1941, for the army. Enno felt frustrated because he stayed so very long. Clint Gardner joined us so late that the political and public place of Camp probably never became clear to him. And on it goes.

During the twelve months and longer, which followed the government camp, it was the same as it had been during the six months which preceded Sharon. Ever since Robert O'Brien went up to Tunbridge and met Lawrence Bowen, the steps of every day have been taken with the full risk of failure.

The period which I have called retreat, also was one of discovery, since it became necessary to add new features to the Camp simply in order to survive. Hence, we improved in many ways far beyond the previous government standards.

The contacts with the towns became, for a time, much closer. The girls joined and gave to our group the representative character which nothing ever has which is either purely male or purely female. The retreat of the government led our friends forward. This was true even in December, 1940, during our stay at the foresters' house. It was then and there that the James family came and sealed our enterprise's name. The Greene's and all our other friends became really active *after* our defeat in Congress.

The forms of daily life were much better discovered in the risky situation of continuous danger. Innumerable adaptations, inventions, and improvisations had to be made, and these enlarged the sphere of our work service.

I do not know if the details will ever be recorded, either of the daily routines, or the Alaska adventure, or of 'devolution week.' Perhaps they should not. However, one thing should remain with us, and that is the 'non-educational,' the *real* character of the period.

I solemnly deny the thesis that the Camp had the purpose of informing people about social problems, or of any other rationalistic mysticism of teaching. It was a unique and risky situation, mastered from day to day by a group living on a higher plane than we, as individuals, could live. It had no 'purpose,' unless it was a purpose to create an experience and a record of what real life is, and what it entails. That such a way of life spread new hope and faith in the future of the town and the people participating, is simply a by-product of any life lived fully. The real life is always devoted to its own reproduction. Anything which is good wants to last, and nothing lasts mechanically, by mere 'elongation.' It only lasts by grooming successors, devolving functions, encouraging more and more people to take a hand. That which does not spread has no life. Growth is not a matter of choice, but of vitality. And of all this, the various phases of Camp bore ample witness. They proved that we only get our third wind if, as members of the community, we know that nobody else will come to our rescue. These remarks should make it clear that the later phases of Camp were no less inventive and formative and paradigmatic than the official part.

Perhaps you can invite the reactions of some of our friends to this sketch. From it, you will see that such towns as Sharon and Strafford have as much of a claim to the site of 'Camp William James' as has Tunbridge. You will also see that this one and unique experiment definitely is ended. This may be painful to you as a farmer in Tunbridge. I have said nothing, however, about Camp as a precedent. Nothing about a revision of its pattern. We are too deeply in the war to be interested right now in the final pattern of a world at peace. All that I or you may be convinced of is that the impetus of Camp belongs to the world and to society after this war. It came too late to influence things; and it also came too early. But if it had not happened, it would be impossible for larger solutions on a world-wide scale to reach down far enough into the hearts of the people. Nothing can come true which has not been promised and prophesied. Most people do not know this; and fewer people believe this. However, nothing has ever had a lasting effect without being done by volunteers first, without any hope of a personal career or profit. We are often deceived into thinking that the life of generations can be improvised by makeshifts, thought up from moment to moment. The result is that the generations remain ignorant of one another, and consequently, nothing has the dignity of being more serious or lasting than the fads and fashions of any one day.

The energies which the war has unleashed are lasting energies, and they must be mobilized and put to use in every generation. Your group has shouldered the spade first and the rifle later. The classes after you, when they return, will have to do things in the opposite sequence. But in the long run, our education will have to cease training 'civilians.'

The experience of 'Camp William James' shows that the concept of society which thinks of two separate worlds—one of mere soldiering in the army, the other of mere studying in academic, playlike fashion—should not recur. The division of the soldier and the civilian has produced two mentalities, which are both unreal. Of the two, the soldier's faith is the better faith, since he at least knows that a man lives in two different times: *for* the duration, and *after* the duration. Every G.I. knows more of life than many a college man because he distinguishes between 'for the duration of the war' and 'peace.' He who does not make this distinction between these two fundamental attitudes does not know what life is like.

To face this double aspect of peace and war, peace in war, and war in peace, is the quality of the educated heart. The blending of the soldier's faith and the civilian's polish, remains the task. We cannot promise you to return to Tunbridge. But the real question, it seems, is: will enough people look out for *their* Tunbridge, *their* Sharon? And how do we go about encouraging people to do so?

Best wishes for your own health.

As ever,

Eugen

The reader may have wondered, long before this, why I have steered such a detailed course in following the history of the Camp. Certainly, many incidents were unspectacular, and should hardly bear repetition in print. Why, then, are they here? There are two answers to this question.

The first is a rather prosaic one. I pointed out in the Foreword that, while I may have allowed my own conception of what was important to crowd out non-essential items, I did wish to establish the main facts of the record. People do have different standards of judgment of matters of this kind, and I do not presume that my personal interpretations have been universally correct. But I have used such information as I could coherently get into the narrative, and which was substantiated by records or recollections available to me. Any further qualitative discrimination has been left up to the reader. This attempt to be inclusive, and at the same time selective, might appear to be contradictory in its effects. However, I have tried to steer a course between the two, in the belief that they need not be mutually repellent. I also feel that the validity and the presentability of the story has been better served.

Walking the tightrope of being choosy and yet impartial, leading as it may to a possible sacrifice of style and continuity, brings me to my second answer, which is perhaps more difficult to explain. It revolves around my feeling that any "true life" experience contains many moments of dullness and passivity. To portray human existence as a constant series of purposeful, crystal-clear adventures is to ignore reality. To make the point concrete, all one need do is to add up the number of hours in a lifetime which are spent in shaving, dressing, washing dishes, riding to work, shovelling snow, cleaning windows, etc., to say nothing of the approximately twenty years which the average person devotes to sleeping. This impressive mass of habit and functional rote would almost be enough to make us reject the idea of being born—if we had the choice. Hence, it is probably true that we all hate boredom because we ourselves are so boring. Consequently, the urge for excitement and for departure from routine is strong within us because it is rarely achieved.

I readily admit that the above description of human existence is a conscious over-simplification. For we do not carry about a rigid yardstick of values which we constantly apply to our own daily lives. Such a procedure would soon become unbearable, and would culminate in complete frustration. Biologically, as well, our bodies could not long endure an unslackening stream of high-intensity physical and emotional experiences. We need our "valleys" of inertia just as much as our "mountains" of activity. Indeed, without the valleys there would be no mountains.

It follows that one of our prime adjustments as individuals in society is to accept this necessity for peaks and depressions, and to benefit by the acceptance. I am not now speaking of economic cycles, but of human cycles. Applying this criterion of oscillation to the history of the Camp as a living group, we can readily discern the periodic ups and downs. We can also see that to have presented the reader with only the highspots would have been a deception by omission, and we would thereby have fashioned a distorted historical image. For it is quite important to realize that the very struggles, dissensions, and aimlessness which unceasingly plagued the Camp helped to make it genuine and meaningful. Insofar as the group reflected the frailties, as well as the virtues, of its members (i.e. humanity), in that measure can it be said to have been "true life." This is to say that human beings may not categorically renounce their personal weaknesses; they can only bear with them and, in concert, try to overcome them. The history of the Camp shows that any weakness, when it does not have to be suffered in isolation, can often be turned into an asset. The reciprocity of social relationships is what makes this possible. It also shows that we fictionalize our lives whenever we try to be unremittingly strong.

I believe that this cyclical idea performs a vital social service. For one thing, it eliminates the ice water of perfectionism from both the performance and analysis of human conduct. In addition, it exposes mechanistic uniformity as being a cultural mirage. For every situation in society is made up of a conglomeration of allies and antagonists, predictables and unpredictables, knowns and unknowns. Society implies life, and life implies movement—inexorable and frequently erratic movement, which does not wait upon the intellect for its expression.

I have emphasized the matter of "true life" because this book has not been concerned with just telling a story. I have wished, albeit optimistically, that the reader might project himself imaginatively into the Camp. I hoped that he might visualize himself doing and saying what was done and said. I was not desirous of merely re-creating characters and events, but preferably of transposing them onto a common keyboard for everyone to play in his own way. This precluded any private romanticizing or edification of what the Camp may have accomplished. In fact, as I look back over the story, after having written it, I find myself less positive about some aspects of it than I was at the beginning. Strangely enough, this is not displeasing. I have retraced the road which the Camp took, and I find it to be a trail similar to others I have followed. The "valleys" and the "mountains" have a familiar look, because they remind me of some I have seen elsewhere. This sort of parallel is what I hope the reader has been able to discover—some linkage between what has at one time or another happened to him, and what happened, for instance, to one or another of the forty-two members of the Sharon camp.

These last few pages have all been part of the second explanation of why this book was written the way it was. Possibly it can be summed up in the word "identification." I have had the notion that if I could get most people to feel that the Camp was within their private range of thought and action, then I might encourage them to do something about it. The problem has been—how to establish contact. And if I have chosen a fumbling and uncoordinated method, it is because I have a hunch that in the end it will prove to be the most productive.

* * * * *

Having now made my excuses, and displayed some prejudices, I would like to set forth my own evaluation of "Camp William James," in terms of 1950.

There were so many cross-currents at work in the Camp that often no direction at all is apparent. The reader will recall that at the end of the first chapter of the book I proposed to leave to his opinion whether or not the Camp achieved its goals. At this present moment, probably the most affirmative reaction I could expect would be one of perplexity, for perhaps the goals were never clearly defined.

On the other hand, if one took the negative view, there would be plenty of supporting evidence at hand. The record is certainly black with regard to the accomplishment of such aims as resettlement, reform of the CCC, and influencing the country's educational system.

Locally, the Camp's dream of starting the rehabilitation of Vermont's farm economy fell dreadfully short of the mark. Aside from the labor contributed largely by individual members on private farms, and the temporary resuscitation of the Rivers place as a headquarters, there were almost no lasting economic and political conquests of regional problems. Of course, this was due somewhat to the sacrifice of government support of the Camp as a consequence of World War II. However, the precise extent to which the war was responsible for these failures is hard to determine. For in addition to the war, we must lay part of the blame upon the nature of the experiment itself. It was forced to pursue its own uncharted way upon a hostile political sea, and it is not surprising that it eventually foundered. Moreover, the task of welding the Federal government, the State government, the communities, the colleges, and the Camp into a cohesive and jointly helpful unit was a complex one. Its accomplishment would have taken a tremendous amount of time and effort, even under the most favorable circumstances, and would have given rise to many errors. There was simply no means at hand for catalyzing such a unity. This being so, the long-range projects of the Camp never moved past the theoretical stage, and it is quite obvious to us now that they had virtually no chance of advancing much farther. Nevertheless, it was extremely irksome and dangerous for the Camp to foster the assumption (at least among the Vermonters) that establishing these projects involved little more than working out the plans on paper, and filling in the details later. There was a smack of duplicity about it. The dilemma was quite evident, for instance, in the difference between the resettlement program, as Nathan Dodge thought of it, and the idea of "permissable" work under the CCC statutes, which the Department of Agriculture had in mind. As we have noted previously in the text, the members of Camp knew that these two approaches were irreconcilable, and that a time would soon come when a choice would have to be made. Yet everyone was spared the embarrassment of a show-down because the Sharon camp broke up before any profound clash occurred. With respect to their favorite projects, then, the Vermont communities were really "whistling in the dark." And in their relations with the townspeople, the Camp thought it best to "whistle" along with them.

On the national level of reorganizing the CCC, the roles of the Federal government and the towns were essentially reversed. This line of development for the Camp, as a proving ground for new ideas and administrative techniques, was more in keeping with the desires of the men in Washington, whereas it meant comparatively little to the Vermont farmers. The Camp was supposed to uncover fresh leadership and to originate routines for eventual transmission to the entire Corps. Actually, it had very little practical understanding of how to go about these jobs. The many divergences of thought and action among the Harvard and Dartmouth groups exemplified this confusion of objectives. With several more months of grace at Sharon, the cross-purposes and anarchy which were prevalent might have been brought under control. But we have no evidence that this improvement was under way, nor even foreseeable. Until its sudden collapse, the government-sponsored camp remained more concerned with negating old rules and regulations than it was in formulating new ones. This process may well have been a necessary prelude to constructive suggestions, but there again we are in the realm of conjecture. And so, in the category of improving an existing national agency, the Camp had hardly made an impression on its chosen problem. Its major accomplishment in this field was that it *did* bring together the only truly diversified enrollment in the CCC's history, and thereby demonstrated that the barriers of social stratification and segregation could be removed. In retrospect, I am inclined to say that this may well overbalance the lack of achievement in other kinds of CCC reform.

The third relationship, that between the Camp and the educational structure of the colleges (principally Dartmouth and Harvard), was even less definable than the other two we have mentioned. There had never been any designated groups or persons in the colleges who could enter into a *rapport* with the Camp. This situation channelled all contacts with the students onto a purely individual level. Those undergraduates who were interested in the Camp expressed themselves, as it were, at their own risk and peril, especially if they had any intentions of joining up. True enough, the colleges felt a responsibility for preserving their integrity, unfettered by entanglements with Federal and local governments. They were also required to maintain order and discipline in their own establishments, particularly during the national emergency. But their consistent refusal to formally recognize the pleas and efforts of their alumni and students alike, represented a measure of repudiation of those pleas and efforts. On its part, the Camp appealed to the students "over the heads" of the college authorities. This practice was generally construed by the latter as an attempt to usurp their function and position. Such was not the Camp's intent, at least as I see it, but the results proved the method to have been a poor one. If it did nothing else, the direct invitation to the students to leave school, with or without official sanction, precluded any open support of the Camp by the college administrations. I want to say here that I neither condone nor condemn the Camp for its lack of success in collaborating with the colleges. I believe that the failure was amoral, the reason being that the Camp was, at the time, insufficiently developed to be fitted into any major phase of academic operations. Perhaps underlying differences would have made integration forever impossible, but here again, we should not proceed beyond the facts which are available, and the question must remain unanswered.

Finally, we have already spoken enough times of the internal strife in the Camp to show that there was little unanimity on the membership level, either. There was a good deal of bitterness and disagreement among various cliques and individuals, and there was seldom a moment when someone was not disgruntled or offended. Even the peripheral members of the larger group circle, the friends such as Dorothy Thompson, Mrs. Greene, Dean Landis, and Nathan Dodge, could not totally divorce themselves from these feelings. Certainly, the record would not support any pretense of blissful happiness and unbounded cooperation within the Camp itself.

In view of all these shortcomings, how can we maintain that the Camp had any constructive value? When we left it, in September, 1942, its very name had been removed from the public record of the State of Vermont. Could any defeat have been more thorough? In a purely tangible sense, probably not. As Huessy pointed out in his letter to Goldsmith in 1945, this one experiment was irrevocably ended.

But in spite of the physical burial, I believe that something else had lasted. Perhaps, for each member of the Camp, that "something" belongs to him alone, and he could not articulate it if he wanted to. Yet if there were nothing more than this private residue, no one could claim that the Camp stood for a universal appeal. By regarding it as an individual affair we would negate one-half of its duality. Its own diminutive form had to be balanced by its breadth of principle. We said at the very beginning of our story that the Camp could not have survived its tribulations without such a dual form. We pointed out that the Camp had to extend beyond its own earthly timespan. Carrying this thought further, we may state that one of the necessary tests for the validity of ideas is that they must be "communicable," just as we have stated that valid human experiences must be "identifiable." Likewise, I believe that the communication of ideas does not simply mean an understanding of words and phrases. It also means *acting* in terms of them. Ideas which are not forerunners of action are of very little use in society. They may afford academic pleasure, in the manner of a hobby, but they will rarely be a social force.

My chief point is that "Camp William James" embodied a communicable set of ideas, and that they were good ones. The Camp did not indulge in righteous moralizing. It led its members along paths which they selected for themselves. The weight and number of its material disasters were appalling, especially when the Alaskan and Mexican expeditions were added to the deficiencies already mentioned. But these temporal setbacks could be, and *were*, surmounted. There was an ingredient of faith in the fibre of the Camp which enabled it to conquer almost any kind of finite difficulty, save the draining away of its members. This ingredient was seldom isolated, if ever it could be, but its presence was always felt, particularly in moments of crisis. For example, Alfred Eiseman recognized it in the lives of the Vermonters when, during his early days as a hired hand, he marvelled at the ability of the farmers to overcome any obstacle or disappointment and still keep going. Another instance of this doggedness was the evacuation of the Sharon camp in the face of hopeless odds. This "something," this assertion of the human will, was powerful enough to carry the boys over every valley of despair they had to face while the Camp was being reconstituted in Tunbridge. The conclusion is that the "moral equivalent" of war, as the Camp signified it, could not have been a communicable idea if it had been unable to withstand the shocks and the drudgery of everyday life. If all the Camp had tried to do had been materially successful, its results would not have been "worldly" — a quality often easier to feel than to describe. It would have been a controlled laboratory success, but it would never have been a social success. For in any realm of human endeavor, we would never be able to identify a victory if there were no defeats with which to compare it. Opposites supplement and clarify each other.

Therefore, I would say that the Camp, through its own valid experience, has proved that the idea of a "moral equivalent of war" is attainable in both a practical and a spiritual sense. By so doing, it has communicated this idea meaningfully to future generations.

In most respects, our world of 1950 is not very much different from the world of 1940. Some of us find the parallels are sharp enough to make us believe we are seeing ghosts. Moreover, the outbreaks of destruction which have occurred over the past hundred years have been growing ever wider in scope, and the respites between catastrophic wars have become shorter. If necessary, we may also add that the destructive forces themselves, besides arising more frequently, are now incomparably more potent than we would have thought possible a decade ago. No lonely island or underground fortress is safe. The sanctuaries have evaporated, and we can afford to do no less than to face realities. Conceivably, the planet may disintegrate under our feet. I do not say these things as prophet of doom and despair. I mention them because they are factual possibilities which cannot be brushed aside as mere pessimism or cowardice. It will require considerable maturity on our part to maintain our moral and emotional equilibrium while realizing that we possess the instruments of our own complete effacement. There will no longer be any hiding behind oceans, or tanks, or bombs, or battleships, or mental Maginot lines. The vanguard is everything, and the battlefield is everywhere. We will stop squandering a good deal of time, energy, and money if we recognize that simple truth. Because in recognizing it we will automatically cease worshipping such costly and nonsensical "defenses" as fleets, armies, air forces, and the like. The most ludicrous and unrealistic belief of our era is the contention that the tools of war are the safeguards of peace. Those who trumpet most loudly for "protection" do not seem to comprehend that shooting wars are born of their own fear — fear of weakness. Our whole history of the Camp has shown that weakness is a human characteristic which *cannot be eradicated*. Furthermore, if accepted in its proper place, it is seen to be a necessary component of strength.

The peoples and nations of the world have never admitted this paradox, which is the very basis of Christianity itself. So far, we have managed to get away with our blindness, even though we still attempt to be strong for eternity. But the strain of maintaining an everlasting strength in prestige, power, and weapons causes increasing tension on all social and political levels, and culminates in hysteria and aggressiveness. And so we have war. Can we afford to follow this deadly pattern once again?

A currently popular belief is that war envelops a nation because it is "unprepared," in a military sense, and that a condition of "unpreparedness" is virtual assurance of defeat. In modern politics this has always been an easy doctrine to expound and defend. It also happens to be expediently true, by which I mean that when someone is actually shooting at you, it is a good thing, from the standpoint of self-preservation, to be able to return the fire. The real fallacy of this doctrine is that it assumes the imminence of war or the inevitability of war. If we accept either of these premises we have signed our own death warrant. We should find it significant that the scientists who have been closest to the fantastic weapons and energies which they have unleashed are among the first to recoil from their horrible potentialities. Einstein is undoubtedly much more uneasy about what mankind is going to do with the nuclear bombs than is the average citizen, who only knows what he reads in the newspapers. The scientist knows full well that the prevention of war among nations will never again be an academic problem. It is as urgent for the survival of the human race as having air to breathe and food to eat. Therefore, the kind of short-run thinking which pins its hopes for peace upon being supreme in armaments will, if it remains ascendant, seal the fate of our civilization. We will be like the man on the bicycle who approached a stone in the road, and who became so grimly fascinated with what might happen if he steered into it that he rammed it solidly and broke his neck in the ensuing fall.

Our society is on its bicycle. The road contains not one stone, but many. If we hold to our present course, engrossed in our own fears and worries, building bigger and better bombs for our "security," the end will only be a matter of time. What difference if it is measured in weeks, months, or years. Perhaps a quirk or impulse of one man will be enough to touch off the final Roman candle. We have, in a sense, entered upon a period of suspended life.

What is the alternative? I think you have already seen the general outlines of it. We must first discredit the belief that "security," per se, is our ultimate goal. This is a defeatist belief. But surprisingly enough, we hear many people decry security as a principle of economics, and at the same time worship it as a philosophy of politics. Such inconsistent double-talk is commonplace today.

We need to remember that life is, first and foremost, a risk. The only real peace of mind will come from accepting it as such, and then dismissing the fact as something to be frightened about. This cognizance of risk is the cardinal virtue of the soldier. If he did not accept the possibility of being killed at any moment, he could not perform his duty. This leads us, as civilians, back again to the "moral equivalent of war." Like the soldier, we must gather our spiritual and physical weapons to fight against our real enemies — greed, lethargy, malnutrition, moral degeneracy, and many others. These enemies are encouraged by shooting wars. They lie in wait while mankind exhausts itself in fratricide. During the peace interludes, they assert themselves with renewed vigor and prominence.

If we have any measure of control over our lives, we cannot allow these enemies to prosper. A widespread "moral equivalent of war" must be sought and discovered. In their imperfect way, the members of Camp William James caught a flash of what they were seeking. They could not blueprint it. Within this book I have tried to give you the best glimpse possible of their attempt to live out a substitute for war. But here, almost ten years later, we know that we must try again. The shape and configuration of our objective are not completely clear, but the necessity for achieving it is no less imperative. If we know, even in broad terms, what we are after, we can at least begin to go about getting it. A working combination of faith, knowledge, and determination will give us a fair chance to gain the victory over war.

We may conclude, then, that the failures of the Camp were not the sole criteria of its worth. Emotional crises and physical losses can always be overcome in society. However, their existence is essential in any real life experience. Finally, the core of the Camp's being was its impetus to create new moral and social forms, not by adhering to charts and formulas, but by responding to the needs and drives of mankind.

Epilogue

I am aware that this book has not yet given forth any specific steps which might be taken to establish a "moral equivalent of war." But I do believe we have supplied ourselves with a sound background for doing just that. The exposition of the history of the Camp and the evaluation of its effects upon those who participated in it have once for all removed the subject from the restrictions of pure hypothesis. We are not dealing with utopian panaceas, but with the blood and bone of life. In this respect, I hope that the story has convinced the reader that a "moral equivalent of war" is a desirable and graspable object.

If that much has been accomplished, here are a few suggestions which might help to get things started, at least on the thinking level. The reason I have chosen to put these final remarks off in a section by themselves is because, technically, they are not a part of "Camp William James." They are altogether personal projections. As such, they are distinct from the verifiable experience of the past, although they are certainly an outgrowth of it. This may appear to be an odd distinction, but I wish to preserve it so that the life cycle of the Camp may stand on its own merit, devoid of any ornamentation I might try to hang on it.

I would say that the practical roads we can follow are two in number.

The first route is that which the Camp itself took — the voluntary, almost spontaneous incentive to meet up with a problem and do something about it. This method can assume many shapes, and is difficult to regiment. It comes and goes without any particular pattern or line of march. But although it depends a good deal upon chance and whim, it represents the kind of self-subscription to an ideal which people are usually proud of when they look back on it. It also has a varying emotional quality which might be passionate one minute and stone-cold the next. I rather suspect that there will always be those of us who will live part or all of our lives in the manner of rooting where the acorn drops instead of waiting to be consciously planted. Likewise, ideas which travel in this fashion trickle from one person to another by a kind of educational and experimental osmosis. The trickle is seldom large, but it is a well-spring which never freezes over and never runs dry. It can penetrate anywhere. Perhaps some college, or group of students, or labor union, or Chamber of Commerce, or 4-H club will suddenly get the inspiration to dedicate its strength for a time to an entity bigger than itself — to its nation, or to humanity. It will go somewhere, or invite to its own locality a segment or facet of society which it had hitherto never known intimately. Together, the two elements would engage in some joint act that neither would have contemplated doing alone. The process might take any form, and none would be too incredible. For instance, the sons of a group of mechanics in a Detroit automobile factory might, through the sponsorship of their father's union, contact a corresponding group of Grange farm boys in Nebraska. The two could arrange to go to Georgia to help build a community center or a hospital for some small town which otherwise couldn't afford to have one. The union and the Grange could provide the boys, plus their travelling expenses, and the town where they worked would provide food and lodging. This is just an example. There are literally thousands of variations to it, and through all of them would run a commingling of youthful mind and spirit which could be achieved in no other way.

To carry it a step further, the Federal, state, and local governments, as in the case of "Camp William James," could help share the cost of feeding and housing the boys, and provide technical assistance, tools, and raw materials. Here would be the kind of spending of the taxpayer's dollar which would have more lasting value than a good many appropriations for jet planes and atomic weapons. For it would carry out a primary tenet of the democratic state, namely that it builds, and *is built by,* its citizens, with meticulous concern for the rights and welfare of all. The nation should be both the collective and the individual expression of its people.

Undoubtedly, you will see countless ways in which such work can be done. Somewhere, there is always a wheel which can set the machinery in motion. The main thing is that we must hit upon constructive outlets for restless human energy. Maybe we can call it "selfless interest," which is really nothing more than self interest seen in its proper perspective. Americans have often prided themselves on their ability to push back frontiers and blaze trails. Finding the "moral equivalent of war" is the greatest — and possibly the last — challenge they will ever get.

Road number two is less imaginative, but perhaps more definitive. It may even be thought of as merely widening road number one to include another lane. It involves the formation of an agency which will have public responsibility for administering a national program of service.

Such an agency was actually proposed to the Congress of the United States by the then Representative Jerry Voorhis of California, in August, 1940. His resolution (H.R. 10340), known as the National Service Act, was introduced for the purpose of supplementing, and eventually encompassing military training. The salient features of the bill were:

1) Every young man between the ages of eighteen and twenty-four would be required to give a maximum of twelve months service to his country in one of the designated National Service agencies.

2) Designated National Service agencies:
   - Civilian Conservation Corps
   - Civil Aeronautics Authority
   - National Youth Administration
   - Public Health Service
   - Soil Conservation Service
   - United States Army and Corps of Engineers
   - United States Coast Guard
   - United States Coast and Geodetic Survey

United States Forest Service
United States Marine Corps
United States Navy

Other agencies to be added when desirable.

3) Each registrant would name his first three preferences in order.

4) A National Service Commission, numbering between seven and fifteen qualified citizens, would establish quotas for various agencies, make selections of new agencies, and administer the over-all program.

5) All persons serving under the terms of the bill would be paid $25 per month in civilian agencies, and $30 per month in the armed services.

6) The Commission might, after negotiations with the nations involved, set up work service camps in Central and South America as an adjunct to the United States' policy of friendship and goodwill.

This measure, which would have made the service compulsory, was introduced during the latter part of the last session of the 76th Congress, and was referred to the Military Affairs Committee of the House of Representatives. It was presented too late for any action during that session, and was thus automatically stricken from the record when Congress adjourned. It was not presented again during the "War Congress" of the following year.

In analyzing the resolution, which lost most of its driving power when the Burke-Wadsworth Selective Service Act was passed in September, 1940, we can see much similarity between its provisions and the kind of thing "Camp William James" was trying to do voluntarily in the CCC. It also embodied the logical peace time extension of compulsory military training which Grenville Clark had suggested to Huessy (see page 88) in their exchange of letters. Nevertheless, it did not presume to do more than lay out general concepts.

Enactment of the Voorhis bill, or a similar piece of legislation, would certainly have created a gigantic Federal agency. This fact alone would have posed vast bureaucratic and administrative problems. More than that, it would have touched off a violent public debate on peace time conscription. The majority of the American public have traditionally resisted any kind of compulsion by government, even if there were no better argument than that it *was* compulsion, regardless of any benefits which might result from it. Opponents of military conscription during the last war were not scarce, and their resistance did not diminish until the United States was physically attacked. After the war, they continued the fight with vigor.

However, we may wonder whether the practice of unmitigated opposition to government activity is in itself a healthy phenomenon, and whether it leads to a logically tenable political attitude. A considerable number of people who are violently against government "bigness," per se, are not in the least hostile to economic "bigness." Yet why should we regard one as morally bad and the other as morally good?

This curious "ethical" division of thought explains why any Federal, or even state measure which puts a claim upon the individual American's time or fortunes is branded immediately as Fascistic, Communistic, socialistic, or what have you. People forget, from one generation to another, that causes which their forbears either steadfastly resisted, or else championed to the death are today accepted as commonplace, or were casually discarded long ago.

A case in point is our system of compulsory public education. There was a time when required attendance at a public school was regarded as a gross infringement upon human rights, and a violation of the sacred duty of parents to be solely responsible for bringing up their children. Today, practically no one advocates seriously the abolition of the public schools. In fact, we have been concerned with making them better and more numerous. Attendance at school is not regarded as simply a discipline to which every child is subjected, but is rather the fulfillment of an obligation which society *owes* to its future citizens. Knowledge and literacy are certainly two fundamental components of good citizenship. However, this integration of the compulsory school idea into the fabric of democratic life did not happen overnight, nor was it painless.

Taking our cue from this illustration, we may expect any proposal for a compulsory and inclusive work service in this country to evoke a storm of protest in many quarters. It is a safe bet that the amount and vehemence of the criticism would surpass the tirade engendered by military conscription alone. This situation is natural, and should not cause any anxiety. If we are willing to assume that the individual owes some moral and physical debts to society, and that such debts are unreservedly assumed as part of citizenship, then we can make some headway against short-sighted arguments and synthetic bogey-men. At the same time, we need to remember that being "in the service" should not be a phrase confined to the personnel of the armed forces. The words should apply equally to those engaged in building roads, fighting floods, controlling erosion, or clearing slums. For love of country neither begins nor ends with shooting her human enemies. To a much greater degree it consists of fighting a never-ending battle against her *natural* enemies — the disease, the ignorance, the poverty, the animosity which are all around us. This new status for civilian service may well require an innovation in our educational thinking and the material expression which grows out of it. It is paramount to realize that the nation requires a constant flow of non-profit service from its people which will give them a sense of belonging to the whole unit.

Unfortunately, about the only way in which this can be even remotely achieved in America today is by membership in the military or naval forces. And even these services are being advertised to the youth more and more as "profitable careers." The basic idea of service has been replaced by a frank appeal to the individual desire for prestige and economic advancement. Because of this potential destructive power, the peace time existence of the man in uniform always seems rather grotesque, in addition to being a waste of human resources. From the nature of his position, the fighting man cannot gain his full stature or justify his existence without doing just that — fighting. As I see it, our job is to give our regenerative civilian services the same esprit de corps, the same identification with the preservation and vitalization of the nation which, so far, only the warring soldier holds.

We should rid ourselves of the notion that *quantity* of legislative compulsion alone is the criterion of the worth of an objective. To adopt this notion leads to inconsistencies which will only create further confusion of values. Freedom from restraint is not an inherently desirable end in itself. It can just as easily be a component of anarchy as of democracy. If we accept the idea of a work service as right and proper, and as having a dignity of its own, we will have taken a long step toward the sober consideration of how to apply the service to our daily lives. The inevitable political hue and cry will not then throw us off the track.

I believe that some kind of national service act, as presaged by the Voorhis bill, is a sound means of attacking the problem of war at its roots. Such a law, applicable to all, is the necessary counterpart of the spontaneous private and individual activities which have already been outlined in this section. To unify these two propositions, I have used the history of "Camp William James" to convert the discussion into practical terms. The Camp's economic, governmental, and organizational crises are forerunners of the problems we shall now have to tackle on a tremendous scale. They have given us a priceless preview of what to expect in the arena of social relations, and they have provided some solid factual ground upon which we can put our feet.

I do not say, of course, that the Voorhis bill was anything more than a harbinger, or that it should now be revived in its original format. The real point is that harbingers are an indispensable ingredient of progress, and that in this instance they *have been made.* The directional signposts are established. Out of the microcosmic history of "Camp William James" can come a living moral equivalent of war. The main task right now is to plant the seeds wherever and whenever we can—without delay.

Footnotes

CHAPTER 1

1. "Moral Equivalent of War." Wm. James. 1910.
2. "Moral Equivalent of War." Wm. James. 1910.

CHAPTER 2

1. Pamphlet, Civilian Conservation Corps, "Standards of Eligibility and Selection for Junior Enrollees." June 15, 1939.
2. Letter from Frank Davidson to James J. McEntee. October 5, 1939.
3. Letter from Frank Davidson to E. Rosenstock-Huessy. October 20, 1939.
4. Letter from Ambrose W. Vernon to Frank Davidson. November 13, 1939.
5. Author of the definitive two volume work "The Thought and Character of Wm. James."
6. From a report written by Alexander Fanelli and Edward Chalfant, both Dartmouth Class of 1942.
7. Excerpt from report, unsigned.
8. Excerpt from report, unsigned.
9. Excerpt from report, unsigned.
10. Excerpt from report, unsigned.
11. Letter from Frank Davidson to E. Rosenstock-Huessy, undated, but probably in March, 1940.
12. From an address, "What We Shall Make Them Do," delivered to Area Conference of CCC Educational Advisers, Hanover, N. H., May 23, 1940.

CHAPTER 5

1. New York City
2. Letter from Frank Davidson to E. Rosenstock-Huessy, undated but probably around September 15, 1940.
3. Which had been "suggested" by the President.
4. Letter from Paul H. Appelby to Paul V. McNutt, October 9, 1940.
5. National Youth Administration.
6. Fred Morrell, Chief of U. S. Forestry Service, and Department of Agriculture representative on the CCC Advisory Council.
7. Report made by Enno Hobbing of meeting of Committee on CCC Personnel, October 14, 1940.
8. A "Life" photographer had spent several days in Tunbridge at the time of the rally. The story referred to was never published.

9. This line of procedure was suggested by Davidson.
10. Letter from Dorothy Thompson to President Roosevelt, October 18, 1940.

CHAPTER 6

1. Not to be confused with the Committee on CCC Personnel, whose proceedings have been discussed in some detail on preceding pages.
2. Letter from Fred Morrell to James McEntee, October 22, 1940. It should be noted that any mention of resettlement projects was scrupulously avoided.
3. Eiseman, Preiss and Schlivek.
4. Letter from E. Rosenstock-Huessy to W. W. Alexander, November 6, 1940.
5. Letter from Alfred S. Eiseman, Jr., Jack J. Preiss, and Louis B. Schlivek to John Fox, November 8, 1940.
6. Farm at which he worked during the summer.
7. Letter from Arthur Root to E. Rosenstock-Huessy, November 14, 1940.
8. Notes taken by Arnold Childs of meeting at "Four Wells," Norwich, Vermont, November 22, 1940.
9. Notes by Roy Chamberlin of Meeting of Council of the Eight Townships, November 21, 1940.
10. Notes by Roy Chamberlin of meeting of Council of Eight Townships, November 21, 1940.
11. Dr. Harry Gideonse, President of Brooklyn College, New York, N. Y.
12. Newspaper columnist and author of the pamphlet, "All Out for Democracy."
13. Signed at the rally on September 25th.
14. Huessy forwarded the invitation a few days later. Letter from Frank Davidson to E. Rosenstock-Huessy, November 27, 1940.
15. From letter from Grenville Clark to E. Rosenstock-Huessy, December 3, 1940.
16. Letter from Ernest Martin Hopkins to E. Rosenstock-Huessy, May 21, 1940.
17. From a petition to Dartmouth Defense Council, November 11, 1940.

CHAPTER 7

1. Which we have already noted on page 87.
2. Bill introduced by Representative Jerry Voorhis of California (H.R. 10430). This bill, if enacted, would have laid the groundwork for a compulsory U. S. Work Service.
3. See page 88.
4. The story of this event is best described in a letter from Enno Hobbing to Mrs. Greene, who, although invited with her husband, was unable to attend.
5. The third son, Henry James of New York, was absent.

6. McKaye was with the Forestry Service, and had achieved wide recognition in agricultural circles for his conservation work. He was also a New Englander, and a man of warmth and understanding. O'Brien and Preiss had known him during their senior year at Dartmouth and had been much impressed with his technical knowledge and personality. His choice as commander was made by the group largely on their recommendations (Huessy also knew him). This unanimous agreement was an outgrowth of Department of Agriculture pressure to have someone appointed before January 1st. It did not mean that the group at the foresters' house subscribed to the principle of designating a commander at that time.
7. Letter from Enno Hobbing to Mrs. Henry C. Greene, December 16, 1940.
8. These notes, describing the two weeks at the Sharon foresters' house, were pieced together from the diaries and letters of many of those who were present. Used chiefly were those of Frank Davidson, Enno Hobbing, Arnold Childs, Roy Chamberlin, and Jack Preiss.

CHAPTER 8

1. Huessy had applied for United States citizenship through regular naturalization channels.
2. Reference to a letter from E. Rosenstock-Huessy to Roy Hendrickson, December 12, 1940.
3. CCC liaison officer, subordinate of Morrell.
4. Gilbert Klos, a candidate for superintendent who was not acceptable to the Camp.
5. Letter from Roy Hendrickson to E. Rosenstock-Huessy, December 18, 1940.
6. Presumably because of age.
7. He was still under the impression that McKaye was available.
8. Letter from Frank Davidson to E. Rosenstock-Huessy, December 27, 1940.
9. Letter from E. Rosenstock-Huessy to Frank Davidson, December 28, 1940.

CHAPTER 9

1. Landis may have gotten this impression from Hendrickson, after the latter had received Huessy's letters in December.
2. Letter from Frank Davidson to Mr. Henry Greene, January 7, 1941.
3. Letter from James M. Landis to Frank Davidson, January 10, 1941.
4. Camp members mentioned in this book are marked with an asterisk in the index.
5. Letter from Arthur Root to E. Rosenstock-Huessy, January 11, 1941.
6. The Committee was now officially composed of Appleby, Morrell, Olmstead, Lasswell, Huessy, Nat Sage, of Massachusetts Institute of Technology, Dorothy Thompson, and Hendrickson, himself, as Chairman.
7. Many of the unfamiliar names which appear in these diaries are those of noncollege enrollees who joined the Camp in Sharon.

8. Excerpts from diaries kept by Enno Hobbing.
9. The Dartmouth and Harvard groups.
10. Letter from Claude Wickard to Representative Albert J. Engel, January 24, 1941.
11. Quoted in Associated Press dispatch in the New York *Herald Tribune*, January 23, 1941.
12. Letter from A. Courtney Parker to E. Rosenstock-Huessy, January 25, 1941.
13. Letter from Roy Hendrickson to Nathan Dodge, January 28, 1941.
14. Wickard's letter to Engel.
15. Letter from Roy Hendrickson to E. Rosenstock-Huessy, January 28, 1941.
16. An Assistant to President Roosevelt.
17. A native Vermont boy recruited from the Poultney CCC camp by Eiseman, Preiss and Schlivek.
18. Excerpts from diaries kept by Enno Hobbing and Page Smith.

CHAPTER 10

1. Jay C. Hayden.
2. Statement in the Senate by Senator George D. Aiken of Vermont, February 3rd, 1941. Later inserted in the *Congressional Record*.
3. Reporter Frederick R. Barclay, of the *New York Times*, in an article dated February 8, 1941.
4. From a statement "A Balance Sheet," by E. Rosenstock-Huessy, February 15, 1941.
5. Letter from James J. McEntee to Fred Morrell, February 17, 1941.
6. Headline in the *New York World Telegram*, February 20, 1941.
7. Letter from George D. Aiken to Nathan P. Dodge, February 24, 1941.
8. From a letter from James F. Curtis, Secretary of the Council of the Nine Towns, to E. Rosenstock-Huessy, March 1, 1941.
9. Benjamin L. Hinckley.
10. Letter from E. Rosenstock-Huessy to Harold Lasswell, undated, but probably sometime in February, 1941.
11. From a speech by Nathan Dodge, welcoming new enrollees to the Sharon Camp, January 10, 1941.
12. From a speech by Dorothy Thompson, delivered at Dartmouth College, Hanover, N. H., March 3, 1941.

CHAPTER 11

1. Letter from Robert O'Brien to Percy Brown, February 13, 1941.
2. Letter from Paul H. Appelby to Nathan P. Dodge, March 26, 1941.

CHAPTER 12

1. Which was what the Greenes had stated they hoped it would be.
2. Letter from Dorothy Canfield Fisher, circulated to Henry James, Mrs. Greene, Huessy, and others, dated April 19, 1941.
3. Letter from Ramon Beteta, Mexican Under Secretary of the Treasury and the Interior, to Arthur Root, March 7, 1941.

CHAPTER 13

1. From column, "My Day," by Eleanor Roosevelt, June 24, 1941.
2. Letter from George Phillips, Russell Greenlaw, and Charles Davidson to "Camp William James," undated, but probably about the middle of August, 1941.
3. Letter from George Phillips to "Camp William James," September, 1941.
4. Letter from John Clark to Arthur Root, September 25, 1941.
5. Letter from James Tierney and Paul Keefe to Arthur Root, October 10, 1941.
6. Letter from Clinton Gardner to Frank Davidson, October 6, 1941.
7. Letter from Mrs. Rosalind Greene to Robert O'Brien, October 9, 1941.
8. Letter from Clinton Gardner to Frank Davidson, November 12, 1941.
9. Telegram from Lee Knowles to Mrs. Greene, December 21, 1941.

CHAPTER 14

1. Interview with Albert DeVivo, by the author, October 15, 1949.
2. Letter from Arthur Root to E. Rosenstock-Huessy, January 13, 1942.
3. Minutes of the annual meeting of Council and Camp, Inc., submitted by Enno Hobbing, February 8, 1942.
4. Letter from Enno Hobbing to Katherine Taylor, May 19, 1942
5. This letter accompanied the donation of $1000 to buy the farmhouse as a center for the Camp.
6. Letter from George Phillips to Percy Brown, August 1, 1942.

CHAPTER 15

1. McEntee was a former trades union official, who had presumably been appointed to his CCC job as part of the general patronage plan which most administrations used to reward their supporters.

Index

All members of "Camp William James" mentioned in this book have been marked with an asterisk.

Aiken, George, U.S. Senator from Vt., ix, 43, 139, 145, 162, 204, 250
Alaskan Expedition, 184, 187, 189, 190, 192, 226, 235
Alexander, Will W., Chairman of the National Defense Commission, 50-61, 68, 69, 125, 248
Allen, Dr. Bush, 20
Allen, Fred, 13
American Council on Education, 55
American Friends Service Committee, 55
American Youth Commission, A.Y.C., 55, 56 60, 191, camps of, 55, 56
Amos, Glen, Superintendent of C.W.J. of the Forestry Service, 119-123, 128, 129, 132, 133, 134
Anderson, Ralph, 97, 121, 122, 131, 132
Appleby, Paul, Under Secretary of Agriculture, 16, 19, 21, 23, 39, 50, 53, 59, 162-164, 247, 249, 250
Arnold, Bob, 17, 18
Austin, Senator from Vermont, 162

Bagby,* Phil, 92, 98, 101, 116, 117, 120-122, 132
Barstow, Robbins, 153
Baz, Dr. Gustav, Mexican Minister of Public Assistance, 176, 177, 192
Beteta, Ramon, Mexican Under Secretary of the Treasury, 174-176, 192, 251
Bingham*, Mary, 181, 189
Bernstein*, Daniel, 166
Blaine*, Nancy, 174, 179, 181, 194, 197, 221, 222
Blood, Robert, 91
Bourdelais*, Bob, 122
Bowen, John, Morell's liaison officer in Boston, 102, 103
Bowen, Lawrence, of Tunbridge, Vt., 25, 35, 37, 41, 85, 86, 108, 112, 155, 226
Boy Scouts, 69
Brener*, John, 97
Brocklebank Hill Project, 101, 107, 110, 112, 118, 123, 131, 135, 221
Bronston*, Jack, 181
Brooklyn College, 87
Brown, Percy, Director of the "Edward Filene Good Will Fund," 159, 160, 166, 169, 198, 206, 207, 212, 213, 215, 216, 219, 250, 251
Burbank, Lyman, of Chelsea, Vt., 85, 86, 173

California Conservation Corps, x
"Camp William James"
autonomy, 106
collaboration with the community, 221
dedication, ix, 100-102
essence of "Camp William James," 224, 225
female division, 174
general, ix-xv, 78, 86, 87, 89, 90, 93, 98, 99, 144, 146, 147, 150-156, 158, 159, 162, 164-166
at Mentzer's farm, Tunbridge, Vt., 155, 156, 158, 161, 165
organization, 116, 117
relationship between Camp and College, 233, 234
at Rivers' farm, 169-173, 183, 209-212, 231
Chalfont, Edward 153, 247
Chamberlin*, Roy, 78, 81, 85, 86, 92, 94, 99 101, 102, 117, 133, 181, 184, 248, 249
Childs*, Arnold, 42, 67, 73, 78, 93, 112, 175, 248, 249
Churchill*, Louis, 181
C.I.O., Congress of Industrial Organizations, 221
citizenship, definition of, 222, 223
Civilian Conservation Corps: CCC, established 1933
administration, 9, 125-127
Camps at Bellows Falls, Vt., 93, 143, 144, 156
Denby-Poultney, 70-72, 102, 117
Maryland, 11-13
central organization, 16
CCC boys (enrolees), x, 18, 19, 71, 72, 89, 93, 94, 96-99, 102, 157
general, ix, x, 8-24, 32-42, 49-51, 53, 54, 56-61, 64, 65, 67, 69, 70, 74, 76, 79-83, 90, 93, 103, 108, 109, 112, 116, 117, 121, 125-127, 140-148, 151-158, 161-163, 186, 209, 222, 223, 232, 243
model (demonstration camp), 52, 56-58, 125
qualifications for enrollment, 9, 10, 15, 165, 233
Clark*, Bob, 130
Clark, John, Coordinator of Inter-American Affairs Office, 191, 251
Clark, Grenville, 88, 94, 243, 248
College Boys, x, 25, 120, 121, 126, 131, 134, 138-140, 158
Conant, James Bryant, President of Harvard, 22
conscription, 3, 4, 88
conservation, ix, 9, 11, 16, 18, 60

Coolidge, Calvin, U. S. President, 140
Council and Camp, Inc., 118, 119, 148, 159, 160, 163-165, 169, 170, 173, 178, 184, 198, 205, 206, 208-211, 213, 214, 217, 218, 220
Council of the Eight (Nine) Townships in Vermont, 63, 74, 75, 85, 86, 89, 97, 109-112, 118, 128, 141, 144, 146-148, 162, 164, 173, 184, 187, 199
Coy, Wayne, Assistant Federal Security Administrator (McEntee's superior officer), 39, 49, 50, 53, 54, 58, 59, 61, 66
Corwin, Grant, 186, 200
Cueva, de la, Licenciado Morio, President of the National University of Mexico, 175
Curtis, of Sharon, Vt., 63, 85, 86, 94, 250

Daniels, Joseph, American Ambassador in Mexico, 180, 185
Dartmouth College, xiii, 7, 17, 19, 23, 31, 36, 39, 42, 61, 70, 83, 85, 89, 90, 94, 99, 100, 151, 153, 154, 156, 186, 194, 233
Dartmouth boys, students, graduates, ix, 25, 32, 36, 64, 67, 69, 78, 85, 158, 208
Dartmouth Defense Group, 90, 93, 248
Dartmouth group, 32, 34, 75, 188, 232, 249
Davis, Richard, 10
Dell*, Charles, 181
Dies Committee, 146
DeVivo*, Albert, 181, 187, 196, 203
Davidson*, Frank, xii, 6-8, 10-16, 19-24, 32-34, 39, 40, 49, 50-62, 67, 74-83, 85, 87, 93 96, 98, 101, 106-109, 111, 112, 114, 115, 120, 122, 123, 135, 161, 162, 177, 181, 185, 186, 188, 196, 199, 212, 247-249, 251
Davidson*, Charles, 131, 187, 189, 190, 195, 251
Dodge, Nathan, of Tunbridge, Vt., 31, 35, 39, 57, 63, 64, 66, 85, 86, 109-112, 118, 119, 128 133, 145, 150, 155, 160, 163-165, 170-173, 179, 182, 184, 186, 196-198, 200, 202, 205-207, 212, 217, 221, 224, 232, 234, 250
Draft, draft-boards, 88, 157, 204
Dumas*, Ralph, 97, 117, 134
Dupras*, Allan, 116

ecology army, x
Eiseman*, Alfred, 25-27, 38, 42, 66, 67, 69, 73, 78, 82, 83, 99, 101, 102, 106, 122, 132, 133, 170, 177-179, 197, 235, 248
Elliott, William G., professor, 15, 16
Engel, Albert J., Representative U. S. Congress, from Michigan, 124, 125, 127-129, 137-144, 250
experimental leadership training camp, x, 39, 44, 60

Fanelli, Alexander, 247
Farm Security Administration, 104, 135, 145, 161-163 (Mr. Hudgens), 173
Faure, Roger, Frenchman killed in the Battle of France, 169
Federal Government, 89, 106, 148, 163, 184, 212
Federal Security Administration, 62, 125
Federal Security Appropriation Act, 103
Edward Filene Good Will Fund 159-161, 165-167, 169, 173, 198, 201, 206-208, 211, 217, 218
Fisher*, Bud, 122
Fisher, Dorothy Canfield, ix, 33, 41, 119, 127, 160, 170-173, 186, 251
Fisk, The Reverend, from Hanover, N. H., 121
Flanders, Ralph, U. S. Senator from VT., ix, 43
Flint, Edward, of Tunbridge, Vt., 35, 39, 43, 116, 140, 165, 170, 171, 179, 184, 197, 198, 206, 210, 212, 215, 217, 221, 224
Flint*, Neal, 116, 133
Flint*, Stanley, 116, 120, 135
Flowers*, George, cook of Sharon, 92, 104, 122
flood control, 9, 30, 36
Fox*, Jake, 181, 187, 196, 200, 202
Fox, John A., Secretary of Commerce, 54, 57, 59, 60, 62, 69, 76, 77, 145, 248
Frank, Waldo, 174-176
Frankfurter, Felix, Justice of the Supreme Court, 162
Fuchs*, John, 132

Gardner*, Clinton, xii, 153, 181, 187, 196, 199, 200, 207 226, 251
Gentille*, Sam, 122, 123
Gibson, of Sharon, Vt., 85, 86
Gideonse, Dr. Harry, President of Brooklyn College, New York, 87, 248
Gilman, 100
Goldsmith*, Daniel, xii, 166, 185, 186, 196, 199, 200, 206-208, 215, 216, 219-221, 234
Goldsmith*, John, 196, 200
Goodman, Benny, 13
Grafton, Samuel, newspaper columnist, 87
Great Depression, 1929, ix, 8, 223
Greene, Mr. and Mrs. Henry Copley, 7, 8, 13, 83, 99, 100, 114, 115, 166, 169, 173, 200, 207, 208, 217, 226, 250
Rosalind, 53, 100, 114, 115, 132, 156, 159, 172, 194, 197, 198, 201, 202, 209, 212, 234, 248, 249, 251
Greenlaw*, Russell, 187, 189, 190, 195, 208, 210, 212, 221, 251
Guyette*, Gus, 117, 134

Hall*, Fred, 121
Harris*, Cynthia, 181, 221
Harvard College, 7, 10, 13, 15, 17, 22, 94, 99, 127, 151, 153, 181, 233
Harvard group (students, friends), ix, 32, 34, 35, 45, 46, 56, 64, 72, 75, 188, 232, 249
Hendrickson, Roy F., Director of Personnel, Department of Agriculture, 75-77, 85, 87, 92, 93, 96-100, 103-109, 119, 128, 129, 147-149, 156, 162, 249, 250
Hill*, Royal, 123
Hitler, Adolf, 7, 138-140
Hobbing*, Enno, 15, 32, 33, 39, 53, 55-60, 67, 75-78, 80-82, 92, 98, 100, 101, 116, 117, 120-122, 131-136, 181, 186, 202, 226, 247-249, 251
The Hobbings, 190, 192, 202, 205-208, 210-213, 221
Holland, Kenneth, 55, 57, 58
Hopkins, Ernest Martin, President of Dartmouth College, 89, 90, 248
Huessy, Eugen Rosenstock, xi, xii, 7, 8, 10, 11, 14, 16, 17, 19, 20, 22-24, 31-33, 39, 50, 54, 55, 58, 61, 62, 66, 68, 69, 72, 74, 76-78, 82, 83, 85, 87-90, 92-100, 103, 105-107, 110-112, 114, 118, 122, 123, 128, 129, 131-136, 138, 139, 141, 147-150, 154, 155, 162-164, 172, 174, 177, 187, 193, 197, 200, 203, 205, 207, 209-214, 220-228, 234, 243, 247-251
Huessy, Hans Rosenstock, 91
Huessy, Margrit Rosenstock, 13, 221
Hurlburt*, Russell, 153, 181

immigration, 23, 24
isolationists, 124

Jacobs*, Wendell, from Barre, Vt., 97
James, Alexander, 99-101, 212
Henry, 163, 248, 251
William, viii, ix, 1-5, 100, 138, 158, 163, 209, 211, 212, 222, 223
William, Jr., 99-101, 212
family, ix, 226
James, Edward Holton, 41, 42, 44
Jones*, Paul, 132, 135, 136

Keefe*, Paul, 121, 122, 133, 177, 179, 180, 192, 193, 195, 251
Kennedy, John F., U. S. President, x
Knowles*, Lee, 181, 187, 196-198, 200-203, 205, 206, 211, 251

Lamb*, Herb, 134
Landis, James, Dean at Harvard, 32, 34, 39, 50, 53, 54, 57-60, 114, 115, 149, 234, 249
Land Use Coordination Office, 20 (Eisenhofer and Stauber), 21, 23
Lanigan, James, 32, 34, 39, 114, 115, 132, 133, 145
Lasswell, Harold B., professor Yale Law School, 39, 50, 54, 57, 58, 87, 249, 250
Larkin, Ed, of Tunbridge, Vt., 73, 121
Lash, Joseph, Head of International Student Service, 191
Lazare, Norman, 194
Leitch*, Clarence, 121, 134
Lend-Lease Program, 123, 124, 223
Le Seur, Jon D., 91
Lincoln, Abraham, U. S. President, 31
Little, Edward, 153
Lowry, William, 85, 91, 153, 156
Lukens, Fred, Chief Educational Adviser for New England, 16

McEntee, J. J., Director of the CCC, 10-13, 21-23, 32, 39, 51, 54, 59, 67-69, 74, 76, 77, 79, 93, 96, 98, 104, 106, 111, 124, 127, 129, 138, 141-149, 152, 163, 164, 223 247, 248, 250, 251
McKaye, Benton, of the Forestry Service, 101, 104, 107, 108, 112, 119, 249
McKenzie, of Norwich, Vt., 63, 85, 97, 212
McNutt, Paul, Federal Security Administrator (McEntee's superior), 16, 39, 51, 53, 54, 98, 247
manual labor, 10, 13, 25, 26, 37, 175
Mattison, of South Strafford, Vt., 10[illegible]
Mellor*, David, 166
Merrill, Perry, Vermont State Forester, 52, 96, 98, 101, 104, 116
Mexican expedition, 177-180, 185, 191, 192, 193, 194, 235
Porfirio Guzman, Hector Duenas, Alfredo Isais, Roberto Vasquiz, 192
Miller, Richard, 153
Miltimore*, Eleanor, 181
Morell, Fred, Head of Forestry Service, Department of Agriculture, 20, 21, 52, 59, 103-105, 107, 110-112, 143, 147, 1[illegible]2, 163, 247-250
Mogan*, Joseph 135
Moral Equivalent of War, ix, xi, 2-5, 1[illegible]8, 219, 223, 224, 235, 236, 238, 240, 242, 246
Murray, Fred, assistant to Head of Forestry Service, 20
Myers*, Charles, 134

National Youth Administration (N.Y.A.), 58, 67, 69, 75, 242
NYA meeting, 74
NYA camp, Waterbury, Vt., 72, 73, 83, [illegible]17
New Deal, ix, x, 9, 95
New York State Power Commission, 15

Noyes' Farm, 41, 42
Mrs. Noyes, 101

O'Brien*, Robert, 25, 26, 38, 66, 67, 73, 78-83, 85, 86, 101, 102, 117, 119, 120, 122, 123, 135, 160, 165, 169-173, 177-180, 185, 186, 194, 197, 198, 201, 206, 212, 214, 226, 249, 250, 251
O'Dell*, Robert, 181
Olmstead, Ralph W., assistant to the Under Secretary of Agriculture, 75-77, 85, 87, 92, 93, 96-100, 103, 107, 114, 161, 249

Parker, Courtney A., 128, 250
Parsley*, Harold, 123
Parties, political; non-partisan flexibility, 35, 46, 47, 127
Peace Corps, x
Pearl Harbor, Dec. 7, 1941, 200, 209, 210, 224
Perry, Ralph Barton, biographer of William James, ix, 53
Phillips*, George, 15, 32, 49, 53, 67, 83, 120, 170, 171, 173, 179, 181, 187, 189, 190, 195, 202, 206, 208, 209, 212-217, 251
Phillips Exeter Academy, 181
Plumley, Representative U. S. Congress from Vt., 145, 162
Press
  Agar, Herbert, "Louisville Courier", 122
    "Free America" 142
  Barclay, "New York Times," 141, 250
  Berger, Myer, "New York Times", 132, 133, 138
  Chase, Stuart, "Survey Graphic", ix, 225
  Cunningham, Bill, "Boston Herald", 164
  "Daily Dartmouth", 90
  "Dartmouth Pictorial", 93
  Hayden, Jay C., "Boston Globe", 138, 250
  "New York Herald Tribune", 124, 126, 250
  "New York World Telegram", 144
  "Washington Post", 129
Preiss*, Jack, xi-xv, 25-27, 38, 42, 66, 67, 69, 73, 78, 79-83, 94, 99, 100-102, 106, 122, 136, 156, 170, 177-179, 197, 214, 248, 249
Project's inner strife, conflicts and rifts, 44-46, 66, 234

"Real Life", 227, 229, 230
Reardon*, Bob, 121
Reeves, Floyd W., Director of American Youth Commission (AYC), 54-60, 69
Rehabilitation & resettlement of abandoned farms in Vermont, 63-65, 95-97, 99, 101, 106, 107, 110, 119, 135, 155, 160, 184, 231
Request for a hearing, 36-38, 139
Reid*, Richard, 208, 209, 214, 215
Roberts*, Lloyd, 134
Rock*, Stanley, 97
Roosevelt Administration, x, 123-125, 146
Roosevelt,
  Mrs. Eleanor, ix, 34, 39, 40, 49, 50, 93, 113-115, 127, 140, 162, 186, 187, 191-193, 251
  Franklin D., U. S. President, ix, x, 21, 32, 39, 40, 49-51, 54, 60-62, 64-67, 74, 87, 88, 93, 123-125, 139, 140, 153, 223, 248
Root*, Arthur, 25, 35, 42, 67, 72-74, 78, 80-83, 94, 117, 118, 132, 134, 174-177, 179, 180, 185, 191, 193, 197, 204-207, 215-217, 248, 249, 251
Rowe, James, White House Assistant, 87, 114, 133, 145
Rullman*, Johnny, 121, 132-135
Rural Resettlement Administration, 53
Russian Revolution, 222

Sage, Nat. of M.I.T., 53, 148, 162, 249
Schlivek*, Louis, 25, 38, 67, 69, 78, 80-83, 94, 98, 99, 102, 116, 117, 121, 133, 177-179, 197, 248
Selective Service Act of Sept. 1940 (Burke-Wadsworth), 38, 89, 94, 243
"selfless interest", 242
segregation of segments of population, 8, 19, 38, 233
service
  compulsory versus voluntary, 244, 245
  to the country, ix, xi, 11, 38, 88, 142, 186, 225
  national, in time of peace, x, xi
  universal work service, x, 4, 186
  voluntary environmental, x
Sharon, Vt. camp and project, 17, 19-24, 32-37, 39, 44, 49, 50-53, 55, 56, 60-69, 74-77, 81, 83, 85, 89-93, 96, 98, 102, 103, 105-107, 109, 110, 113, 124-129, 138-140, 143-148, 154-156, 158-163, 183, 184, 196, 230, 232, 233, 237
camp commander, 75-78, 84, 94, 96-98, 104, 106, 107, 119, 126, 146, 148, 149
Klos, Gilbert, 104, 249
Hinkley, Benjamin L., 148, 250
honorable discharge, 147, 148, 156, 162
Washington Supervisory (Advisory) Committee, 53-61, 68, 69, 98, 103, 106-108, 114, 115, 119, 145, 147-149, 162, 163, 223
Shriver, Sargent, Director of Peace Corps, x
Shutler, Phillip, Vt. State Planning Commissioner, 36
Simmons, Virgil W., 54, 57, 58
Skidmore College, 181
Slater, of South Royalton, Vt., 85, 86, 187
Smith*, Fremont, 123, 131, 134, 155, 156
Smith*, Page, ix-xi, 67, 83, 94, 99, 101, 116, 117, 120-122, 131-136, 153-155, 169, 222, 226, 250

Smith, Dr., 121
Smith*, Winslow, 181
Soil Conservation, control of soil & erosion, 67, 98, 162, 220
  project, 131
  Soil Conservation Service (SCS), 67, 98, 162, 242
  White River Junction District, C. K. Webb Chairman, S. L. Trisley, 67, 134
Stollard*, O. B., from Ohio, 120, 132, 134
Stone, Harlan Fiske, Justice of the Supreme Court, 162
Stone, of South Strafford, Vt., Judge, 100

Taylor, Katherine, 173, 174, 197, 198, 200, 202, 206, 207, 209, 213, 216, 217, 251
Tierney*, James, 121, 133, 177, 179, 180, 192-195, 251
Tierney, Lieutenant, 96, 97, 100, 104, 109, 116, 120-122, 130, 132
Tibbets*, Norris, 181
Thompson, Dorothy, ix, 33, 39, 41-44, 49, 56, 60, 61, 74, 82, 93, 99, 105, 113, 127, 138, 150-155, 162, 204, 205, 234, 248-250
Townly*, Charles, 181
Tunbridge project, 41, 59-62,
  versus Sharon camp, 80-82
Tunbridge Rally, 36, 39-44, 49, 63, 66, 90, 140, 196
training program for camp leaders, 50, 54, 110, 125, 165, 224
Tunbridge Group, 30-32, 35, 36, 38, 40, 42-45, 52, 56, 59, 65-68, 72, 74, 75, 77, 85, 89, 90, 93, 96, 97, 109-111, 113, 118
New Tunbridge Group, 157, 158, 161, 163, 164, 166, 169, 197
Tunbridge, Petition to the President, 43, 44, 57, 87, 140

unemployment, ix, x, 8, 15
  unemployed as assets or outcasts, 23, 224
Uptegrove*, William, 26, 38, 91, 153, 179
United Service Organization (U.S.O.), 190
U. S. Army, 9, 16, 50, 57, 59, 96, 97, 133, 141, 143, 144, 167, 190, 210, 242, 243
U. S. Congress, x
U. S. Coast Guard, 11, 242
U. S. Department of Agriculture, 16, 19-23, 34, 39, 53, 54, 59, 61, 62, 67, 68, 74-79, 82, 83, 85, 94, 96, 97, 102, 104-108, 114, 115, 125, 126, 129, 138, 141-143, 145, 149, 162-164, 223
U. S. Department of the Interior, 16, 20
U. S. Department of Justice, 103
U. S. Department of War, 9, 59, 62, 74, 125, 143
U. S. Employment Service, 59, 60, 204
U. S. Forestry Service, 97, 98, 243
U. S. Marines, 11, 243
U. S. State Department, 185, 191, 193

Vermont Forestry Department, 52
Vernon, Ambrose W., 14, 247
Visitors to the Camp
  Bullocks from Norwich, 122
  Hanbury-Sparrow, Alan, 99
  Mr. Kenlon, Chief CCC inspector, 131
  Jim O'Donnell, 132
  Frank Welsh, 132
Volunteer Land Corps (land-army corps), 204-207, 209, 210, 213-217, 221
volunteers, role of, 227
Voorhis Bill, (Jerry), (H. R. 10340), Aug. 1940, National Service Act, 94, 242, 243, 246, 248

Wainwright, General, on Bataan, 226
Wales*, David, 181
Wallace, Henry, 162
war, xiii, 2-4, 6, 175, 223
Watson, Edwin M., Secretary to President Roosevelt, 52
Washington, D.C., political front, 14-16, 22, 32-35, 40, 45, 49, 64-66, 78, 82, 87, 88, 95, 96, 102, 105, 108, 112, 113, 120, 123, 130, 143, 145, 146, 152, 154, 157, 161, 18-
Washington group, 75
Weimar Republic, 7, 55
welfare agencies, 59
Wickard, Claude, U. S. Secretary for Agriculture, 124-127, 129, 250
Welles, Sumner, U. S. Secretary of State, 193
Wilson, Stanley, former governor of Vermont, 101, 102, 106, 118, 122, 170, 171
Wilson, Woodrow, U. S. President 1913-1921, 222
Winces*, Red, from Maryland, 132, 135, 136
Wolfe, Glen, Of Forestry Service, Department of Agriculture, 115, 116, 119, 120
World War II, x, 188, 194, 200-202, 210, 212, 216-218, 222, 225, 227, 231
World Wars, 222
Work camps, 7, 8, 20, 36, 38, 138, 139, 142, 143
work projects for camp, 115, 122, 133-136
work (labor) service, xi, 4, 68, 69, 142, 246
  environmental, x
  on globe-wide scale, 5
  voluntary, 15, 31, x

Yale University, 181
Young*, Robert, 196, 221, 222
Y.M.C.A., 69